Origin and Originality in Renaissance Literature

Origin and Originality in Renaissance Literature

Versions of the Source

DAVID QUINT

Yale University Press
New Haven and London

Published with the assistance of
the Frederick W. Hilles Publication Fund.

Designed by James J. Johnson
and set in Palatino Roman type.
Printed in the United States of America by
BookCrafters, Inc., Chelsea, Mich.

Library of Congress Cataloging in Publication Data

Quint, David, 1950-
  Origin and originality in Renaissance literature.

Revision of thesis (Ph.D.)—Yale University.
  Includes index.
    1. European literature—Renaissance, 1450-1600—
History and criticism. 2. Originality (in literature)
I. Title.
PN721.Q54   1983   809'.031   82–24789
ISBN 0–300–02894–6

10 9 8 7 6 5 4 3 2 1

*For my mother, Eleanor Dolsky Quint, and
in loving memory of my father, Howard H. Quint*

Contents

Preface

Ernst Robert Curtius writes that when new literary topoi emerge they provide "indications of a changed psychological state, indications which are comprehensible in no other way." From Plato's *Phaedo* and Virgil's *Fourth Georgic* Renaissance authors derived the topos of the *source*, the confluent origin of the rivers of the earth. Given an expanded meaning and emphasis in their writings, this locus of origin, both a literal geographical place and a symbolic commonplace, becomes a distinctive reflection of the literary and cultural preoccupations of the age. The realization that one is dealing with a topos—and with a tradition that overlays the classical idea of a global river system with Judaeo-Christian meanings—may in turn justify new readings of the literary works in which depictions of the source appear. My own readings vary in approach according to the individual genres, rhetorical strategies, and thematic concerns of the works in question. To discuss the episode of the source in Tasso's *Gerusalemme liberata*, for example, it is necessary first to examine a passage in Ariosto's *Orlando furioso* which Tasso's episode consciously is rewriting. The interpretative chapters (2–6) of this study form a series of largely discrete essays; together these chapters illuminate the common use which different Renaissance texts make not only of the source topos but of other recurrent thematic motifs: the story of Orpheus, the typological figure of the morning dew, ideas about praise and poetic apotheosis.

But my readings of individual texts also contribute to a larger argument, one that tests Curtius's statement in a way that Curtius's own largely ahistorical concept of the literary topos does not, and so the book's emphasis shifts repeatedly from literary explication and the history of ideas and symbols to problems of literary and intellectual history. The source topos emerged at a moment when, under the impact of a new historical consciousness, the Renaissance literary text was seeking to reexamine—and represent—the source of its fictions' authority. That consciousness allowed the text to be read as the exclusive creation of its historical human author and could thus question the claims to a nonhistorical transcendent truth which had been advanced for the text by traditional modes of allegorical reading and writing. Renaissance writers self-consciously debated the status of their fictions in light of these alternative allegorical and historicist readings of the text: ultimately at issue was the question whether those fictions were dependent upon systems of revealed truth or belonged instead to an autonomous secular domain.

My first chapter argues that this literary issue was embedded in a larger Renaissance conflict between tradition and modernity. It maintains that the positing of authorizing origins acquired urgency in a culture which had gained a new historical awareness. On the one hand, there was a kind of epistemological anxiety, heightened by nostalgia, in the task of depicting a source which sanctioned what were otherwise "counterfeit," purely man-made fictions. On the other hand, Renaissance culture valorized the human creativity which it had newly come to recognize, and it could only define the individuality of the creator in historical terms. My final chapter, an epilogue which considers the case of Milton, suggests that a shift in literary values had taken place by the end of the Renaissance, so that the writer's originality would replace a transcendent allegorical origin as the literary text's principal criterion of worth. Among the writers considered in the book Rabelais is the one who appears best able to resolve these conflicting impulses of Renaissance literary creation, to reconcile the claim to participate in a source of authorized truth with the full expression of authorial individuality. For this reason the chapter on the Rabelaisian books is removed from a sequence which treats the writers in chronological order and placed at its end. This arrangement helps to shape my argument: since the first chapter defines the issues of the study in Erasmian terms derived from a reading of *The Praise of Folly*, it is not surprising that a "solution" to those issues is found in the works of a writer as deeply imbued with Erasmianism as Rabelais.

This study revives ideas about Renaissance culture that ultimately go back to Burckhardt and his description of the rise and development of Renaissance individualism. Those ideas, I believe, have been modified but not superseded by interpretations that emphasize the persistence of medieval culture and piety in an age which Burckhardt saw pervaded by a new spirit of secularism. The work of Eugenio Garin has redefined this spirit as one of historical criticism, born from Renaissance humanism and its philological study of classical culture; and I have followed Garin and characterized the essential cast of humanist thought as "historicist," without wishing to confuse such thought with its distant descendent, the scientific historicism of the nineteenth century. In doing so I have elided the philological and rhetorical constituents of the humanist cultural program: no less than the attempt to reconstruct the historical context of ancient writings, the humanist conception of the text as a rhetorical performance argued that it indeed *had* a context, a mesh of contingent human occasions.

The central role which Garin assigns to humanist philology in the evolution of Renaissance thought and culture also suggests the centrality to that culture of a literature that criticized its own claims to truth. The gradual relinquishment of the literary text's allegorical sanctions and the eventual acknowledgment of literature's cultural autonomy was an important stage in a more general criticism of the authority of the text itself, and of a culture in which the text remained the principal instrument of knowledge. When, in the second volume of the *Paralelle des anciens et modernes* (see chapter 2, note 3), Charles Perrault singled out for his withering criticism the Platonic description of the universal source of rivers, he contrasted that classical "fable" with modern scientific observation. The subject of the volume is eloquence, and Perrault's argument momentarily shifts ground from a comparison between ancient and present-day orators; in the face of a new epistemology, eloquence itself—as a bookish method of organizing and explaining the world—appears to be obsolete. His choice of the source topos is significant, for the topos which posits an original unity underlying multiplicity can be read as the emblem par excellence of the tendency of a bookish culture to impose on experience the closed form and internal coherence of a book: what Bacon, criticizing philosophical systems, would label as "Idols of the Theater." If Renaissance literature still belongs to such a bookish culture, it could simultaneously perform a critical examination of that culture's textual sources of authority that would ultimately challenge all forms of received truth. The issue remains very much under debate in Renaissance literature and thought, but that debate constitutes a moment of crisis and transition in which a culture organized by belief and by the written word finds itself about to be superseded, eventually to yield to the authority of scientific reason and empiricism.

With the exception of verse passages and the text of *The Praise of Folly*, all citations from Latin authors are translated into English in the main text. Latin texts of the Renaissance works cited are included in my notes. Citations from the Bible are given in the translation most likely to have been used by the author under discussion.

It is a pleasure to acknowledge and thank others who have contributed to my studies and who have guided the writing of this book. My first debt is to my teachers. Thomas M. Greene supervised the Yale University doctoral dissertation that has formed the basis of the book, and he has continued to offer invaluable support and criticism of my work. John Freccero's study on Dante and the source topos originally suggested the subject to me. A. Bartlett Giamatti and James Nohrnberg encouraged and enriched my study of Renaissance literature. I am also grateful to Paula Berggren, Fred J. Nichols, Michael O'Loughlin, and the late Richard S. Sylvester. Many generous friends and scholars have read and commented upon manuscript versions of the book. Michael Murrin has read the manuscript in all its various stages; his criticism, often adversarial, has always been fruitful and constructive. Dennis J. Costa and Margaret W. Ferguson have commented incisively upon earlier drafts. My chapter on Virgil has benefited from readings by my Princeton colleagues Robert Fagles, J. Arthur Hanson, and Froma I. Zeitlin. I am also thankful for the suggestions and advice of Paul Alpers, Salvatore Camporeale, Elizabeth Cropper, John D'Amico, Philip Damon, Charles Dempsey, Maria DiBattista, Robert F. Durling, Alban Forcione, Anthony Grafton, Robert Hollander, William Kennedy, Ronald Levao, John Logan, John Marino, Earl Miner, Glenn W. Most, Annabel Patterson, François Rigolot, Thomas P. Roche, and Michael Seidel. I have incorporated valuable insights from my Princeton students Tanya Kazanjian and Alex Sheers.

The research and writing of this book have been generously supported by a Danforth Graduate Fellowship, a Fulbright-Hays Traveling Fellowship, a fellowship to the Harvard Center for Italian Studies at Villa I Tatti, by grants from the American Council of Learned Societies and the Leopold Schepp Foundation. I wish especially to thank Cipriana Scelba and Luigi Filadoro of the Commissione per gli Scambi Culturali fra l'Italia e gli Stati Uniti, and Craig Hugh Smyth and Dante della Terza, the directors of Villa I Tatti.

I wish to thank Carol Szymanski, who prepared the manuscript, and Barbara Folsom of the Yale University Press, who has expertly edited it. I have enjoyed and appreciated the courtesy and savvy efficiency of my editor, Ellen Graham.

1

The Counterfeit and the Original

FORGERIES

The problem of how Renaissance culture was to define its own individual creativity with respect to a classical tradition that it at once posited and sought to displace as a source of authority and value is the subject of a witty anecdote in Vasari's life of Michelangelo. In a biography that reads more like a hagiography, one of the first miracles performed by the young Florentine artist was to sculpt a sleeping Cupid after the ancient manner. When the work was shown to him by Baldassare del Milanese, Pierfrancesco de' Medici suggested that if it were buried and properly tricked up, it could be sent to Rome and sold as an antique. Michelangelo obligingly entered into the scheme.

> It is said that Michelangelo fixed it up in such a way that it seemed to be antique; nor is this to be wondered at, for he had the talent to do this and better things. Others maintain that Milanese brought it to Rome and buried it in a vineyard of his, and then sold it for two hundred ducats to the Cardinal San Giorgio. Others say that an agent of Milanese sold it to the Cardinal, and that Milanese wrote to Pierfrancesco to give Michelangelo thirty scudi, saying that he had received no more for the Cupid, tricking the Cardinal, Pierfrancesco, and Michelangelo. But the Cardinal, later learning from someone who had seen it that the Cupid had been made in Florence, managed to have an envoy of his find out the truth, and he made the agent of Milanese repay the money and take back the Cupid, which came into the hands of Duke Valentino and was given by him to the Marchioness of Mantua, who took it to her city where it still is seen today. This matter did not pass without the Cardinal San Giorgio being blamed for not recognizing the value of the work, which consists in perfection, since the moderns are as worthy as the ancients so long as

1

they are excellent, and the behavior of those who pursue the name rather than the works themselves is mostly vanity: such men are found in every age, who esteem appearances more than reality.[1]

This pointed anecdote places Vasari within a tradition of Renaissance thought that would develop a century later into the quarrel of the ancients and moderns.[2] Already at a tender age Michelangelo has shown himself equal in skill to the classical sculptors by passing off as an antique original what was first intended merely as an imitation of their style. He is well on his way to becoming the universal artistic genius who will surpass the ancients ("aveva *ingegno* da far questo, *e meglio*"—italics mine) with his own style. Cardinal San Giorgio is excoriated not for being duped, as a Roman, by crafty Florentines— which seems to Vasari merely to be in the nature of things—but, in spurning the counterfeit antique, for having given up an authentic Michelangelo. The connoisseur must not, like the cardinal and foolish collectors of all epochs, place too much value on the label of antiquity ("al nome") attached to the work of art, but should consider instead the work's intrinsic merit ("i fatti").

No sooner, however, has the Renaissance master established his claim to individuality than he himself must be wary of imitation. While writing the second part of *Don Quijote*, Cervantes was distressed to see appear in print a continuation of his novel authored by one pseudonymous Avellaneda. In chapter 72, Cervantes has his hero and squire encounter Don Alvaro Tarfe, a character from Avellaneda's sequel. Having read Avellaneda's book, Don Quixote remembers Tarfe's name and demands an explanation of the lies it tells about himself and Sancho Panza. Amazed, Tarfe realizes that he has not heretofore known the real Cervantine knight and squire but two other personages who bear their names, and he swears out an affidavit to that effect.

Cervantes's novel may be juxtaposed with Vasari's biography inasmuch as the defense against false Quixotes rests on the same intrinsic criteria that made Michelangelo's counterfeit Cupid into a genuine article. Cervantes comments that his characters received too much comfort from Tarfe's affidavit.

> . . . como si les importara mucho semejante declaración y no mostrara claro la diferencia de los dos Don Quijotes y la de los dos Sanchos sus obras y sus palabras.[3]
> [. . . as if this same declaration were of great importance to them and as if

their deeds and words did not demonstrate clearly the difference between the two Don Quixotes and the two Sanchos.]

Resembling the Cardinal San Giorgio, who judged the work of art by
its nametag, Quixote and Sancho Panza look for proof of their literary
authenticity in something extrinsic from the characters with which
they have been endowed by their author. Outside documentation is
neither necessary nor even useful to distinguish the two versions of
Don Quijote. Cervantes, in fact, goes a step further than Vasari, whose
Vite serve the purpose of authenticating works of art the authorship of
which may not be self-evident on stylistic grounds. The passage
implies that had Avellaneda possessed the wit and skill to make a
successful imitation of the *Quijote*, there would be little to choose
between his and Cervantes's works. Like Michelangelo, Avellaneda
would have come up to his model, and his counterfeit would be equal
in worth to the original.

Nor can Cervantes defend the authenticity of his fiction on the
basis of outside historical fact. As a fiction, the *Don Quijote* of Avellaneda is as true as the *Don Quijote* of Cervantes, who admits as much by
giving Avellaneda's character, Don Alvaro Tarfe, an existence within
his own narrative as "real" as those of Don Quixote and Sancho. On its
literal level, Cervantes's book does not accuse Avellaneda of having
written a false history, but of having written about *another* Don
Quixote and Sancho Panza. For were Avellaneda's history false,
Tarfe's presence would cast doubt upon the veracity of Cervantes's
own "true history," and Quixote himself has earlier declared that lying
historians should be burned like coiners of false money ("los histo-
riadores que de mentiras se valen habían de ser quemados, como los
que hacen moneda falsa.")[4] Insofar as both texts are fictional artifacts,
well or indifferently made, they are both counterfeits, and the reader
can only choose between the two on the basis of their respective
literary merits. There can, then, be little use in a document affirming
the authenticity of Cervantes's book when that document is itself part
of the book's fiction.

By insisting that aesthetic judgment should rest upon the intrinsic
qualities of the work of art, Vasari and Cervantes separate the work's
prestige from a historically prior origin. This works to the advantage of
Michelangelo, the Renaissance latecomer. He surpasses the achievements of the ancients, who can no longer be regarded as preeminent
simply because they came first. Vasari's *Proemio* to the *Vite* points out

that the ancients themselves were preceded by even more ancient artists whose works and names are lost.[5] The claim to historical priority is vitiated since no human work of art is absolutely prior, originating outside of history. Rather, the artist's individual greatness confers upon him an *originality* which makes him seem to transcend history. Vasari gives Michelangelo the epithet "divino," and represents his birth as a second Nativity, the coming of a messiah to God's chosen people of the arts, the Tuscans.[6] However hyperbolic, this language nevertheless describes a reality which, like the Christian revelation itself, is historically structured. Michelangelo's achievement is both apparently singular in its perfection and simultaneously the fulfillment of the history of Italian Renaissance art since Giotto. This history, which in relationship to Michelangelo's career assumes the character of an evangelical preparation, is the subject of Vasari's *Vite.*

For Cervantes, however, there is as yet no certainty that his novel will culminate the literary history in which it takes its place. On the contrary, the recognition of his own historicity deprives him of priority with respect to the literary history that continues beyond him as Altisidora's dream (2. 70) of an endless proliferation of books, including Avellaneda's sequel, satirically describes. The distinction of being the first to write about Don Quixote does not guarantee that he will be the last or the best to do so. Cervantes had, in fact, incautiously laid open his work to imitators by ending part 1 of the *Quijote* with Ariosto's verse, "Forse altri canterà con miglior plettro" (*Orlando furioso* 30.16.8), an invitation to other writers to continue the story of Angelica which, by Cervantes's time, had produced three Italian and two Spanish sequels.[7] And Cervantes knew that the *Orlando furioso* was itself a continuation of Boiardo's *Orlando innamorato,* and that Ariosto had decidedly overgone his predecessor poet.

The originality of the Renaissance artist was thus to be measured not only against the past but also the future. To assert the value of individual divergence from a canonic tradition, particularly from the imposing models of classical antiquity, became possible only when that tradition was historicized and ceased to function—on account of its priority—as an absolute standard. The tradition's historicity is recognized in its imitability. When Michelangelo turns his imitation into a forgery, the ancient originals he imitates may be perceived as *forged* in another sense of the word—they are something made or wrought by men. By mastering the style of the ancients, the Renaissance man recognizes his common humanity with them and his own potential for stylistic creativity.

The comparison of ancients and moderns thus opposes two specific historical periods, each with its respective style or styles, and here the modern may have the advantage that his age can produce something new. But by locating his own work in history, the Renaissance artist deprives it, no less than the works of the ancients, of absolute priority with respect to subsequent imitation. The authentic originality of the *Quijote* lies not merely in its invention but in its *inimitability*, and can only emerge from the test of history, from a perspective unavailable to its author. Avellaneda's copy fails to rise to the Cervantine standard and he is eventually dismissed by literary history as a second-rate imitator. In Vasari's *Vite*, the Mannerist imitators of Michelangelo experience a similar failure that confirms the uniqueness of his genius.[8]

As a concept of value, originality is the byproduct of a historicist criticism which considers the work of art within its historical context without necessarily assigning value to the context itself. The comparison of the work to other similarly evaluated works measures what is distinctive and inimitable in it alone. Originality thus becomes virtually identical to the intrinsic strengths of the work of art. It comes into play when no single work of art or set of works is considered absolutely original, when, to the contrary, all works are considered counterfeit—man-made and a part of history. For all the appearance it may lend the work of art of escaping the relativity of human history, originality is itself a relative quality.

The emergence within Renaissance culture of the kind of historical relativism necessary for the appreciation of originality had detectable beginnings in the rhetorical and philological program of Italian humanism.[9] The humanist grammarians, seeking to renew an ancient style, the Latin of Cicero and Virgil, undertook a philological reconstruction, which, as Cicero himself had proclaimed of the Twelve Tables, leads to "a portrait of the past, since both an archaic language may be understood and the kinds of proceedings reveal as well the customs and ways of life of our precursors."[10] The humanists similarly acquired a sense of the relationship of literary style to its historical context. The classical authors wrote according to the norms of their age which could be historically recovered and successfully imitated. At the same time, the humanist student of the classics acquired the capacity—to cite Angelo Poliziano as he, in turn, cites Quintilian—"to

6

remove from their family as illegitimate those books which seem to be falsely attributed."[11] One way in which the central period of the Renaissance might be dated would be to take the years between the detections of two major literary counterfeits—the first in Latin, the second in Greek—between Lorenzo Valla's exposure, on stylistic and historical grounds, of the Donation of Constantine in 1439 and Isaac Casaubon's similar detection in 1614 of the second-century origins of the reputedly hoary doctrine of Hermes Trismegistus.[12]

The detection of literary forgeries resulted from an awareness of stylistic difference. This awareness was rarely value-free. Almost all humanists agreed that scholastic Latin, in its violation of classical usage and syntax, represented a fall into "gothic" barbarism and darkness. A broad Ciceronian current within the humanist ranks, whose principal exponents included Paolo Cortesi, Pietro Bembo, and Mario Nizolio, held up the prose of the Roman orator and the verse of the Augustan poets as the highest achievement of Latin letters and the sole, timeless model for imitation.[13] The Spanish humanist, Juan Luís Vives, whose attitude on imitation was considerably more complex, nevertheless confirmed Cicero's Latin as the cultural standard and commented that the writings of later Roman authors "are more like counterfeits and semblances."[14] The Ciceronians were opposed, however, by humanists more insistent upon the historical relativity of style: Poliziano, Gianfrancesco Pico, and the Erasmus of the *Ciceronianus*. In what would become a kind of litmus test for Renaissance supporters of literary innovation and still later a defining element of baroque style, Poliziano defended the later writers of the post-Augustan period. Borrowing an argument of Tacitus, he reasoned that the departure from a Ciceronian standard did not represent a decline but rather a historical change to another mode of expression with its own particular norms and merits: "For if we rightly look into the matter, we will realize that their eloquence, rather than corrupted and debased, had changed its style. Nor should we call that which is different necessarily altered for the worse."[15] Because, Poliziano continued, "nothing in human nature is blessed with perfection in every respect," no one style should be followed as an absolute model, and different styles may be valid each in its own way.[16] Poliziano's championship of later Latin poetry might thus include the latest Renaissance poet, and he elsewhere defended his own ability, through a judicious and catholic imitation of many models, to found a personal style for self-expression.[17] By expanding the canon to be imitated, he might eventually take his own place within it.

The humanists did not draw a line between the form and meaning of the literary text. Rather, they insisted upon their interrelationship. Consequently, beyond its stylistic and aesthetic implications, their philological method could have far-reaching epistemological consequences in an age that still saw the text as the principal instrument of human knowledge. In the attempt to analyze *how* the text produces its significance and to break it down into its component parts, the humanists made meaning itself into a historical problem. As they perceived stylistic differences among the classical authors, they noted differences in thought as well. As the ancients were revealed as individual authors whose opinions and doctrines varied and sometimes contradicted one another, they gradually lost their collective authority. The new Renaissance appreciation of individual creativity and human differences could thus have its unsettling consequences. For if the individual author was to be defined historically, his creation fell into the realm of historical contingency, at a remove from any timeless or fixed standard of truth. Historically delimited, the meaning and authority of the text might be just as relative as its literary style.

It is in reaction to such potentially subversive implications of a humanist model of rhetorical and philological analysis that Poliziano's friend, Giovanni Pico della Mirandola, wrote his famous letter in defense of scholastic philosophy to the Venetian humanist Ermolao Barbaro.[18] Pico offers an alternative model based on metaphysics. His argument separates style and meaning, rhetoric and philosophy, in order to assert philosophy's claim to reveal transcendent truths. Countering the traditional humanist complaint against scholasticism—that the schoolmen wrote inelegant and incomprehensible Latin—Pico argues that rhetorical style is mere theatrical trapping, appropriate perhaps to the world of man's historical activity, politics and the lawcourts, but not to philosophy, which contemplates timeless realities. In their pursuit of the contemplative rather than the active life, Pico asserts, the philosophers "sought what was contrary to and what was in agreement with nature, they did not care meanwhile what the Romans may have thought about it."[19] Nature, conceived as the repository of eternal, unchanging truth, is opposed to the historical opinions of the Romans which the humanist grammarian may be able to define through painstaking philological study. Similarly, Pico continues, "We do not ask of money with what coinage it is stamped, but of what kind of metal it consists. Nor is there anyone who would not prefer to have pure gold under a German coinage, than a counterfeit Roman coin."[20]

Pico is willing to admit a preference of style—the Latin of the (German) scholastics is less pleasing than classical (Roman) Latin—but style itself is unimportant. His disjunction of form and content allows him to focus exclusively on content, the pure gold of philosophical truth. This truth is conceived as single and originary, and is the basis of Pico's syncretism, his attempt to demonstrate the unity of philosophy and the concordance of pagan wisdom with Christian revelation.[21] His solution to the relativism inherent in the awareness of historical difference is to assert that all true philosophical texts agree on metaphysical principles. For the gold remains the same immutable truth regardless of its coinage, the literary style subject to historical fluctuation. Pico refutes the disturbing idea raised by humanist philology that both style *and* meaning are relative, that the coinage is all that really exists. It was this idea which produced the anxiety underlying his criticism of humanist method. From Pico's point of view, the historicism of a Valla or a Poliziano threatens not merely to expose designed impostures like the Donation of Constantine, but to reveal all human texts, insofar as they make claims to metaphysical truth, as counterfeits.

THE PRAISE OF FOLLY

Pico perceives an unhealthy relationship between the historical relativism fostered by humanist philology and the humanists' concern for stylistic elegance. He worries that in a world without an absolute standard of meaning texts will be judged by their seductive rhetorical form rather than on the basis of any philosophical or moral truths they may contain. He cites the dangerous example of Lucretius, whose polished verse cloaks an abhorrent Epicurean doctrine. The humanist focus upon the meaning which man makes for himself may allow that meaning to replace a divinely given significance.

Pico's worst fears are confirmed in the world of human culture portrayed in *The Praise of Folly* (1511).[22] Here counterfeit meaning is understood within the context of Christian doctrine as a form of idolatry: man worships his own creations rather than his Creator. As the leading humanist of his generation, however, Erasmus does not, like his predecessor Pico, view humanist method as the cause of cultural crisis. By posing the problem in traditional Augustinian terms, Erasmus rather suggests that humanist criticism for the first time allows men to become fully aware of a crisis which has been

present all along. Erasmus's defense of his method as an instrument of
self-knowledge emphasizes the historicism of humanist philology
over the formalism of humanist rhetoric.[23] This historicism becomes a
pietistic weapon that resists the rhetorical seductions of the letter and
strips away the false appearances of human culture: Folly's Lucianic
satirical perspective is consistently identified as the perspective of
history. Furthermore, when Folly concludes her oration by returning,
through Christian allegory, to a true origin of meaning, she incorporates a historicist criticism of the scriptural sources of revelation as a
necessary control against allegorical excess. *The Praise of Folly* demonstrates the double role Erasmus proposed for humanist method in his
religious program. The method lends itself alternately to the destruc-
tive criticism of human idols and the critical reconstruction of God's
Word. These two activities are mutually consistent in their common
goal, the separation of the human counterfeit from the divine original.

In the cultural marketplace described by *The Praise of Folly*, counterfeits are taken at face value.

Si cui sit uxor egregie deformis, quae tamen marito, vel cum ipsa Venere
certare posse videatur, nonne perinde fuerit, ac si vere formosa foret? Si
quis tabulam minio lutoque male oblitam, suspectet, ac demiretur,
persuasum habens, Apellis aut Zeuxidis esse picturam, nonne felicior
etiam fuerit eo, qui eorum artificum manum magno emerit, fortassis
minus ex eo spectaculo voluptatis percepturus? Novi ego quemdam mei
nominis, qui novae nuptae gemmas aliquot adulterinas dono dedit,
persuadens, ut erat facundus nugator, eas non modo veras ac nativas
esse, verum etiam singulari atque inaestimabili pretio. Quaeso, quid
intererat puellae, cum vitro non minus iucunde pasceret et oculos, et
animum, nugas, perinde ut eximium aliquem thesaurum, conditas apud
sese servaret? Maritus interim et sumptum effugiebat, et uxoris errore
fruebatur, nec eam tamen sibi minus habebat devinctam, quam si magno
empta donasset. Num quid interesse censetis inter eos, qui in specu illo
Platonico variarum rerum umbras ac simulacra demirantur, modo nihil
desiderent, neque minus sibi placeant? et sapientem illum qui specum
egressus, veras res adspicit?[24]

[To that man, who has a notably ugly wife, who nonetheless seems to her
husband as though she could compete with Venus herself, isn't it just the
same as if she were really beautiful? If someone admires and wonders at a
canvas badly smeared with red and yellow, persuaded that it is a
painting by Apelles or Zeuxis, won't he be happier than he who has paid
a lot for the works of those masters, but perhaps receives less pleasure

from looking at them? I knew a person of my name, who gave his new wife some counterfeit gems, persuading her, for he was an able trickster, that they were not only real and genuine, but also of an exceptional and priceless value. I ask, what difference did it make to the girl, if she fed her eyes and soul no less happily upon glass and kept them hidden beside her as if they were some extraordinary treasure? The husband meanwhile both avoided expense and enjoyed his wife's error, for he bound her to him in gratitude no less than if he had given her very costly gifts. Nor do you think that there is any difference between those who in that cave of Plato's admire the shadows and images of various things, desiring nothing more and no less pleased with themselves, and that wise man who, leaving the cave, gazes on real things?]

In contrast to Vasari's story in which Michelangelo's forgery had value not as the antique it posed as but in itself, Folly seems to take the point of view of Vasari's butt, the Cardinal San Giorgio, happy so long as he could be persuaded that he possessed an ancient original. The muddy daub in Folly's example has no intrinsic value and gives pleasure through its bogus attribution to Zeuxis or Apelles. As Vasari complains, the nametag replaces the work of art as the standard of value. Folly, however, goes on to question the distinction between counterfeit and original if the name attached to the fake is sufficient to provide the deceived collector with as much or even more enjoyment as the owner of a genuine old master may receive. The story of Thomas More giving his wife a glass jewel makes the same point. In both cases, the counterfeit object is cherished not for itself but for what its owner has been led to believe about it.

He believes, however, only what he wants to believe. The line between the deception of the counterfeit and self-deception is a thin one, as Folly's first example attests: the man who cajoles himself into believing that his ugly wife is beautiful. Beauty is in the wishful thinking of the beholder. If there is no fixed outside standard by which to judge the intrinsic value of the object, Folly argues, the place of such a standard will be assumed by the self, flattered by the idea of owning an object of value. The possessed object becomes an extension of its owner, whose self-esteem rises the higher it is appraised. (The final logical step may be the plagiarism which Folly, later in her oration, will advise the aspiring writer to undertake; in this case, the object is passed off as the creation of its owner, who replaces the authenticating nametag on the title page with his own: the plagiarized book is intended to be judged by its cover.) A relativistic concept of value will ultimately leave value free-floating, dependent less on the qualities of the object than on the subjective mind of its judge. In Folly's version of Plato's myth of the cave—which excludes any outside perspective from those it confines—the prisoners are perfectly pleased ("modo nihil desiderent") with the shadows cast upon the cave wall, as well as with themselves ("nec minus sibi placeant"). The syntactic coupling suggests that the satisfaction of desire in the shadow images is a form of Philautia, self-love, whom Folly calls her sister in merit ("mihi merito germanae est vice") and who is virtually interchangeable with Folly in the first part of her oration.[25] Once the shadow is turned into a mirror of the prisoner's desire, it no longer matters whether it reflects an exterior reality or not: whether the painting signed as a Zeuxis is original or counterfeit, whether the jewel thought to be genuine is a precious stone or glass.

Plato's cave, however, is a smaller model of the world of history and matter. Folly's analysis of the self-love that allows the counterfeit to pass for the real thing can be extended to all human existence. The real things ("veras res") are metaphysical truths which the wise man seeks outside the cave. To continue Plato's analogy, the shadows are temporal objects—more precisely, the sensible perceptions of those objects. According to Folly, these objects are transformed by the human mind into signs from which it constructs a system of cultural meaning. The prisoners of the cave are the willing prisoners of their culture, a culture that answers and flatters their desires. Contented with the sensible sign, the prisoners never leave the cave of history and remain unaware of the realm of timeless meaning which lies beyond its confines. Instead, they attribute timelessness and truth to the only meaning they know, the meaning they have created for themselves. Self-love precludes the self-awareness that would make man conscious of his own historicity and the historicity of his culture. This narcissistic oblivion to history is identical to the gift of perpetual youth which Folly, herself the daughter of Youth, claims to bestow upon her devotees at the opening of her oration.

Folly, in fact, claims to be the principal benefactress of humanity, and argues that it is vital to preserve the illusions which satisfy human desire so well rather than to inquire too curiously into their substance. She illustrates her point with one in a series of reappearing theatrical analogies.

> Si quis histrionibus in scena fabulam agentibus personas detrahere conetur, ac spectatoribus veras nativasque facies ostendere, nonne is

fabulam omnem perverterit, dignusque habeatur, quem omnes e theatro
velut lymphatum saxis eiiciant? Exorietur autem repente nova rerum
species, ut qui modo mulier, nunc vir: qui modo iuvenis, mox senex: qui
paulo ante Rex, subito Dama: qui modo Deus, repente homunculus
appareat. Verum eum errorem tollere, est fabulam omnem perturbare.
Illud ipsum figmentum et fucus est, quod spectatorum oculos detinet.
Porro mortalium vita omnis quid aliud est, quam fabula quaepiam, in qua
qua alii aliis obtecti personis procedunt, aguntque suas quisque partes,
donec choragus educat e proscenio? Qui saepe tamen eumdem diverso
cultu prodire iubet, ut qui modo Regem purpuratum egerat, nunc
servulum pannosum gerat. Adumbrata quidem omnia, sed haec fabula
non aliter agitur.[26]

[If someone should try to strip away the costumes and characters from
actors performing a play on the stage and show them to the audience in
their real, genuine appearances, wouldn't he spoil the whole play, and
wouldn't it be right for all to throw stones at the madman and drive him
out of the theater? Things would suddenly emerge with a new appearance: who was formerly a woman would now be a man; formerly young,
now old; shortly before a king, now a servant; a former God would now
suddenly appear to be a tiny man. Indeed, to take away that illusion is to
ruin the whole play. For those fictions and illusions are what hold the
gaze of the spectators. And what else is the whole life of mortal men
except a kind of play, in which different people enter in others' costumes,
and they each act their parts, until the stagemaster leads them off the
stage? He often orders the same man to come on in different costumes,
and he who once acted the king in purple robes now plays a servant in
rags. Everything is a shadowy fiction, but otherwise this play cannot be
acted.]

Pico declares to Barbaro that true philosophical discourse is opposed
to all that smacks of the theater, to rhetoric and its outward shows. The
philosopher has no place in Folly's world, where men are not merely
captivated by the external trappings of their culture but become actors
as well as audience in the play of life ("fabulam"), a play whose flashy
costumes and masks bear no necessary relationship to the actor who
wears them. Aware of this disparity, the wise man does not wish to
play along and is unable to adapt to his society; like Cato the censor
who was forced to leave the theater because his grave presence spoiled
the show. If the pleasure of the theatergoer requires merely the
suspension of disbelief, human happiness, Folly argues, depends
upon a positive belief in the fictions of culture—that is, a lack of
awareness that they are fictions. Such belief is upheld by self-love,

without which, she asserts, "the actor, with all his gesturing, will be hissed from the stage" ("explodetur cum sua gesticulatione Histrio"); to be self-conscious about playing a cultural role will ruin the performance.[27]

At the level of culture, egocentrism produces ethnocentrism, and Folly notes that self-love makes men happy with their differing national cultures; elsewhere she catalogues the claims which each nationality makes for its superiority to all others. According to Folly, the cultural fictions which unify societies and states have their origin in flattery; and the lyres of Amphion and Orpheus, the poet-orators who first gathered primitive peoples into cities, are the emblems of adulation. But while they appeal to the self-love of the masses, these fictions ("fabulosis inventis") are, in fact, produced by demagogic politicians like Minos and Numa in order to make the masses serve their rulers' interests.[28] In attributing to Folly the rise of cities and empires, Erasmus appears to refer directly to the end of Book 14 of *The City of God* and to Augustine's definition of the earthly city founded in the love of self, where "the lust for dominion has dominion over its princes as well as over the nations they subdue."[29] In the same well-known passage, Augustine quotes Romans 1:22–23 on the worldly-wise of the city of man: "stulti facti sunt et mutaverunt gloriam incorruptibilis Dei in similitudinem imaginis corruptibilis hominis et volucrum et quadrupedum et serpentium." The foolish become idolaters, in love with their own human fictions: this Augustinian-Pauline formula encapsulates the argument of Erasmus's treatise on folly.

The ultimate dangers of a culture which substitutes show for substance is revealed when Folly examines the present state of Christianity in the hands of literalizing scholastic theologians. Erasmus invokes the traditional doctrinal opposition of letter and spirit to demonstrate the dissimilarity between the schoolmen's religion and the original devotion of the apostles. The latter worshipped

in Spiritu, nihil aliud sequentes, quam illud Euangelicum, spiritus est Deus, et eos qui adorant eum in spiritu et veritate oportet adorare. Verum haud apparet eis tum fuisse revelatum, una eademque adoratione adorandam imagunculam carbone delineatam in pariete, ut Christum ipsum, si modo duobus sit porrectis digitis, intonsa coma et in umbone qui adhaeret occipitio, treis habeat notas.[30]

[in the Spirit, following no other doctrine than that Evangelical one: God is a spirit and those who worship him should worship him in the spirit and in truth. Indeed, it scarcely seemed to have been revealed to them that a little image outlined with charcoal on a wall was to be worshipped with the same adoration as Christ Himself if two fingers are extended, the hair is unshorn, and there are three rays in the halo attached to the head.]

As the counterfeit Apelles, intrinsically worthless, is valued for the painter's nametag, the image of Christ is reduced to a series of authenticating iconographic rules which replace any inner, spiritual content: it becomes an idol. Working in the same vein is the Scotist who finds that everything that can be said about Christ is contained in the letters ("ipsis litteris") of His name, a cabbalistic exercise which turns the Word of God into a mere word.[31] A counterfeit, man-made religion is now worshipped in place of its divine Founder. The satirized schoolmen, of course, *think* that they teach true religion and are unaware that their adherence to the doctrine they have made up is a form of idolatrous self-love, a self-love through which they imagine themselves—like the first theologian Paul—already rapt to the third heaven ("dum felices sua Philautia perinde quasi ipsi tertium incolant coelum").[32] The theologians, moreover, preach what they practice, and thus their religion of externals is transmitted to the people as a form of theater. After Folly analyzes a typical sermon as a kind of five-act play, she argues that either the preachers have learned their tricks from players or the players from preachers ("Quamquam utrique alteris usque adeo sunt similes, ut nemo dubitet, quin aut hi ab illis, aut illi ab his rhetoricen suam didicerint").[33]

So long as man remains an unconscious actor within the play of culture he merely adds to its theatricality. His ethnocentrism prevents him from acquiring Folly's outside, satirical perspective, which sees the play as play, a scenario of man's own making, and reveals the human reality beneath its shows and finery. Folly describes this perspective in vertical terms, the heavenly vantage point of which the schoolmen's imagined rapture is a perverse parody. First she considers how man would view his existence if, like Jove, he saw it from a high watchtower ("specula"):

> quot calamitatibus hominum vita sit obnoxia, quam misera, quam sordida nativitas, quam laboriosa educatio, quot iniuriis exposita pueritia, quot sudoribus adacta iuventus, quam gravis senectus, quam dura mortis necessitas. . . .[34]

> [to how many calamities is the life of man subject, how wretched and sordid is his childbirth, how wearisome is his upbringing, his boyhood

exposed to how many injuries, his youth compelled to how much labor
and sweat, how heavy is his old age, how harsh and inevitable is his
death. . . .]

A list of specific misfortunes attendant upon human life follows, but
Folly makes her point by outlining each of the painful ages of man. The
god's perspective is, above all, historical, while the greatest illusion of
Folly's adherents is their obliviousness, which they take to be an
immunity, to history. Jove perceives man in the grip of a temporal
process leading necessarily toward death. The same pessimism reappears when Folly again invokes the perspective of the Olympian gods
who sit and watch the human drama like spectators at a theater ("quod
theatrum est illud, quam varius stultorum tumultus?").[35] By the end of
her description of the earthly performance, the "stultorum tumultus"
has become a "mortalium . . . tumultus," extending folly to all mortals—and insisting upon the human fools' mortality.

> In summa, si mortalium innumerabiles tumultus, e Luna, quemadmo-
> dum Menippus olim, despicias, putes te muscarum, aut culicum videre
> turbam inter se rixantium, bellantium, insidiantium, rapientium, luden-
> tium, lascivientium, nascentium, cadentium, morientium. Neque satis
> credi potest, quos motus, quas tragoedias ciat tantulum animalculum,
> tamque mox periturum. Nam aliquoties vel levis belli, seu pestilentiae
> procella, multa simul millia rapit ac dissipat.[36]
>
> [In sum, if you were to gaze down from the moon, as Menippus once did,
> on the innumerable commotions of men, you would think that you were
> seeing a swarm of flies, or gnats, quarrelling among themselves, war-
> ring, plotting, pillaging, playing, wantoning, being born, falling, dying.
> Nor would you be able to believe what broils, what tragedies such a little
> animal stirs up, even though he is so soon to die. For now and then even
> a light outbreak of war or pestilence seizes and wipes out many thou-
> sands of them at once.]

The long series of present participles—themselves the grammatical
emblem of process—concludes with the basic facts of human life:
birth, aging, death. The middle term *cadentium* is especially witty,
since it can mean "newborn" as well as "perishing"; man is already
dying at the moment he comes into the world. The focus now falls
upon the fatal "choragus" who, in the earlier description of the human
theater, had led the players off its stage. And whereas in that passage
the actor stripped of his costume was revealed as a "homunculus,"
here he is further reduced to an "animalculum" at the mercy of
historical and natural forces which threaten to annihilate him. It is

from the perspective of history—the external view of the spectator which is unavailable to the actors—that Folly exposes the play of culture as a series of pleasing fictions of the self. Conversely, her tracing of cultural fictions back to an origin in self-love is another way of indicating their human historicity. Erasmus's Augustinianism and his humanist method have merged.

By turning history upon human culture, Folly merely reveals the antithesis upon which culture is built. For culture provides stable structures of meaning precisely in order to protect men from historical contingency and change. Culture is, in this sense, inherently conservative, and attempts, insofar as possible, to disguise or allay the effects of history. Folly strips away this illusion of cultural stability: cultural meaning is itself part of the historical process it seeks to mask. Yet the god's vision of human existence which she offers may be too terrible for man to bear. The grim alternative of history only confirms the necessity for culture: a position which Folly has argued all along and which qualifies the more traditional *contemptus mundi* theme of her oration. If only death lies beyond the human play, it is no wonder that Folly advises her audience to keep their delusions and to accept counterfeit meaning as better than no meaning at all. Man may as well remain happy within his theatrical existence—even if, in her example of the Greek madman who remained happy in an empty theater under the illusion that fine dramas were being acted out on the bare stage, that existence is reduced to a purely autonomous fiction of the self with no correspondence to reality. The madman only complains when he is cured, and Folly asks whether it is really wise to leave the comforting prison of Plato's cave.

The pietistic argument of *The Praise of Folly* does not, of course, strip away human cultural defenses so that the reader may simply return to them but, rather, in order to rebuild culture on a new foundation. This foundation, as the second part of Folly's oration will demonstrate, is not new but has been available all along. An original dispensation of meaning may yet be recovered from the discredited structures of human culture, even from the masks and costumes of the play of life. It is, in fact, a reversal of Folly's theatrical metaphor which signals the major shift in Erasmus's book, a recourse to allegory. Casting her satirical eye upon the dissolute and corrupt king, Folly compares the man to his regalia.

> Deinde addite huic torquem auream, omnium virtutum cohaerentium consensum indicantem, tum coronam gemmis insignitam, quae quidem

admoneat eum heroicis omnibus virtutibus oportere caeteris antecellere. Praterea sceptrum, iustitiae & undecumque incorrupti pectoris symbolum. Postremo purpuram eximiae cuiusdam in rempublicam caritatis indicium. Haec gestamina si princeps sua vita conferret, equidem futurum arbitror, ut plane pudescat ornatus sui, vereaturque ne quis nasutus interpres, totum hunc tragicum cultum, in risum, iocumque vertat.[37]

[Then give him a golden chain, indicating the joined harmony of all virtues, then a crown set with gems, which admonishes him that he ought to outdo everyone in all heroic virtues. Then a sceptre, the symbol of justice and of a totally uncorrupted heart. Then his purple robes, indicating his exceptional love for his country. If the prince compared his own life with these regalia, I think that he would be clearly ashamed of his attire and he would fear lest some satirist should turn all this noble finery into laughter and ridicule.]

The play of human culture, it now turns out, is to be taken seriously. The finery of kings and princes, as will also turn out to be the case with the vestments of cardinals and popes, are signs pointing to moral and uplifting meanings. Unfortunately, men rarely live up to the duties of the offices prescribed by their insignia. They are happy merely to see in their apparel the sign of their worldly power and importance or to enjoy the aesthetic qualities of the finery itself. The behavior of the rulers is symptomatic—this is literally true within a Renaissance theory of kingship where the king is the object of his subject's imitation and where, as Folly points out, his faults will be transmitted down the social scale like a contagion ("gravis . . . pestis")[38]—of the way in which cultural signs, potentially full of meaning, are characteristically abused. The problem should again be posed in terms of letter and spirit. The literalist's appropriation of the sign for his own purposes suppresses its inherent spiritual significance and allows a "nasutus interpres," the Lucianic satirist which Folly has hitherto embodied, to insist, mistakenly, that signs and self-love are all that exist. Similarly, the moral of Folly's second, revised version of Plato's cave is that, while the masses of mankind admire most those things which are most fleshly and think them near to being the only things which are ("vulgus hominum ea quae maxime corporea sunt, maxime miratur, eaque prope sola putat esse"), the wise man knows differently.[39] Folly's oration now maps the way for the spiritual journey outside the cave.

The understanding of the sign's spiritual sense requires allegory, the removal of the sign from the historically specific context of its usage. The structure of this allegory, nonetheless, remains historical: it is conceived as a restoration or a reconstitution of an original meaning, a meaning which exists temporally prior to the sign itself. In practice, the allegorical sign will point to an earlier history of meaning, and the final section of Folly's oration self-consciously demonstrates its own allegorical structure when she turns to outside literary authorities upon which to rest her case. These previous texts are also constituted by human signs, and the allegorical process could go on forever, an infinite regression in which one sign is continually substituted for another, were there not an originary sign subtending all signs. Christianity posits this sign in the Incarnate Word of God. Folly skips quickly from classical authors to the authority of scripture, to the dispensation which makes true meaning possible.

The Incarnation unites divine significance with a fully historical, human sign, and its scriptural witness is contained in historical, literary texts. Paradoxically, Folly's allegory reads signs out of their human, historical context in order to refer them back to an original meaning which must be reconstructed within the historical context of Christ's ministry. The necessary reintegration of historicism into the quest for an allegorical source of meaning is, of course, the purpose which Erasmus's application of humanist philology to biblical scholarship seeks to fulfill.[40] Folly refers to Erasmus, the textual critic of the New Testament, by name, and proceeds to defend his method by contrasting it to the scriptural exegesis practiced by scholastic commentators. With the use of syllogism, the favorite tool of scholastic logic, she herself offers a nonsensical interpretation of Ecclesiasticus 20 : 33, "Melior est qui celat insipientiam suam, quam homo qui abscondit sapientiam suam." Her conclusion that the scriptural author praises folly over wisdom not only defies common sense but ignores the context: an injunction to put wisdom to active use. Folly suggests that the schoolmen follow the example of Paul, who deliberately wrenched a few words from their context on the Athenian altar to the unknown god (Acts 17 : 23) in order to transcend their pagan letter and use them as an argument for Christianity. But she criticizes the practice of this method on scripture where Paul's very words will seem contradictory if they are not understood in context ("cum apud divum Paulum pugnent Divinae Scripturae verba, quae suo loco non pugnant").[41] The reader of scripture must strive for a full contextual understanding of the letter before proceeding to spiritual allegory. The literal sense acts as a control against an overly free allegorical interpretation: the allegorist may otherwise read as he wishes, and his reading in the name of seeking divine meaning is likely to reflect his own human preoccupations. Again a paradox: neglect of the scriptural letter will produce a more literalist understanding both of the Bible and of Christianity. This proves to be the case with a commentary by the scholastic exegete, Nicholas de Lyra, which Folly holds up to ridicule. By interpreting the "gladium" of Luke 22 : 35 as a literal sword rather than—as Erasmus insists—the sword of the spirit, de Lyra, in fact, repeats the misunderstanding of Christ by His apostles (22 : 38)—at what they take to be His bidding they produce two swords and are gently rebuked—and ignores the fact that, still a few more verses later (22 : 51), Jesus orders that swords be put away.[42] Only after this abusive scholastic exegesis has been satirized does Folly return to the text of the Bible with the proper philological method and find the allegorical key to the meaning of her own name in Paul's discussion of wisdom and folly in 1 Corinthians 1–4. Allegorically understood, Folly becomes identical with spiritual Christianity itself— as opposed to the wisdom of the world—and finally with a state of ecstatic vision that is both the authentic version of the Pauline rapture affected by the self-loving theologians and a true refuge, unlike the theatrical illusions of the Greek madman, from earthly troubles.[43] With this discovery of a folly worthy to be praised, and with an exhortation to live in the spirit which the letter contains, the oration comes to an end.

Folly's argument presents two alternative methods of reading the cultural sign, a double reading which is a typical feature of Renaissance thought. The first method corresponds to the new historicism fostered by humanist philology: it regards culture as an exclusively human creation, whose meaning is determined by the historical circumstances and individual dispositions of its authors. At first, Folly celebrates man's capacity to make the fictions by which he lives. Her ability to recognize human creativity, however, depends upon a historical perspective which at the same time discloses the contingency of those man-made fictions. At the point when all meaning seems to be autonomously human, and the possibility of any true meaning in the face of history is about to disappear, Folly introduces a second reading which recovers an original dispensation of divine meaning that once authorized and continues to authorize the cultural sign. This second reading takes the form of *allegory* and this term,

Sperua

broadly defined, may characterize any reading which points beyond the historically determined meaning of the sign. Allegory in this sense is an intrinsic element in all interpretation, for the reader always brings his own subjectivity to bear upon what he interprets. Renaissance allegory, however, normatively posits a metaphysical source of authority for its meaning—as if God were the ideal reader as well as the ultimate author of the sign.[44] This divine source is named in the very final paragraph of Folly's oration, even though it is simultaneously revealed to lie outside the limits both of her discourse and of the wordless Augustinian rapture with which she identifies her name. It is "fontem illum aeternae felicitatis," the eschatological goal of which the Christian believer seeks a kind of foretaste.[45]

There is, for Erasmus, a continuity between the two methods of reading, historicist and allegorical, which *The Praise of Folly* isolates. The operation of allegory entails a genuinely historical understanding of the sign's meaning, traced back to an original context in the Christ event—a philological reconstruction which Erasmus describes throughout his other writings as a return to the sources ("ad fontes") of revelation.[46] These, in turn, attest to a more primary source. The figure of the divine fountain at the end of *The Praise of Folly* subtends an argument which, retracing the origin of its own meaning and of all meaning, moves in a logical trajectory from the exclusively human to the exclusively divine.

But the double reading of *The Praise of Folly* cannot reconcile the human creativity which the historicist Folly identifies, admires, and criticizes with the authorized source of truth which the allegorist Folly seeks to reconstruct. Erasmus elsewhere describes an individual creativity sanctioned by Christian truth: the creativity of the scriptural interpreter who applies the meaning of the Christ event to his own personal disposition and experience, an inner process by which he himself is interpreted and spiritually transformed by the Gospel text.[47] But *The Praise of Folly* concentrates its satire upon a creativity that is not grounded in the Word of God. When perceived from a strictly historicist viewpoint as the autonomous creation of human individuals, culture turns into a series of idols of the self. To be *original* in this context, the human creator is apt to set himself apart not only from the historically prior traditions of culture, but from an absolutely prior, authorizing origin. The imprint of his own individuality and historicity upon his creations reveals the counterfeit nature of their meaning, a man-made significance that stands in place of divine truth. (There is no way, Folly further argues, to choose between equally inauthentic counterfeits, and the absence of a metaphysical standard entails a relativism of cultural value so thoroughgoing that originality itself becomes meaningless: once value is measured by man alone, it quickly degenerates into the reflection of each human subjectivity.)

The opposition which *The Praise of Folly* thus sets forth between the individual human author and authorized truth is felt in its own text. Erasmus's literary creativity adopts the mask of Folly and deprives itself of authority in the same way that Folly announces from the beginning of her oration that she is a sophist and makes her speech, prompted by the interested motive of self-praise, into a model of the cultural idols which it will dissect. As long as Folly remains the original fiction of her human author, her oration and his text are limited to a corrosive satire that empties human life of significance. The positive, allegorical movement of the text toward the recovery of true meaning is accompanied by a gradual relinquishing of Folly's distinctive voice for a conventional language of piety and by the identification of Folly herself with a preexistent scriptural typology.

THE SOURCE

If the double reading which *The Praise of Folly* performs on Renaissance culture as a whole applies equally well—and in an exemplary fashion—to its own text, this may be due to the nature of the text as a literary fiction. Imaginative literature is self-consciously aware that it is something *made-up*—opposed, as Cervantes playfully demonstrates, to historical fact. Since Plato, the burden of proof that poetry speaks the truth has rested with the poet. The literary text might, then, more readily fit the definition which the historicist criticism fostered by Renaissance humanism was beginning to apply to all texts and products of culture: it might more readily be conceded to be the creation of an autonomous human author. Plato's war against poetry, however, was not one-sided. The poets and their champions resorted to allegory as their first line of defense against charges that literature was a mere aesthetic plaything or, worse, as in the case of Pico's Lucretius, a dangerously seductive lie.[48] This traditional practice of allegory persisted and reached its last great flowering in Renaissance fiction, at times in pointed opposition to a new historicism and the skeptical attitudes toward literary authority with which it could appear to be allied. The Renaissance literary text was thus particularly predisposed to readings that were alternately historicist and allegorical because these readings easily conformed to opposing sides in an age-old argument over the nature of literature itself. By the same token, the implications of that argument in the Renaissance went beyond the merely literary and reflected the divisions which humanism introduced into the mentality and larger culture of the age.[49]

The double reading of the Renaissance text found different criteria by which to judge its value. The historicist reading, focusing exclusively upon the craftsmanship of the human author, categorized his work according to traditional genres and evaluated it in comparison with the work of other authors; this reading thus described an autonomous, essentially secular domain of literature with its own particular set of standards and values. Such a comparison, moreover, revealed what was unique and individual to the text alone, and eventually this originality could be considered valuable in itself. The allegorical reading, by contrast, valorizes the literary text as an extension of a metaphysical or religious system of truth. Allegory locates the text's value in a source of truth and authority that lies outside the text itself—normally in an earlier text or series of texts that have been granted an authoritative or sacred status.[50] To the extent that allegory defined the value of the literary text to consist in a truth for which it is dependent upon another text, it could devalue the text's independent literary identity and the originality of its author. Allegory thus presented the Renaissance author with a parent text which, even more than the prestigious models of classical literature, could inhibit his claims to individual self-expression, a text from which he could not declare his own creative autonomy without an accompanying sense of religious anxiety or some acknowledgment of his fiction's relative lack of authority. *The Praise of Folly* suggests how the literary text which both wants and claims allegorical sanctions may find it difficult to assert the value of any independent—hence unauthorized—creativity of its own.

By the end of the Renaissance, a shift in literary values had occurred, both reflecting and contributing to a general secularization of culture. This shift is felt when Cervantes asks that *Don Quijote* be judged on the basis of its intrinsic qualities as a literary work of art, perhaps ultimately for its inimitable originality. In one sense, literature had lost a round in its war with Plato, for the text gradually ceased to be valued as the vessel of a transcendent, revealed truth, and allegorical claims to such truth were less and less frequently advanced. But, in another sense, literature had won, gaining its own share of the cultural marketplace, a sector governed by its own rules and standards. Erasmus's Folly had predicted a collapse of cultural value once man and not God was made the measure of things. But humanism filled the potential vacuum with specialist experts who produced treatises and laid down norms—not only for the poet, but for the family, the governor, the courtier, the prince, the schoolmaster, even for the angler. Among its other revivals of ancient culture, the Renaissance reinvented the literary critic.

It may not be possible to map out a sequential development for the process by which a historical understanding of the text and the literary values it generated came eventually to replace the practice and values of allegory. This process, however, defines a large corpus of Renaissance literature, works with varying thematic preoccupations, written at different stages in the developments of their respective national literatures. In common with one another, these works self-consciously stage a debate over the extent to which an awareness of the literary text's human historicity may or may not be reconciled with the claims it makes to transcendent truth, over whether the text's source of meaning and locus of value lie in the literary originality of its author or in an extratextual, authorized origin that subtends its discourse. This debate over the origins of textual authority and value found a means of expression in a symbolic figure of origin—the river source or fountainhead, which, in the version that Renaissance authors found ready-made for them in Virgil's *Fourth Georgic,* appears so regularly in their writings as to constitute a distinctive topos.[51]

The versions of the source in the literary works discussed in the following chapters (as well as in the writings of other sixteenth- and seventeenth-century authors, among them Bembo, Folengo, Marino, Opitz, and Grimmelshausen) attest to its appeal as a figure of timeless origin for a culture which had begun to discover its own historical nature.[52] The idea of a single, timeless, originary truth stands in a dialectical relationship to the growing and often anxious Renaissance awareness of historical multiplicity and of a proliferation of human meaning which we have seen expressed in the motif of the counterfeit—that which, by definition, lacks an authorizing source. *The Praise of Folly* contrasts a counterfeit man-made culture, in which all meaning is generated from and therefore dependent upon the contingent situations of human history, to an authentic culture which can trace its institutions and meanings back to the sources of the Christian dispensation and to a godhead characterized as an eternal fountain. The opposition between the human counterfeit and the divine original contains a temporal opposition to which the source figure gives a spatial representation. The source is temporally anterior to the river which it generates. If placed in opposition to the river, the Heraclitean emblem of history and flux, the source, conceived as pure unchanging origin, will be outside of time itself.

But the source figure not only points up but may also bridge this opposition, for the source and river are continuous with one another. For the Renaissance writer, this image of continuity between the time-bound and the timeless could be transferred to suggest the possibility of a link between the products of human history, including his own literary text, and a transcendent or divine source of meaning. The source figure afforded him an occasion to discuss the source of his text's capacity to signify—whether that capacity derives from an authorized source beyond the historical text or whether it is generated autonomously within the text itself. The Renaissance author who acknowledges the temporal distance separating his text from a timeless source of truth must either determine how the text can still participate in that truth or face the possibility that it has cut itself off from such truth altogether. The recognition of this temporal distance is necessary, however, if the author wishes to assert an individuality that can only be fully defined in historical terms. The source figure could thus describe what alternately historicist and allegorical readings of the Renaissance literary text might characterize as its double movement—away from the source to the original self-expression and historical identity of its author, back to the source and its authorized truth.

The way back to the source is revealed in Pierre de Ronsard's *Ode à Michel de l'Hospital* (1552), which provides an exemplary Renaissance version of the topos.[53] Ronsard's fiction is explicitly about the origins of its own poetry and puts forward a theory of inspiration that expresses the ideals of the poets of the Pleïade. It describes how the Muses, having reached their seventh birthday, ask their mother Memory to bring them for a visit to Jupiter, the divine creator and their own father. Led to the shores of the ocean, they plunge into its depths until they reach its welling source.

> Sourdoyent de milles fontaines
> Le vif sourgeon per-ennel.[54]   [129–30]

[welling with thousands of fountains, the living, eternal source.]

This is the eternal origin not merely of one, but of all the rivers of the world, which flow away from and back to their source.

> Là les Tritons chassant les fleuves,
> Sous la terre les escouloyent
> Aux canaux de leurs rives neuves,
> Puis de rechef les r'appelloyent.   [141–44]

[there Tritons, driving the rivers before them, make them flow beneath the earth to the channels of their new banks, then recall them once again.]

The model for this confluent source in the midst of the ocean lies in Virgil's *Fourth Georgic* and will be the subject of my second chapter. Ronsard follows Virgil by identifying the source as the primordial origin of all material creation, where Nature has placed "Les semences de toutes choses" (139). It is also the seat of divinity, for Jupiter keeps his court there. The return of the Muses, guided by Memory, back to the source figures an allegorical movement back through time, a kind of Platonic anamnesis which recovers a divine origin outside of time itself.[55] In the presence of their father, the Muses, in fact, sing about events at the very beginning of creation and time, the war between the Olympians and the Titans imitated from Hesiod's *Theogony*. Pleased with their performance, Jupiter grants the Muses the power to inspire men, the original act which authorizes poetry. He carefully distinguishes authentic poetry, the Muses' divine gift, from mere human art, the product of an analyzable and learnable *techné*.

> Vostre mestier, race gentille,
> Les autres mestiers passera,
> D'autant qu'esclave il ne sera
> De l'art, aux Muses inutile.
>   Par art le navigateur
>   Dans la mer manie et vire
>   La bride de son navire.
>   Par art plaide l'Orateur,
>   Par art les Rois sont guerriers,
>   Par art se font les ouvriers;

> Mais si vaine experience
> Vous n'aurez de tel erreur,
> Sans plus ma sainte fureur
> Polira vostre science. [395–408]

[Your profession, noble race (of poets), will surpass all other professions, because it will not be the slave of art, art that is useless to Muses. By art the navigator handles and turns the bridle of his boat. By art the Orator pleads; by art Kings become warriors, by art craftsmen do their work. But if you do not vainly pursue that erroneous course (of art), my sacred furor will by itself polish your poetic skills.]

> Cest art penible et miserable
> S'eslongnera de toutes parts
> De vostre mestier honorable
> Desmembré en diverses parts,
> En Prophetie, en Poësies,
> En mysteres et en amour,
> Quatre fureurs qui tour-à-tour
> Chatouilleront vos fantasies. [425–32]

[This laborious and wretched art will be totally removed from your profession, divided into different parts, into Prophecy, Poetry, Priestly mysteries, and Love, four furors which by turns will excite your fantasies.]

Ronsard opposes the poet-as-maker—who is no poet at all—to the inspired poet, whose *furor poeticus* was grouped by the fifteenth-century Neoplatonist Marsilio Ficino with three other divine furors— those of the prophet, priest, and lover.[56] Renaissance thinkers who advanced claims for the divine origins of poetry argued that prophecy, both biblical and sibylline, as well as the first liturgical hymns of Hebrew and ancient Greek religion, first took the form of verse. Ronsard's ode repeats the argument of the *Phaedrus* (245a), which lies behind all such Neoplatonic discussions of poetic furor.

> But if any man come to the gates of poetry without the madness of the Muses, persuaded that skill alone will make him a good poet, then shall he and his works of sanity with him be brought to nought by the poetry of madness, and behold, their place is nowhere to be found.[57]

The failure of a consciously crafted and exclusively man-made poetry ever to be more than a still-born and graceless art confirms that "les vers viennent de Dieu,/Non de l'humaine puissance" ("verses come from God, not from the power of man;" 475–76).

Although Ronsard's Jupiter bases his decree on the best Platonic authority, he may be protesting too much. The literary history which the ode goes on to detail describes a progressive humanizing of an originally divine poetry and the increasingly diminishing activity of the Muses upon the earth. The first Greek poets, the "poëtes Divins" who consorted with the Muses and practiced a poetry without art, and who include Homer, Hesiod, and the "Orpheus" of the Orphic hymns along with some purely legendary poets (Musaeus, Linus), are succeeded by a new breed of versifiers.

> Apres ces Poëtes saints,
> Avec une foulle grande
> Arriva la jeune bande
> D'autres Poëtes humains
> Degenerant des premiers:
> Comme venus des derniers,
> Par un art melancholique
> Trahirent avec grand soin
> Les vers, esloignez bien loin
> De la sainte ardeur antique.   [637–46]

[After these holy poets, another young band of human poets arrived in a great throng, degenerating from the first ones: as if they were latecomers, by a melancholy art they betrayed verses with their painstaking care, quite far removed from the ancient sacred ardor.]

Aeschylus, Aratus, Theocritus, Apollonius Rhodius, Lycophron, Sophocles, Euripides, Aristophanes—all poets who belong to a literate, historical culture—have betrayed and distanced themselves from the Muses by interjecting their careful artistry into the making of verses. The situation only worsens with the Roman poets, who still, but only barely, retain some trace of the Muses' inspiration.

> Non pas comme fut la premiere
> Ou comme la seconde estoit,
> Mais comme toute la derniere
> Plus lentement les agitoit.   [663–66]

[Not like the first or second group, but as if the very last, (inspiration) shook them more gently.]

This steady historical movement of poetry away from its divine source reaches a catastrophic end with the barbarian invasions of the Roman Empire and the onset of those "Dark Ages" which Renaissance men now saw separating them from antiquity. The Muses desert the earth and flee to heaven.

28   Ronsard confidently announces that the Muses have returned to human history with the birth of Michel de l'Hospital, whose literary productions and patronage of the poets of the Pleïade have caused the renaissance of poetry in France. When the poet addresses his own Muse at verse 693, he indicates that the *Ode* itself is proof of the return of an inspired, divine poetry. The *Ode* thus traces a recovery of a lost source that is analogous to the progress of *The Praise of Folly*. Whereas Erasmus's book depicts a culture which, through a history of human appropriation, has separated itself from its original Christian foundations, the *Ode* describes the historical alienation of poetry from its inspired source and its degeneration into a human art. The remedy to both situations is to reunite present history with the divine source. This process involves the return, through the historical tools of Renaissance humanism, to an ideal past—and to an earlier text from that past. For Erasmus, the recovery of the religious purity of the apostolic community can be accomplished through a correct philological understanding of Scripture. Ronsard and the ideal Pleïade poet he describes claim to reinherit the inspired, prophetic mantle of the Greek bards. The basis for this claim, on closer examination, rests on little more than a return to Greek poetic models: adapting the form of the Pindaric ode, imitating Hesiod's accounts of the creation.

Such imitation of classical models requires, however, precisely the kind of conscious poetic craftsmanship and care that Ronsard declares to be opposed to true poetic inspiration. The self-authorizing fiction of the *Ode* itself has raised the alternative of a purely human art that is a kind of counterfeit double to inspired poetry: it has exposed itself to a reading that might see it, too, as work of art and reject its claims to prophetic authority. In the process of depicting the allegorical source that subtends its poetry, the *Ode* reveals a potential double reading that is both allegorical and historicist. Ronsard acknowledges a historical break in the tradition of inspired poetry, and indeed a steady decline of inspiration as poetry enters recorded history and moves away from its prophetic origins. His recovery of those origins is accompanied by an awareness of his own historicity that questions whether such a recovery is possible at all.

As it upholds the inspired poet, who draws from a divine source, the *Ode à Michel l'Hospital*, moreover, downgrades the original poet, the human maker who measures his place in literary history. Yet, as the *Ode* itself suggests, Ronsard was acutely conscious of his own historical contribution to the rebirth of French letters. In his *Response aux injures et calomnies de je ne scay quels predicantereaux et ministreaux de Genève* (1563), he proudly proclaims his achievement.

> Adonques, pour hausser ma langue maternelle,
> Indonté du labeur, je travaillay pour elle,
> Je fis des mots nouveaux, je r'appellay les vieux
> Si bien que son renom je poussay jusqu'aux Cieux.
> Je fis, d'autre façon que n'avoyent les antiques,
> Vocables composez et phrases poëtiques,
> Et mis la Poësie en tel ordre qu'apres
> Le François fut egal aux Romains et aux Grecs.   [951–58]

[Therefore to elevate my maternal tongue, undaunted by work, I labored for her. I made new words, I recalled old ones—so well that I exalted her fame to the heavens. I made, in other fashion than the ancients had, compound words and poetic phrases, and put Poetry in such order that the Frenchman was equal to the Romans and the Greeks.]

Here the elevation of French verse to parity with the poetry of the ancients does not depend upon the recovery of prophetic inspiration but on the hard work of the skilled poet. Ronsard goes on to assert that his accomplishments have made possible the very verse of his Huguenot detractors and that their attacks on him through the medium he has perfected is an act of disloyalty which, in the context of the poem, is analogous to their religious and political schism.

> Tu ne le peux nier, car de ma plenitude
> Vous estes tous remplis, je suis seul vostre estude,
> Vous estes tous yssus de la grandeur de moy,
> Vous estes mes sujets, je suis seul vostre loy.
> Vous estes mes ruisseaux, je suis vostre fonteine,
> Et plus vous m'espuisez, plus ma fertile veine,
> Repoussant le sablon, jette une source d'eaux
> D'un surgeon eternel pour vous autres ruisseaux.   [967–74]

[You cannot deny it, for you are filled with my plenitude, I am your only study. You have issued from my grandeur, you are all my subjects, I am alone your law. You are my streams, I am your fountain, and the more you drain me, the more my fertile vein, pushing away the sand, jets up from an eternal wellspring a source of waters for your other streams.]

Ronsard himself has turned into the source—a "surgeon eternel" as compared with the "surgeon per-ennel" of the *Ode*—and the figure now stands not for a divine poetic origin but for the poet's own potent originality: his uniqueness (note the repetition of "seul") and his generative role in French literature. But this assertion of originality is accompanied in the *Response auz injures et calomnies* by a general retreat from the positions advanced in the *Ode*. The artlessness of the inspired poet which the *Ode* had opposed to conscious poetic craftsmanship now becomes an attribute of that craftsmanship: the Horatian art which conceals art—"Ils ont un art caché qui ne semble pas art" (810). More strikingly, Ronsard denies any prophetic authority to poetry—"Ny tes vers ny les miens oracles ne sont pas" (853)—and states categorically that the sole aim of verse is to give pleasure (858). Poetry has lost the sacred status it enjoyed in the *Ode:* it is now celebrated as the product of that human art which the *Ode* disdains, and is little more than an aesthetic toy.

Ronsard may find himself forced into this reductive position by the religious controversy in which he is engaged: the claim of prophetic inspiration for his verse might resemble the spiritual claims of his Protestant adversaries and leave him open to the same charge of arrogance he levels against them. Nonetheless, the juxtaposition of the two Ronsard poems and their two versions of the source suggests the divided aspirations of a poet who desires both to ground his verse in an authorized source and to establish his own individuality as a literary creator: to be a source for other poets. For Ronsard, these dual aspirations appear to be antithetical—the claim of poetic originality seems to come at the expense of a desacralization, even a trivialization of poetry—and they find expression in two separate, perhaps mutually exclusive, poetic statements.[58]

Ronsard locates the source of literary meaning and value alternatively in an authorized divine origin or in the originality of the human author. In the first case, he reads the literary text allegorically as the vessel of transcendent truth; in the second, he reads the text as a historical, exclusively human creation. This double reading typically comes into play when Renaissance authors invoke the topos of the source; their attempt to posit an allegorical origin for the meaning of the literary text is accompanied by a new understanding of the text's historicity. The opposition allegory/history is repeated in different ways by each of the authors whose version of the source is analyzed in the following chapters: Sannazaro's opposition of epic authority to pastoral autonomy, Tasso's Platonic response to Ariosto's attack on allegory, Bruno's abolition of history in favor of allegory, Spenser who conversely makes allegory dependent upon and thus vulnerable to the events of history, the Rabelaisian poetics of the Spirit which counter the threat of Babelic autonomy and historical dispersion. These authors make the source of their texts' authority the explicit subject matter of their fictions: as is the case in *The Praise of Folly*, the way in which the text claims to produce its meaning is an inseparable, often central part of the meaning it produces. These versions of the source, as they try to distinguish an authorized literary meaning from a counterfeit one, reveal cultural and intellectual pressures which, by the close of the Renaissance, would lead to a cessation of allegory and to the recognition of literature as an independent entity, separated from systems of revealed truth. In turn, such literary questions point to a larger problem of the age: the gradual loss of transcendent sanctions felt by Renaissance culture as it undertook to discover its own human origins.

2

The Virgilian Source

The writers of the Renaissance modeled their depictions of the source—the confluent origin of the rivers of the earth—upon a passage in the Aristaeus-Orpheus epyllion that ends Virgil's *Fourth Georgic*. This epyllion brings with it a problematic legacy from the criticism of late antiquity. The fourth-century commentator Servius asserted that Virgil introduced the mythological episode in order to replace a panegyric in praise of his fellow poet, C. Cornelius Gallus. Gallus, who *is* celebrated as a character in Virgil's *Tenth Eclogue*, had been Roman governor in Egypt where his conduct in office lost him the political favor of Augustus. His subsequent suicide in 26 B.C., according to Servius, necessitated the change in Virgil's poem. Much critical ingenuity has been expended in unconvincing attempts to read the Aristaeus-Orpheus story as a topical allegory of Gallus's disgrace and death. A second school of modern classical scholarship, led by Eduard Norden, has questioned the credibility of Servius's account and, perhaps more pertinently, insisted upon the integral relationship of the epyllion to the *Georgics'* great themes of natural process, death, and regeneration.[1] The present reading reexamines this relationship, focusing upon Virgil's oceanic source myth and upon the metaliterary themes of the epyllion. In order to portray the personality which separates man from the rest of nature, Virgil explores the link between poetry and human identity. His fiction distinguishes two kinds of poetry: a divine, vatic poetry, personified by Proteus, which is joined to the sources of natural creation; the human poetry of Orpheus, which originates in the individual experience of mortality and loss.

The subject of the *Fourth Georgic* is apiculture, and its controlling metaphor is found in the analogy between the community of the beehive and human society. The analogy is partly playful and satirical, for the anthropomorphic bees suggest mankind's pettiness, but it culminates in a famous passage (219–27), in which the bees together with men and all forms of life, are seen to participate, touched by divinity, in the eternal generative cycle of creation. The bees' death is described as "casus . . . nostros" (251). Yet, as the epyllion which concludes the book will demonstrate, it is precisely in death that the analogy breaks down and that the difference between apian and human experience emerges.

The epyllion is an explanation of the origin of the *bugonia*, a method for generating bees spontaneously out of the carcass of a bull. It is first performed by the rustic demigod Aristaeus, whose apiary has become extinct. Aristaeus is so upset at the loss of his bees that he rejects his hard-earned accomplishments as a farmer.

> en etiam hunc ipsum uitae mortalis honorem,
> quem mihi vix frugum et pecudum custodia sollers
> omnia temptanti extuderat, te matre relinquo.[2]   [326–28]

[even this honor of my mortal life, which, with all my efforts, the skillful tending of crops and herds had scarcely squeezed out for me, I relinquish to you, mother.]

Aristaeus's despair is another version of the impasse reached at the end of the *Third Georgic*, where mortality, the plague which threatens to extinguish both the herds and their human masters, jeopardizes the program of cultivation outlined in the four books of the poem. The *bugonia* which ends the *Georgics* as a whole guarantees the continuation of the species and signals the triumph of agriculture in a general resumption of the natural life cycle.

Aristaeus calls upon his mother, the sea nymph Cyrene. The scene is imitated from the meeting of Achilles and Thetis in the eighteenth book of the *Iliad* (34 ff.), where the hero mourns for the fallen Patroclus and learns of his own impending death. In the contrast between the extinction (and eventual renewal) of the collective bee community and the individual human loss in the Homeric model, the epyllion announces its general theme and anticipates its subsequent opposition of Aristaeus to Orpheus.

Anguished by the fact of death, Aristaeus is led down into the source of life. His return to his mother takes him to the very womb of the earth. Cyrene's cave lies at the origin of the world's rivers.

> iamque domum mirans genetricis et umida regna
> speluncisque lacus clausos lucosque sonantis
> ibat, et ingenti motu stupefactus aquarum
> omnia sub magna labentia flumina terra
> spectabat diuersa locis, Phasimque Lycumque,
> et caput unde altus primum se erumpit Enipeus,
> unde pater Tiberinus et unde Aniena fluenta
> saxosusque sonans Hypanis Mysusque Caicus
> et gemina auratus taurino cornua uultu
> Eridanus, quo non alius per pinguia culta
> in mare purpureum uiolentior effluit amnis.   [363–73]

[and now he went gazing at the home and watery realms of his mother, at the lakes enclosed in caves and the echoing groves, and, amazed at the huge movement of waters, he gazed at all the great rivers flowing beneath the earth, separated in their places; Phasis and Lycus and the fountainhead whence deep Enipeus first breaks forth, whence father Tiber and whence the Anio's streams, and rocky, roaring Hypanus and Mysian Caicus, and the golden Po with its bull's face and twin horns, than which no other stream flows more violently through rich fields into the purple sea.]

This is the cave of Ocean. Virgil is following Plato's description of the earth's underground water system in the final pages of the *Phaedo* (11d ff.).[3] According to the Platonic myth, all the earth's springs, rivers, and seas have their source in Tartarus, through which flows the great river Oceanus which encircles the globe. There, too, are the rivers of Hell: Acheron, Pyriphlegeton, Cocytus, and Styx. Plato's map of the underworld introduces a discussion of expiation and reincarnation; purged after death by the infernal rivers, human souls are returned to earth in new bodies. Virgil's fiction and Plato's myth share a common derivation from Homer, who declares that the river Oceanus is both the the source of the earth's rivers, lakes, and springs (*Iliad* 21.195–97) and the father of the gods and of all things (*Iliad* 14.200–01, 244–48). Virgil would also have known the passage in the *Metaphysics* (983b) where Aristotle debates whether the latter epithets which Homer applies to Oceanus contain a very ancient reference to the doctrine that water is the animating principle of material life, a doctrine which Aristotle attributes to Thales of Miletus.[4] In the epyllion, Cyrene orders her sister nymphs to pour a libation to "Oceanumque patrem rerum" (382).

The nymphs of the oceanic source are weaving, an activity associated with classical myths of creation and birth.[5] Appropriately, their work is accompanied by a genealogy of the gods.

> inter quas curam Clymene narrabat inanem
> Volcani, Martisque dolos et dulcia furta,
> aque Chao densos diuum numerabat amores.　　　[345–47]

> [among whom Clymene was telling about the vain precautions of Vulcan, and of the tricks and sweet secret loves of Mars, and was cataloging the many loves of the gods from Chaos on.]

Clymene recites nothing less than universal history. The gods characteristically embody cosmological forces in classical thought, and theogonic myths contain cosmogonic meanings. One such myth is the adultery of Venus and Mars, sung by the minstrel Demodocus in the eighth book of the *Odyssey* (226–66). The Homeric allegorist Heraclitus, who wrote either during or shortly after Virgil's lifetime and whose work is a compendium of earlier sources which were probably available to the Roman poet, identified the goddess and war-god as personifications of the Empedoclean principles of Love and Strife. Their union, caught in the net forged by Vulcan, produces the cosmic harmony which makes for order and creation.[6] Before Virgil, Lucretius had used the myth to express a similar meaning at the opening of the *De rerum natura*. Clymene's catalogue of the loves of the gods traces creation history back to its origins in primeval Chaos.

Here in this natural matrix, Aristaeus's quest should logically come to an end. Cyrene's cave of origin is the repository of the secrets of creation, of the type of knowledge of first things embodied in Clymene's song. Cyrene herself instructs Aristaeus in the technique of the *bugonia* at the end of the epyllion. From the strict viewpoint of plot, the ensuing consultation of the seer Proteus has struck critics as unnecessary.[7] But Virgil's narrative, in its very digressiveness, has a Homeric model.

Virgil seems to have understood that the *Odyssey* pairs Menelaus's capture of Proteus (4.351–587) with Odysseus's visit to the dead in book 11, and he imitates both passages in his own Proteus episode.[8] Circe sends Odysseus to consult the shades of Hades in book 11, after which he must return to her to obtain the necessary information for his homecoming. Like Cyrene, Circe has known what to do all along.

In both cases, the hero (Odysseus/Aristaeus) must learn from the seer (Tiresias/Proteus) the name of the deity he has offended and to whom he must offer a piacular sacrifice (Poseidon/Orpheus, the Nymphs). The underworld episode of the *Odyssey*, in fact, *both* furnishes a narrative model for Aristaeus's visit to Proteus and will be quoted directly during Orpheus's descent to the underworld, providing another link between the interrelated stories of the epyllion. But Virgil's digression is thematic as well, for the relationship between Proteus and Cyrene is conceived in terms of a displacement from the source.

The transformations of the Old Man of the Sea are related twice for the reader. First, Cyrene warns her son what to expect from Proteus; then the poem describes the seer's efforts to escape the grasp of Aristaeus.

> fiet enim subito sus horridus atraque tigris
> sqamosusque draco et fulua cervice leaena,
> aut acrem flammae sonitum dabit atque ita uinclis
> excidet, aut in aquas tenuis dilapsus abibit.   [407–10]

[for he will suddenly become a bristly boar or a fierce tiger, a scaly serpent, or a lioness with a tawny mane, or he will make the fierce sound of fire and thus escape his chains, or he will depart dissolved into fleeting water.]

> ille suae contra non immemor artis
> omnia transformat sese in miracula rerum,
> ignemque horribilemque feram fluuiumque liquentem.   [440–42]

[not forgetting his arts, he counters by transforming himself into all the miraculous shapes of nature, into fire, a horrid beast, and a flowing river.]

In both cases the flowing river appears to be Proteus's ultimate defense against intruders. But this last of his metamorphoses defines Proteus's status with reference to the cave of Cyrene. The flux of the river matches the elusive changeability of Proteus and distinguishes his mutable and manifold nature from the original oneness of the timeless source. If, on the cosmological level, the Oceanic cave represents the origin of life in prime matter, ancient allegorical interpretation identifies Proteus as matter advanced to the stage of form or disposition to form. His many shapes reflect the infinite forms which matter may assume.[9]

Aristaeus sees at first hand the eternal generative process of nature, from the beginnings of life at the self-renewing source to the panoply of creation. The trip from Cyrene to Proteus is thus an allegorical doublet to the *bugonia* by which Aristaeus will succeed in regenerating the species of his bees. But Proteus now proceeds to tell the story-within-a-story of Orpheus, in which the human individual is excluded from nature's cycle. After Eurydice dies, bitten by a serpent while fleeing from the erotic pursuit of the self-same Aristaeus, Orpheus ventures not to the source but to the dark underworld. His attempt to resurrect Eurydice fails, and Proteus's narrative ends with the head of the dismembered poet being carried away upon the river Hebrus, the waters not of generation but of temporal flux and oblivion. The opposition of human mortality to natural palingenesis is the obvious starting point for an interpretation of the epyllion. What remains unexplained, however, is why the tragic protagonist of human loss should also be the archetypal poet, how poetry links together the Aristaeus-Proteus and Orpheus-Eurydice stories. One link may be found in the double identity of the oracular Proteus, who, if he is a figure for a manifold nature, is also a classical figure of the poet-orator. Through Proteus, natural regeneration is made analogous to poetic representation and particularly to a divine, truthtelling order of poetry. The problem of a natural renewal which excludes and alienates the human individual is reproposed in the opposition of two rival versions of poetic creation, the shape-changing of Proteus and Orpheus's song.

In his essay on Demosthenes, Dionysius of Halicarnassus uses the example of Proteus to praise the orator's range of expression:

> It thus had a character not at all unlike that of Proteus as portrayed by the mythological poets, who effortlessly assumed every kind of shape, being either a god or superhuman, with the power to deceive human eyes, or a clever man with the power to vary his speech and so beguile every ear: the latter alternative seeming the more likely, since it is irreverent to attribute mean and unbecoming appearances to gods and superhuman beings.[10]

Dionysius's distinction takes special care not to pay Demosthenes a backhanded compliment. The figure of Proteus is as morally ambiguous as the art it is used to describe. The orator's persuasiveness must be separated from the sophist's deception. Behind Dionysius's passage lie several Platonic texts. In the second book of the *Republic* (381d), Socrates attacks the Proteus myth, among others, because it suggests that a divinity could be capable of multiplicity.

> Then God is altogether simple and true in deed and word, and neither changes himself nor deceives others by visions or words or the sending of signs in waking or in dreams.[11]

"There is no lying poet in God," Socrates remarks in the same passage. Misrepresentation by figures and words is the source of opinion as opposed to truth. In the *Euthydemus* (288b) and the *Euthyphro* (15d), those dealers in opinion, the sophists, and sophistical reasoners are dubbed with the name of Proteus.[12] The figure also appears at the end of the *Ion*. Socrates has deflated the claims of the rhapsode Ion to speak knowledgeably on all subjects.

> you will not even tell me what subject it is on which you are so able, though all this while I have been entreating you to tell. No, you are just like Proteus, you twist and turn, this way and that, assuming every shape, until finally you elude my grasp and reveal yourself a general.[13]

Socrates ironically turns the encyclopedic pretensions of the rhapsode's poetry against him. Used in Dionysius's *second* sense, the skilled human orator rather than the divine trickster, the comparison to Proteus would praise the scope and variety of the verses which Ion recites. But Socrates intends the other sense of the figure and sees in the very multiplicity of poetry the mark of its lack of authority. The two meanings of the figure, Proteus as ideal poet-orator and Proteus as sophist, persist through and beyond the Renaissance.[14]

Virgil assigns to Proteus the title of "vates" (387), which combines the categories of seer and poet. His transformations can be understood as the words and figures of poetic language. The displacement of Proteus from Cyrene's cave would then stand for the temporal distance between poetic representation and a timeless source of meaning. Virgil's allegory operates on two levels and draws an analogy between the cosmological Proteus and the mimetic Proteus. As nature advances watery prime matter—which the eye cannot observe in its original state—into form and the different orders and species of creatures, so a timeless originary meaning is differentiated in time by language and representation. In Cyrene's cave, Aristaeus arrives at a pure origin which, because it is undifferentiated, cannot represent itself and is inaccessible to his understanding.[15] He is detoured instead to Proteus who, capable of an infinite variety of shapes, embodies the principle of difference itself.

Proteus at first takes too many forms and his multiplicity is bewildering. But it is precisely because he stands for a totalized language, comprising all possible modes of representation, that once he is bound—reduced to a syntactically ordered instrument of knowledge—Proteus can re-present an original significance and become a truthtelling "vates." The cosmological analogy still holds good. For Heraclitus the allegorist, the bound Proteus stands for truth, for the truth of nature lies in the constant principles of matter obscured by the mutability of forms.[16] Representation participates in truth as the form participates in the being of material creation, but both lie outside the timeless truth contained in being itself: Proteus is therefore displaced from Cyrene's cave of origin.

But paradoxically, the truth which Proteus proceeds to tell as the embodiment of an ideal, completely adequate language of representation is the story of Orpheus: the hopeless displacement of human poetic language from a truth outside of time and beyond its representation.

In the *Symposium*, Plato sounds a discordant note among the interpreters of the Orpheus myth. Orpheus's underworld descent in search of Eurydice is the gesture not of true love, but of insufficient love.

> And yet the gods sent Orpheus away from Hades emptyhanded, and showed him the mere shadow (φάσμα) of the woman he had come to seek. Eurydice herself they would not let him take, because he seemed, like the mere minstrel he was, to be a lukewarm lover, lacking the courage to die as Alcestis died for love, and choosing rather to scheme his way, living, into Hades.[17] [179d]

Plato asserts (1) that Orpheus does not resurrect Eurydice but rather receives in her place her shadow or mimetic double, and (2) that his venture into Hades actually evades the problem of death. The substitute Eurydice given to an Orpheus singled out and deprecated as a poet indicates that the myth may have been understood in antiquity as an allegory of poetic creation. The Eurydice whom Orpheus obtains *through* his singing would in fact be the re-creation of the dead woman *in* his song. A juxtaposition of the Orpheus-Eurydice myth and the theme of mimetic duplication occurs in the *Alcestis* of Euripides, a passage which Plato may have had in mind. Admetus yearns for the poetic powers of Orpheus in order to restore Alcestis to life (vv. 357–63). His wish follows directly upon verses in which he has expressed his intention to commission a statue of his wife. He will place the image in his room, embrace it, and deceive himself into thinking it is real. Admetus also hopes to see Alcestis in his dreams.[18]

Plato could have found the idea that the infernal gods send up phantasms in the underworld scene of the *Odyssey*. After vainly trying to embrace his mother Antikleia, whose shade flies from his grasp like a dream (ὄυειρω), Odysseus wonders whether Persephone has only sent him an image (εἴόωλον). Odysseus does not descend to Hades but rather summons up the shades of the dead by means of a ritual sacrifice. Homer's description of the dead spirits ascending to earth (*Odyssey* 11.36–43) is imitated in the *Fourth Georgic* when the shades rise up from the depths of the underworld at the sound of Orpheus's song (471–77).

Orpheus summons up Eurydice from where she and her fellow shades are held fast in the waves of the Cocytus and Styx (478–80). These infernal rivers flow from a common source, the river Ocean, in the myth of the *Phaedo*, where death and birth coexist in the cycle of metempsychosis. As Virgil divides features of *Odyssey* XI between the two episodes of Aristaeus and Orpheus so that Aristaeus's consultation with Proteus has overtones of a trip to the underworld, he now separates out the elements of landscape conflated together in his Platonic literary model, making the underworld into a dark parody of Cyrene's source cave. There is thus a carefully established symmetry between the descents of Aristaeus and Orpheus.

But this symmetry points up the differences between the two stories: the transformations of Proteus and the song of Orpheus which summons Eurydice back into being are antithetical models of the poetic act. Proteus is the vessel of timeless, originary truth, to which his divine representation is related as a river is to its source. But Orpheus's song has its "source" in death, that is, within a human history conditioned by mortality. His poetry attempts to recreate and repeat the experience of his love for Eurydice—now part of an irrecoverable past. Wrestled with and bound, Proteus delivers his oracle. But Eurydice speaks only to bid Orpheus farewell and slips out of his vain embrace (494–502): by raising her up again, Orpheus merely confirms the fact of her loss.

While Proteus is capable of endless transformations and shapes, Orpheus's song is circumscribed by his desire, to which only that song can give a name: eventually the song reduces itself to the name of the lost Eurydice, which it endlessly *repeats*, even as his severed head rolls upon the flood. By naming, human language differentiates men one from another, lending them personal identities unavailable in the Protean, anonymous natural order to which the bees of the *Fourth*

Georgic belong. Without the individualizing name, the desire of natural creatures is reduced to an impersonal reproductive drive: the bees
are said to have eliminated desire—and personality—altogether by
procreating asexually (197–202).[19] Although the bees live less than
seven years, their species goes on immortal (208), and the perfectly
stoical bees do not seem to know the difference. But the human name
allows man to recognize the temporality of his desire and alienates
him from the natural process of generation in which he nonetheless
participates. Whereas the bees of Aristaeus may be revived through
the *bugonia,* a collective renewal of the hive, individual human beings,
first Eurydice and then Orpheus himself, are swept away by death. In
the epyllion, the pursuit of sexual desire inevitably leads to a confrontation with mortality and loss. Eurydice flees from the lustful Aristaeus into the deadly jaws of the serpent, just as she will later elude the
grasp of the overly desirous Orpheus and return to Hades. Neither
male can possess her, and both are left with asexual substitutions.
Aristaeus receives the technique of apiculture. Orpheus, in what is the
founding and defining act of human poetry, rejects the love of all other
women (516) and clings to the song which now repeatedly raises up
the object of his desire.

If Orpheus's song is tied to its historical moment of origin—
pointing to the death of Eurydice—the song itself can be repeated. In
contrast to the timeless truth of Proteus's oracle, Orpheus seeks to
console himself with the timelessness of the poetic artifact. For in the
song which persists, unchanged, across time—even beyond
Orpheus's death—Eurydice lives on and Orpheus continues as her
lover. His desire refuses to accept for itself the temporality which her
loss has made all too evident. Perhaps one may understand in this
sense Plato's assertion that Orpheus receives a mimetic substitute
because of his fear of death. Finding a kind of stability in language,
Orpheus attempts to remove his desire from natural and historical
process, though now the desire and the song which names it point to
one another in a narcissistic act of self-definition. In the process of
keeping true to the memory of Eurydice, Orpheus's desire seems to
shift from the dead woman to the memorializing artifact, which
assumes an autonomous existence of its own.[20]

The story of Orpheus indicates a middle ground for human
poetry between a constantly self-regenerating, nameless nature and a
divine language of truth—*both* of which are allegorized in the figure of
Proteus. Man's language gives him an individual identity and an

awareness of time that distinguishes him from the rest of natural creation. Yet that same language does not transcend the historical individuality which it creates and cannot explain a human existence tragically conditioned by historical loss.

As a threnodic coda, the epyllion looks back upon Virgil's four-book poem. The agricultural program outlined in the *Georgics* attempts to recover a unity between man and nature lost at the end of the Golden Age (1.118 ff.). But whatever the success of the farmer Aristaeus in wresting a livelihood from the soil—the culminating *bugonia* merges agricultural technique with the miraculous generative processes of nature itself—in the failure of Orpheus, Virgil acknowledges an inconsolable human mortality. It is in the nature of the poetry of which they are composed—a poetry whose origins lie in human history rather than at the divine source—that the *Georgics* recognize man's irrevocable alienation from the natural order.

Renaissance authors who imitated the *Fourth Georgic* could find in Virgil's fiction of the source a myth about poetic origins and an opposition between rival forms of poetry. The figure of Proteus embodied a vatic poetry that re-presented the truth of a timeless source. The poetry of Orpheus, on the other hand, was the self-expression of its autonomous human creator, a discourse caught in the flow of time and history. Virgil's model was thus already well suited for Renaissance writers who turned to the figure of the source in order to assess the nature and authority of their own fictions, and who tried to measure literature's claim to allegorical sanctions against their awareness that literature was the product of individual, historical authors. For no writer was this model more congenial than for Jacopo Sannazaro who, as my next chapter will argue, defined the possibilities of his literary career between the Virgilian alternatives of Orpheus and Proteus.

3

Sannazaro: From Orpheus to Proteus

EPIC AND PASTORAL

At mihi paganae dictant silvestria Musae
    Carmina, quae tenui gutture cantat Amor.
Fidaque secretis respondet silva querelis,
    Et percussa meis vocibus antra sonant.
Nec tantum populos, nec tantum horrescimus urbes,
    Quantum non iustae saevitiam dominae.
Hoc vitae genus, hoc studium mihi fata ministrant;
    Hinc opto cineres nomen habere meos.
Me probet umbrosis pastorum turba sub antris,
    Dum rogat agrestem lacte tepente Palem.
Me rudis indocta moduletur arundine Thyrsis;
    Et tam constanti laudet amasse fide.
Inde super tumulumque meum, Manesque sepultos
    Tityrus ex hedera serta virente ferat.
Hic mihi saltabit Corydon, et pulcher Alexis,
    Damoetas flores sparget utraque manu.
Fluminibusque sacris umbras inducet Iolas,
    Dum coget saturas Alphesiboeus oves.
Non mihi Moeonidem, Luci, non cura Maronem
    Vincere: si fiam notus amore, sat est.
Quid feret Aeacides nobis, quid cautus Ulysses?
    Quid pius Aeneas, Ascaniusve puer?
Ista canat alii, quorum stipata triumphis
    Musa vagum e tumulis nomen in astra ferat.[1]

[To me let the rustic Muses dictate their sylvan melodies, which Love sings with his delicate throat. The faithful woods answer my secret complaints, and the caves resound, struck by my voice. I do not fear so

44

much people and cities as the cruelty of my unjust Lady. Let the fates afford me this manner of life and this occupation; from it I hope that my ashes will achieve renown. Let me be acceptable to the band of shepherds in their shady grottoes, while they propitiate rural Pales with warm milk. Let rude Thyrsis accompany me on his unskilled Pan-pipe, and let him praise me for having loved with such constant faith. Let Tityrus proffer a garland of fresh ivy upon my tomb and buried remains. There Corydon and fair Alexis will dance for me and Damoetas will strew flowers with both hands. Iolas will spread shade over the sacred rivers while Alphesiboeus drives home the well-fed sheep. O Lucius, it is not my care to vanquish Homer and Virgil; if I become famous through my love, it is enough for me. What is Achilles to us, or prudent Ulysses, what pious Aeneas or the boy Ascanius? Let them be sung by others, whose name the Muse, surrounded by triumphs, carries out of the grave and into the stars.]

Jacopo Sannazaro's elegy recalls similar protestations made by the poets of antiquity, renouncing their aspirations to the lofty genre of epic in favor of humbler poetic veins.[2] However conventional, the opposition of pastoral to epic aptly describes a literary career whose dual achievements are the pastoral "novel," the *Arcadia* (1504), and the *De partu Virginis* (1526), a three-book epic on the subject of the Nativity. The earlier work is written in the *lingua volgare;* the second, in high-style Latin hexameters. The Virgilian pattern of this career, the *rota Vergilii,* is also conventional: more than one Renaissance writer began with the pastoral in order to hone his skills for the more arduous task of epic.[3] But the tension between pastoral and epic continues even within Sannazaro's two major works. The funerary games and the underworld descent in its final two prose sections draw the *Arcadia* toward an "epic" conclusion, while the apparition of the angels to the shepherds of Bethlehem affords the occasion for a pastoral interlude in the third book of the *De partu Virginis*. The question of genre is inseparable from Sannazaro's thematic and poetic concerns. In his fiction, epic and pastoral present conflicting versions of the claims and scope of the literary work.

Pastoral renunciation versus epic aspiration. Where the pastoral is insular, excluding foreign elements from a deliberately restricted literary code, the epic is imperialistic—its usual subject is, not coincidentally, empire—and all-inclusive. The expansionist tendencies of epic, nowhere better evidenced than in a marked taste for catalogues, have led its partisans to claim an encyclopedic status for the genre. Epic swallows up other genres into its own: in order to comprehend the entire range of human experience, the epic poet exploits all literary forms. Hence Tasso, epic's foremost theorist, developed the concept of a mixed style, and hence, too, the frequent inclusion of pastoral oases, as well as dramatic declamations and lyrical set pieces, within the larger epic whole. Epic plenitude—its length, its varied contents, and breadth of style—implicitly equates the epic fiction to the multiplicity of the phenomenal world.

45

But the world of phenomena is caught in time. Epic vastness and variety cannot camouflage the discontinuity between history and the literary text. For even if their aim is an "imperium sine fine," epics, like encyclopedias, go out of date. To counter the threat of obsolescence, epic features conventions by which the divine and the timeless may enter its poetic universe: the heavenly messenger, the underworld descent, the dream, the prophecy. Through such devices, epic announces the interpretation of history which lies at the core of its fiction: it presents itself as a typology that will explain future as well as past and present events. Epic wants to say it all, once and for all.

The timelessness of pastoral is a very different matter. Its literary fiction is grounded in sociological fact. If the action of epic turns around the locus of history and empire, the city—Troy, Rome, Thebes, Paris, Jerusalem, the New Troy, even the New Jerusalem—the pastoral is set in the hinterlands within a peasant culture whose conservatism and resistance to change have been the despair of reformers and revolutionaries alike. Time does not disappear in the countryside, but its measurement according to the shifting course of the seasons, the stuff of almanacs, is the proper subject of the Hesiodic-Virgilian georgic rather than the domain of pastoral. The static quality of rural life, entrenched in custom, apparently self-sufficient and self-contained, inspires the temporal suspension in which so much of pastoral poetry operates. The fiction of timelessness is reinforced in Renaissance pastoral by its association with the Golden Age, that era which is *not* history because it either preceded history or may come again at the end of history. The messianic prophecy of the Golden Age, whose prototype was found in Virgil's *Fourth Eclogue,* recasts the world in pastoral's own image, a "pastoralization" which eventually replaces history with ahistory.

From the vantage point of the bower, history is an external force beyond the pastoralist's control or understanding. The outside political world may be the guarantor of the contentment and security of a shepherd like Tityrus in Virgil's *First Eclogue,* and the pastoral fiction of an unchanging, happy rural status quo can easily be appropriated by a conservative ideology which asserts that a benign relationship exists between the powers that be and the lower, weaker classes of society.[4] But the very powerlessness of the shepherd—of the unlucky Meliboeus who in the same eclogue is driven out of his home in Arcady— generally darkens his view of history, whether it is seen as a capricious political order or, in larger terms, as the plague of time and death, the charnel house of Florence from whose contagion the young people of the *Decameron* retreat to Fiesole. To these ills the pastoral offers no solution but evasion and absorption into its bucolic routine. The pastoralist is too busy setting his own house in order to ponder the dissolution of history or his own mortality. The pastoral retreat may finally be an interior movement toward the self which imposes upon its carefully delimited surroundings a coherence unavailable in the greater world outside the bower.[5] The poetic voice, too, is humble and private. Where the epic poet speaks for the community or nation, and invokes the "divine" voice of a collective history, the pastoral poet speaks for himself.

If history menaces the shepherds at the beginning of Virgil's *Eclogues,* desire proves too much for the pastoral at their end. In the *Tenth Eclogue,* Gallus is driven out of the bower by the love that conquers all. As he bids farewell to Arcady, Gallus fantasizes two versions of pastoral solace for his unrequited passion. In verses 31–43, he imagines a pastoral *locus amoenus* of consummated love in which his beloved Lycoris herself would lie in his embrace. In verses 50–60, however, pastoral activities are suggested as a means of forgetting Lycoris and sublimating his desire. Thomas Rosenmeyer, who suggests an Epicurean philosophical basis for the contentment of Theocritus's shepherds, stresses this second idea—the renunciation of eros. "The naturalness of love is tempered by its lack of consummation; the herdsman either refuses love, or he loves without success. Only in this way can the poet control passion within the boundaries that it needs to observe so as not to dispel the mood of the noon peace."[6] In Virgil's *Second Eclogue,* after a passionate erotic outburst, Corydon simply returns to work and dismisses Alexis from his mind. To turn again to the example of the *Decameron,* despite all the scandalous sexual goings-on in the *novelle,* and although several of its members are known to be in love with one another, the pastoral community in Fiesole remains remarkably chaste. Gallus's first dream of a consummated love, however, never disappears from the pastoral. Its literary beneficiaries include Angelica and Medoro in the *Orlando furioso* and Adam and Eve in Milton's Eden. Consummation and renunciation alternate in the medieval subgenre of the *pastourelle*, where the country maid may or may not bestow her favors upon the amorous knight, and they turn up again as the two opposing positions in the late Renaissance debate between Tasso and Guarini over the pastoral swain's disposition to free love or to chastity.

Insofar as each removes desire, consummation and renunciation are two sides of the same coin, which is why Gallus could attribute both of them to the pastoral Never Never Land in the first place. Sexual desire is the sign of man's participation in the world of generation and history which the pastoral seeks to exclude and to which Gallus—despite his wishful thinking—will return, thereby concluding Virgil's book of eclogues. But desire *of any kind* implies a temporal narrative sequence—which is at odds with pastoral's present tense (and which the pastoral of erotic consummation eliminates by keeping the desired object eternally present to the lover). Denying the existence of wants that cannot be satisfied within the spatial and temporal confines of the bower, the pastoral renounces desire per se.

These themes of pastoral—evasion of history, containment of desire, absorption into a routine—all point to a poetics of autonomy. The closed world of the bower is the thematized model of the literary text which turns in upon itself, creating meaning through a conventional, internally coherent, and deliberately limited code. This purely literary meaning may be termed "intratextual"; it attempts to free itself from any necessary correspondence to, or dependence upon, the world outside its textual structures—structures which are simplified by pastoral to the point where they become transparent.

On the one hand, the impulse toward poetic autonomy leads to literature for literature's sake and the reduction of the pastoral text to a self-contemplating verbal object. But, on the other, pastoral autonomy is frequently accompanied—and perhaps saved from the charges of facile aestheticism and bad faith—by a skepticism toward the literary text which claims authority outside itself, particularly the authority to tell the truth about history.[7] Pastoral retreats from the life and death questions of human history because it acknowledges that it cannot answer them: the pastoral text evades because it cannot transcend its own historicity. Rather than attempt to overcome the discontinuity between the text and history, the pastoral writer chooses to emphasize and make a virtue of that discontinuity, to proclaim the autonomy of his fiction from history. This autonomy is apparently confirmed by the capacity of the text, and particularly of a fixed tradition of bucolic texts, to withstand history and to lend an aura of timelessness to their meaning—not the timelessness of truth, but the permanence of the literary artifact. In the best pastoral literature, history and desire are confronted, reminding the reader that something *does* exist beyond the sophisticated game of meaning which the text plays according to its own predetermined rules. But should the problems of human history become too insistent and demand of the text some other solution than evasion or renunciation, the pastoral fiction confesses its lack of authority and the game comes to an end. The desire contained and quelled within the bower is, in the last analysis, the desire to go outside the text and its conventional structures of meaning.

The reemergence of the epic and pastoral genres in Renaissance literature may be linked to different attitudes toward the authority of the literary text. Pastoral meaning points to the textual structures from which it is exclusively produced; epic meaning claims to derive from a transcendent source outside the text. The turn in Jacopo Sannazaro's career from the *Arcadia* to the *De partu Virginis* reflects a conscious attempt to transcend a self-enclosed, ultimately inauthentic pastoral fiction and to ground the literary text in authorized truth: his epic meditates on nothing less than the Incarnation. Both works thematize the epistemological implications of their poetics with a descent to the source of rivers in imitation of the *Fourth Georgic*, and each emphasizes a different aspect of Virgil's epyllion. The intratextual fiction of the *Arcadia*, acknowledging the inadequacy of its language in the face of history, stresses the poetic failure of Orpheus. The *De partu Virginis*, celebrating in epic verse the fullness of the Word which gives meaning to all history, features the prophetic voice of Proteus.

THE *ARCADIA*

Any discussion of the *Arcadia* must begin with the problem of dating. The first ten eclogues and prose sections of the work can be found in a manuscript of 1489. They also appeared in an inaccurate pirate printing of 1501. The authorized printed edition was published in 1504, edited by Pietro Summonte, the friend of Sannazaro who turns up as a speaker in Eclogue 12. The book now contained twelve eclogues and prose sections and an epilogue in the form of an address to the pastoral reedpipe *(A la sampogna)*. The provenance and dating of the additional material and its relationship to the earlier version of the *Arcadia* have created scholarly controversy and, beyond the controversy, raised serious questions about the nature and meaning of the book.

The problem is complicated by the biography of the poet.[8] In 1501, after a series of wars that began with the invasion and expulsion of Charles VIII and his French forces in 1495–96, the Aragonese king of Naples, Federico II, was deposed and the kingdom fell under foreign hegemony, divided between France and Spain. At the beginning of Prosa 12, the narrator Sincero has an allegorical dream in which he hears the Siren Parthenopea, the personification of Naples, weeping. As he listens to her, a great wave from the ocean overwhelms him, apparently symbolizing a foreign invasion of the city. Finally, he sees a cut-down orange tree (Arangio), an emblem of the House of Aragon. This dream could refer *either* to the events of 1495 or those of 1501.

Sannazaro joined his patron, Federico, in exile in France. Living in retirement away from his native city, the poet fulfilled the typology of his pastoral fiction. This historical coincidence has led some scholars to place the composition of the final two eclogues and prose sections of the *Arcadia* during the years of exile. The unauthorized edition of 1501 may have caused him to reexamine his book. In this case, the return in Prosa 12 to a city of Naples seen under the aspect of death would reflect the post-1501 political realities. Sannazaro, however, did not himself return to Naples until 1505, after the death of Federico and the publication of the twelve-eclogue *Arcadia*.

In an important study, Eduardo Saccone has argued for the unity of the whole *Arcadia* and suggested a date for its final two eclogues and prose sections in the 1490s. Saccone notes that the intervention of history in Eclogue 10, a satiric invective against the times, signals a new departure in the book which cannot be reconciled with the material which has preceded it. Eclogue 10 could not therefore end a "first" *Arcadia*, but rather links the first ten eclogues to the final two, which contain the narrator's return to the historical world of Naples: the twelve-eclogue version would have been implicit from the start.[9]

The present reading of the *Arcadia* accepts the theory of two separate periods of composition, one in the 1480s and one following the poet's exile in 1501. While Saccone is correct in arguing that the final two prose sections and eclogues repeat the concerns of Eclogue 10, unifying the twelve-eclogue *Arcadia*, there is also reason to believe that the ten-eclogue *Arcadia*, attested to in the manuscript tradition and in the 1501 printing, was also an integral and complete artistic conception. The numbers of eclogues involved are significant in themselves. Epics come in multiples of twelve—the *Aeneid* in twelve books, the Homeric poems in twenty-four. The numerical demands of the form seem to have caused the expansion of *Paradise Lost* from ten to twelve books, of the twenty-book *Gerusalemme liberata* to the twenty-four book *Gerusalemme conquistata*. But if the twelve-eclogue structure introduces an epic element into the final 1504 version of the *Arcadia*, ten, the number of Virgil's *Eclogues*, is the preeminent pastoral number. Sannazaro's Eclogue 10, moreover, imitates features of Virgil's *Tenth Eclogue*, the Gallus eclogue, in which the acknowledgement of pressures which will lead the protagonist out of Arcady and back into the historical world signals the end of the pastoral sequence. The disjunction between Eclogue 10 and the rest of the *Arcadia* does not necessarily indicate a new starting point in the direction of the subsequently added eleventh and twelfth eclogues. Rather, it brings the early ten-eclogue *Arcadia* to a conventional Virgilian conclusion.

Before the pastoral tone is broken by Eclogue 10, a thin plot thread has emerged from the *Arcadia's* extended, repetitive descriptions of an idyllic landscape. The narrator Sincero has left Naples because of unrequited love for his childhood sweetheart, yet he finds in Arcadia little of the traditional pastoral solace for unhappy lovers (Prosa 7). He encounters two amorous shepherds who mirror his own state of mind, Carino, once suicidal, but now a hopeful optimist, and the desperate Clonico, who loves in vain (Prosa 8). When some customary pastoral advice on erotic desire, urging the shepherd to return to work in order to forget his passion, fails to impress Clonico (Eclogue 8), he is led before the shepherd wizard Enareto. In the tenth prose section, Enareto gives a long description of the magical rites he will perform either to remove Clonico's desire ("E se uscire da amore totalmente vorrai") or to charm his hardhearted mistress to return his affections ("Ma se più tosto la tua nemica ad amarti di costringere tieni in desio"). Clonico may choose between the pastoral alternatives of erotic renunciation and consummation. The magical "cure" appears to resolve the problem of desire and to conclude the plot which love had set in motion. Eclogue 10 follows as a kind of anticlimax.

This eclogue carefully reverses the pattern of the larger book. The shepherd Selvaggio, tormented by love, leaves the bower and goes to Naples. Attesting to a desire which the pastoral cannot contain,

Selvaggio is reminiscent of Virgil's Gallus. Soon another Gallus figure emerges in the poem, Sannazaro's friend and fellow poet, Gian Francesco Caracciolo, with whose praises Eclogue 10 will end, much as the *Tenth Eclogue* had ended with the celebration of Gallus and his poetry. Selvaggio describes his visit in Naples to the "academy" of learned poets who have gathered around Giovanni Pontano (31 ff.). He singles out Caracciolo's satires for praise, and the greater part of the eclogue is taken up by Caracciolo's song, a furious and frightening invective against the times. Saccone has identified the period of strife and civil disorder which Caracciolo describes with the rebellion of the Neapolitan barons against the central authority of the Crown in the early 1480s.[10] But much of Caracciolo's complaint is phrased in general, and hence all the more cataclysmic, terms: his fear, for example, of a second flood.

> E le nubi spezzate   fan gran suoni
> tanti baleni e tuoni   han l'aria involta
> ch'io temo un'altra volta   il mondo pera.[11]   [90-92]

[And the shattered clouds make great noises, so much lightning and thunder has enveloped the air that I fear lest the world should perish a second time.]

Like Virgil's Gallus, Caracciolo would like to escape from this historical chaos and make for idyllic Arcady, yet forces beyond his control keep him in Naples.

> E, se non fusse che 'l suo gregge affrenalo,
> e tienlo a forza ne l'ingrata patria,
> che a morte desïiar spesso rimenalo,
>   verrebbe a noi, lassando l'idolatria
> e gli ombrati costumi al guasto secolo,
> fuor già d'ogni natia carità patria.   [189–194]

[And if his flock did not restrain him and keep him by force in his ungrateful country which makes him want to die, he would come to us, leaving its idolatry and false customs to the ruined age which has abandoned all native love of country.]

Virgil dramatized the disorder of the world outside the pastoral enclosure through the inner disorder of Gallus's passion. Sannazaro's eclogue, with its two Gallus figures, moves from the private love of Selvaggio to Caracciolo's satiric description of the public world falling in ruin around him.

A satiric view of history is implicit in the pastoral retreat of the *Arcadia*. In Eclogue 6, the shepherds Serrano and Opico discourse at length on a world which goes "di male in peggio" and has been deteriorating steadily since the Golden Age which the pastoral attempts to imitate. Eclogue 10 merely reveals the dark turmoil of history which had lain out of sight and out of mind beyond the confines of the bower. And that historical world appears precisely as a blighted Arcady. Naples and its inhabitants are dressed up as bower and shepherds; the satirist Caracciolo is presented as a swain trying to cure his flocks from an infectious disease. In his song, the pastoral deities and nymphs head up a list of angry gods who have ceased their benign functions in nature and threaten to destroy the world (93–128). The catalogue ends with Astraea abandoning the earth: "La donna e la bilancia è gita al cielo" ("The lady with her scales has gone to heaven"; 156). Sannazaro recalls the flight of Astraea back to the heavens at the end of Ovid's description of the Iron Age (*Metamorphoses* 1. 150); he intends, as did Ovid, an inversion of the "iam redit et Virgo" which begins the Golden Age prophecy of Virgil's *Fourth Eclogue*. Seen under the aspect of history, the pastoral vision disintegrates.

Naples out of joint, then, is the underside of Arcady. Eclogue 10 transfers the autonomy of pastoral discourse to history and the result is satire. As the last good man in his decadent age, Caracciolo is sufficient unto himself alone.

> Et è sol di vertù sì chiaro specolo,
> che adorna il mondo col suo dritto vivere;   [195–96]

[And he alone is such a shining mirror of virtue that he adorns the world with his upright life.]

But the autonomous authority of the satirical text is not so much a choice as a necessity, dictated by the inability to find any source of meaning in the world of dissolution it portrays. The truth which the satirist claims as his own is the absence or inaccessibility of any such source. If the pastoral bower constitutes an area of fixed, conventional meaning in which the private poetic voice can operate, when that voice turns outward to history it discovers its isolation and changes to satire—a voice crying in the wilderness.

The pattern of Eclogue 10—the opposition of pastoral and historical worlds which reveals the negativity latent in the pastoral fiction—is repeated in the eleventh and twelfth eclogues of the later 1504 *Arcadia*.

The twelfth eclogue, set in Naples, reproduces the subject matter of the eleventh, sung in Arcady. Both poems are funeral elegies: death, too, is in Arcady.

53

In his well-known study of the pastoral elegiac tradition in the visual arts, Erwin Panofsky distinguishes between a tragic confrontation with death in Theocritus's *First Idyll* and a much softened, more consoling version of the funeral elegy in Virgil's *Fifth Eclogue*. "Virgil does not exclude frustrated love and death; but he deprives them, as it were, of their factuality. He projects tragedy either into the future, or, preferably, into the past, and he thereby transforms mythical truth into elegiac sentiment."[12] Virgil himself points to his revision of the Theocritean lament by appropriating the name of Daphnis, the departed shepherd-poet mourned by the *Fifth Idyll*. His poetic procedure is highly ingenious and somewhat more complicated than Panofsky suggests. In what begins as a singing match between two shepherds, Mopsus describes the disruptive effects of Daphnis's death upon the Arcadian landscape (36–39)—a recognition of the real threat which mortality poses to the pastoral fiction of timelessness. In response, Menalcas removes that threat by announcing Daphnis's apotheosis. In Menalcas's song, Daphnis has become a pastoral god who sheds a benign influence down upon the bucolic world (56 ff.). We do not need to know that Daphnis may stand for the deified Julius Caesar to appreciate how satisfactory a solution in purely pastoral terms Virgil has provided to a pastoral problem. Daphnis never leaves the bower. His loss is immediately dispelled by his divine presence as a tutelary god, a spirit of the place who looks after the shepherd's flocks and contributes to the pastoral peace. His immortality is an alternate version of pastoral timelessness: death transforms him into one more familiar element of the never-changing pastoral world.

The equation between immortal bliss and the contentment within the bower is explicit in Sannazaro's imitation of the *Fifth Eclogue* in his own Eclogue 5 of the *Arcadia*. The shepherd Androgeo is apotheosized into what is presented quite literally as a second bower.

> altri monti, altri piani,
> altri boschetti e rivi
> vedi nel cielo, e più novelli fiori:
> altri Fauni e Silvani
> per luoghi dolci estivi
> seguir le Ninfe in più felici amori.

54

Tal fra soavi odori
dolce cantando all'ombra
tra Dafni e Melibeo
siede il nostro Androgeo,
e di rara dolcezza il cielo ingombra,
temprando gli elementi
col suon de novi inusitati accenti.   [14–26]

[Other mountains, other plains, other thickets and banks you see in heaven, and fresher flowers: other Fauns and Sylvans pursue Nymphs in happier loves through sweet summer places. So, among lovely fragrances, sweetly singing in the shade, our Androgeo sits between Daphnis and Meliboeus, and fills heaven with rare sweetness, tempering the elements with the sound of new unheard-of songs.]

Rhetorically, with its anaphoric repetition of *altri*, the stanza suggests a transfer to a higher, metaphysical plane beyond the bower, and the language hints that Androgeo may have entered the Christian heaven. But, in effect, the bucolic vocabulary places Androgeo in one of a series of identical bowers: the real emphasis lies not on difference or otherness but on similarity.[13] The pastoral reduces all experience to the terms of its finite code, and triumphs over death by admitting no discontinuity between *the way it describes* the happy existences enjoyed by its living and dead shepherds. In the process, the immortality of the deified shepherd is reduced to a sheerly literary existence. This reduction, however, is not concealed but quite explicitly acknowledged by the pastoral fiction: the shepherd is apotheosized into a literary immortality.

In Virgil's eclogue, Mopsus enjoins the grieving shepherds to build a tomb for Daphnis. On it they are to place a verse epitaph describing the fame the dead shepherd's poetry had earned him, a fame that reached to the stars—"ad sidera notus" (43). Menalcas takes up the task.

nos tamen haec quocumque modo tibi nostra uicissim
dicemus, Daphninque tuum tollemus ad astra;
Daphnin ad astra feremus: amauit nos quoque Daphnis.   [50–53]

[nonetheless, we still sing these verses of ours, whatever sort they may be, with you in turn, and we will raise your Daphnis to the stars. We will carry Daphnis to the stars; Daphnis also loved us.]

Menalcas hyperbolically promises to raise Daphnis to the stars, to confer upon him through his own song the fame which Daphnis has already achieved. Mopsus's reply distinguishes between the dead poet and the living one who celebrates him: "et puer ipse fuit cantari dignus, et ista/ iam pridem Stimichon laudauit carmina nobis" ("and the boy himself was worthy to be sung, and long ago now Stimichon praised these songs of yours to us"; 54–55). Whatever his merits as a poet, Daphnis derives his present fame as a character in Menalcas's verse, whose quality is attested to by the praise of the third person, Stimichon. When, in the next line of the eclogue, Menalcas's song begins with Daphnis looking down upon the floor of heaven, the reader may understand the shepherd's apotheosis as a literalization of Menalcas's earlier metaphor. He has placed Daphnis in the stars and conferred upon him the eternal fame of literary immortality. Sannazaro's imitation seems to grant the dead poet-shepherd Androgeo somewhat more power to immortalize himself: he sits in his heavenly bower between Daphnis and Meliboeus, who here stand for Theocritus and Virgil respectively, poets whose verses will live forever. But at the end of the eclogue, Androgeo's immortality depends upon his being the subject rather than the author of poetry.

> né verrà tempo mai
> che'l tuo bel nome estingua
> mentre serpenti in dumi
> saranno, e pesci in fiumi.
> Né sol vivrai ne la mia stanca lingua,
> ma per pastor diversi
> in mille altre sampogne e mille versi.   [59–65]

[nor will there ever come a time that your fair name will be extinguished, as long as there are serpents in brambles and fish in rivers. Nor will you live only on my weary tongue, but through different shepherds on a thousand reedpipes and in a thousand verses.]

Androgeo lives on in song, whether his own or the verses of others who sing his praise. In both Virgil's and Sannazaro's eclogues, the apotheosis is a transparent fiction created before the reader's eyes by the poet-speakers. But apotheosis is also a metaphor for deathless earthly fame. While the eclogue's speakers acknowledge that they are producing a fiction of immortality about the dead shepherd, they simultaneously assert that their fictions, as permanent poetic artifacts, confer a *real* immortality—preserving the shepherd's memory as long as they are read. Like the pastoral bower it mirrors, the timeless realm in which the apotheosized shepherd dwells is disclosed to be the timelessness of literature itself.

Eclogue 11, the funeral elegy which the shepherd Ergasto sings over the tomb of his mother, Massilia, also follows the pattern of Virgil's *Fifth Eclogue*. Just as the Daphnis eclogue is divided between the disconsolate Mopsus and the consoling Menalcas, so Ergasto's song falls into two parts. He begins with an outburst of grief, modeled largely on Moschus's *Lament for Bion*, calling upon nature to sympathize with his sorrow. After he repeats the refrain, "ricominciate, Muse, il vostro pianto," at verse 114, there is a break. Massilia is envisioned in her celestial seat, and the refrain is changed and put to rest at verse 141: "Ponete fine, o Muse, al vostro pianto." Comforted, Ergasto invokes Massilia to shower down her divine influence upon the site of her pastoral tomb.

The tomb has already been described in a remarkable passage at the end of Prosa 10. Panofsky's study demonstrates how the shepherds' encounter with the pastoral tomb changed in the hands of Poussin from a moment of memento mori to an occasion for elegiac reflection upon the past in which the harsh fact of death has been removed. Sannazaro's verbal picture of Massilia's tomb goes a step further. The work of compassionate shepherds has turned her sepulchre into a garden, replete with sculptures, flower beds, and topiary work. The shepherds recline and sing in the bower that contains her resting place.

> Ove molti olmi, molte querce e molti allori sibilando con le tremule frondi, ne si moveano per sovra al capo; ai quali aggiungendosi ancora il mormorare de le roche onde, le quali fuggendo velocissime per le verdi erbe andavano a cercare il piano, rendevano inseme piacevolissimo suono ad udire. E per li ombrosi rami le argute cicale cantando si affaticavano sotto al gran caldo; la mesta Filomena da lunge tra folti spineti si lamentava; cantavano le merole, le upupe e le calandre; piangeva la solitaria tortora per le alte ripe; le sollecite api con suave susurro volavano intorno ai fonti. Ogni cosa redoliva de la fertile estate: redolivano i pomi per terra sparsi, de' quali tutto il suolo dinanzi ai piedi e per ogni lato ne vedevamo in abondanza coverto; sovra ai quali i bassi alberi coi gravosi rami stavano sì inchinati, che quasi vinti dal maturo peso parea che spezzare si volessono.
>
> [where many elms, many oaks, and many laurels whispering with trembling branches moved overhead; to which was added the murmuring of the hoarse waters which, fleeing rapidly through the green grass,

went in search of the plain: together they made a most pleasant sound to hear. And among the shady branches, the clever crickets wearied themselves singing in the great heat; sad Philomel was lamenting from afar among the thick thornbushes; the blackbirds, larks, and lapwings were singing; the solitary turtle-dove was weeping on the high cliffs; the busy bee flew around the springs with soft murmuring. Everything was redolent of fertile summer: the apples were fragrant, gathered on the earth, and on all sides one saw the ground before our feet abundantly covered with them: above which the low trees with their heavy branches stood so bent that it seemed that they wished to break, overcome by the weight of the ripe fruit.]

The tomb is transformed into a *locus amoenus,* delightful to hearing, sight, and smell. The tragedy of death disappears in this pastoral vision of contentment and beauty, and the tomb itself is almost lost in its lush surroundings. Yet the tomb remains the focal point of the garden, for Massilia's presence is said to be the source that instills peace and loveliness into the idyllic landscape.

It is this presence, transferred into the profusion of the garden-tomb, which Ergasto invokes at the end of his song.

> Ma tu, più c'altra, bella et immortale
> anima, che dal ciel forse m'ascolti,
> e mi dimostri al tuo bel coro eguale,
>   impetra a questi lauri ombrosi e folti
> grazia, che con lor sempre verdi fronde
> possan qui ricoprirne ambo sepolti.
>   Et al soave suon di lucide onde
> il cantar degli ucelli ancor si aggiunga,
> acciò che il luogo d'ogni grazia abonde.
>   Ove, se 'l viver mio pur si prolunga
> tanto, che, com'io bramo, ornar ti possa,
> e da tal voglia il ciel non mi disgiunga,
>   spero che sovra te non avrà possa
> quel duro, eterno, ineccitabil sonno
> d'averti chiusa in così poca fossa;
>   se tanto i versi miei prometter ponno.   [145–60]

[But you, soul lovely and immortal beyond others, who perhaps hear me from heaven and point me out to a fair choir of your peers, beseech grace for these thick and shady laurels, so that they may cover us both, buried here, with their evergreen leaves. And to the sweet sound of the shining waters, let the singing of the birds be added, so that the place may abound in every kind of grace. For, if my life lasts so long that I may celebrate you as much as I wish, and if heaven does not disjoin me from this desire, I hope that that lasting, eternal, and undisturbable sleep which has enclosed you in such a little grave will not keep its power over you; if my verses can make so great a promise.]

The perspective suddenly switches in Ergasto's last seven verses. He ceases to pray for Massilia's intervention, but rather for enough remaining life and an adequate poetic style with which to sound her eternal fame. Massilia ceases to condescend from heaven to create a garden ambience for the poet; rather Ergasto promises to raise her from a solemnly described sleep of death into a poetic rather than celestial afterlife. Once again the pastoral apotheosis makes it necessary to reconsider the relationship between Massilia and the garden which enshrines her presence. The "grazia" of verse 149, Massilia's divine influence which Ergasto implores her to rain down upon the site of her tomb, is supposedly the source of the garden's "grazia," its physical charm, at verse 153. But it may instead be this beautifying rather than beatific grace of the man-made garden which creates the idea that her divine spirit must be immanent within its precincts. At the same time, the gracefulness of the garden attracts the Arcadian shepherds to the tomb, bringing Massilia back to their minds and keeping her memory alive. The garden thus becomes a double for Ergasto's elegy: both are artifacts whose high aesthetic qualities insure their lasting fame and the fame of the woman they commemorate. The evergreen laurel trees of the garden are, in fact, the emblem of eternal poetic fame, and the angelic lady who confers not salvation but literary immortality is the invention of Petrarch, whose Laura is named for the laurel wreath which his verses in *her* praise have placed about *his* temples.[14] Ergasto's prayer is, in fact, imitated from *Canzoniere* 327, where the poet, in turn, promises to bestow everlasting fame on Laura's name. Sannazaro skillfully grafts the poetic circularity of the Petrarchan formula onto the fiction of pastoral apotheosis: the apotheosized Massilia is implored to shed her immortal influence upon the garden and the verses which immortalize her. Ergasto hopes eventually to be enshrined in the same laurel-covered tomb he has built for Massilia, an enduring poetic monument that eternizes both author and subject.

The pastoral apotheosis, replacing the dead with the permanent stuff of poetry, repeats the myth of Orpheus, whose song is substituted for the dead Eurydice. Ergasto appeals to the example of a "felice Orfeo" who recovers Eurydice through his verse (64–68), and he subsequently identifies the restorative power of Orpheus's poetry with its *fame*.

> E se le rime mie non son sì note
> come quelle d'Orfeo, pur la pietade
> dovrebbe farle in ciel dolci e devote.   [73–75]

[And if my rhymes are not as famous as those of Orpheus, at least pity ought to make them seem sweet and devoted to heaven.]

The pastoral idea of a successful Orpheus is derived from the final verses of the *Lament for Bion*.

> Could I but have gone down into Tartarus as Orpheus went and Odysseus of yore and Alcides long ago, then would I also have come mayhap to the house of Pluteus, that I might see thee, and if so be thou singest to Pluteus, hear what that thou singest may be. But all the same, I pray thee, chant some song of Sicily, some sweet melodious country-song, unto the Maid; for she too is of Sicily, she too once sported on Etna's shores; she knows the Dorian music; so thy melodies shall not go without reward. Even as once she granted Orpheus his Eurydice's return because he harped so sweetly, so likewise she shall give my Bion back unto the hills; and had but this my pipe the power of that his harp, I had played for this in the house of Pluteus myself.[15]

The poet invokes the powers of Orpheus twice: first to descend to Hades and listen to Bion's poetry; then to bring Bion back to earth. These aims are one and the same, and when Bion is asked to sing his way back to the hills—an Orpheus who rescues himself from death—his restored presence is to be understood as the lasting fame of his verses. The purpose of hills in pastoral poetry is to echo, and the survival of Bion's verses and his name is assured by their repetition by future lovers of poetry. Bion may be dead, but his song will live on, as will the *Lament for Bion* itself, which, despite its poet's disclaimer, successfully performs the Orphic task of raising up and conserving the memory of the dead.

So, too, the mortal Eurydice lives on, memorialized in a poetry that is immortal, that will last as long as poetry is read. The presence or absence of the literary text replaces the human categories of life and death. The name of Eurydice may point to her absence in a world of human experience outside the poetic text, but *within* the text it announces her indelible presence upon the written page. Death similarly occasions no loss in a pastoral fiction which seals itself off from history in the timeless bower. The spirits of the dead, commemorated in bucolic song, remain present in the bower, enjoying the same literary existence as its living shepherds. So long as the bower is constituted by a closed, intratextual code, it not only retains those spirits, but could not, in fact, exorcise them. Ergasto finds the Orphic solution—with no mention of Orpheus's subsequent fate—a perfectly viable model for the pastoral apotheosis.

Pastoral envisions a happy, consoled Orpheus as part of its preference of literature to life, of its rejection of history in favor of a permanent and self-consciously autonomous literary artifact. The reality of death cannot break through into the *Arcadia* until Sincero goes outside the literary realm of the bower, when he leaves Arcady in the twelfth prose section. His return to Naples compels him to confront the historical dissolution from which the pastoral fiction escapes, those temporal forces from which Virgil's Orpheus attempts to remove his song but which overwhelm him nonetheless. The opposition of pastoral to history at the end of the *Arcadia* is specifically presented in terms of alternate readings of the Orpheus myth: the pastoral Orpheus, who recovers Eurydice and compensates human loss with poetry, and the Orpheus of the *Fourth Georgic*, who is caught in history and whose song only measures the extent of his loss.

In Prosa 12, the narrator, waking from his prophetic dreams, allegories of the Neapolitan political crisis, wanders distractedly beside a river. Here Sannazaro's imitation of the *Fourth Georgic* begins. A nymph emerges from the depths. As the waves part in two to reveal the river bed, she leads Sincero into a watery underworld.

> ove molti laghi si vedevano, molte scaturigini, molte spelunche, che rifundevano acque, da le quali i fiumi che sovra la terra correno prendono le loro origini.

> [where many lakes were seen, many springs, many caves, which poured forth waters, from which the rivers which flow above the earth take their origins.]

Virgil's weaving nymphs of the source are here, too.

> E quivi dentro sovra verdi tappeti trovammo alcune Ninfe sorelle di lei, che con bianchi e sottilissimi cribri cernivano oro, separandolo da le minute arene. Altre filando il riducevano in mollissimo stame, e quello con sete di diversi colori intessevano in una tela di meraviglioso artificio; ma a me, per lo argomento che in sé conteneva, augurio infelicissimo di

future lacrime. Con ciò sia cosa che nel mio intrare trovai per sòrte che tra li molti ricami tenevano allora in mano i miserabili casi de la deplorata Euridice; sì come nel bianco piede punta dal velenoso aspide fu costretta di esalare la bella anima, e come poi per ricoprarla discese a l'inferno, e ricoprata la perdé la seconda volta lo smemorato marito.

[And inside there we saw some Nymphs, her sisters, on green carpets, who with white and very fine sieves were sifting gold, separating it from the tiny sands. Others were spinning it out into a very soft thread, and they were weaving it with silks of different colors into a cloth of marvellous artifice; but for me, because of the story which it contained, it was a most unhappy augury of future tears. For on my entry I found by chance that among their many tapestries they were holding in their hands the woeful story of the lamented Eurydice: how, stung in her white foot by a poisonous asp she was forced to breathe out her fair spirit, and how later her husband descended to Hell to recover her and, having recovered her, the forgetful man lost her a second time.]

The happy Orpheus of the pastoral fiction has been left behind in Arcady. His immediate replacement, an emblem both for Sincero's fate and for the relationship of poetry and history, is the Virgilian Orpheus, who recovers Eurydice only to renew his loss. In his conflation of the elements of the *Fourth Georgic* epyllion, the story of Orpheus is located at the source instead of Clymene's cosmogonic song. Virgil depicted the oceanic source as a locus of the eternal meaning of creation made inaccessible to man in his mortal existence. Sannazaro condenses the Virgilian fiction by turning the source into a nonsource, finding nothing there but the mortality that confounds all human meaning. "Non senza volontà del Cielo fai ora questo cammino" ("Not without the will of Heaven do you now make this journey"), the nymph solemnly tells Sincero, echoing the words of Virgil in Dante's *Commedia* (*Inferno* 21.82) and, perhaps more pertinently, those of the apparition of the dead Creusa in the second book of the *Aeneid* (vv. 776 ff.). Creusa is as irrecoverable as Eurydice,[16] but she extends to Aeneas epic's promise of an ultimate coherence in history as a consolation for her loss. But if the underground journey seems to lead in the direction of epic, it offers no revelation of transcendent meaning to redeem a history presented exclusively in terms of destruction and death. On his way, Sincero finds himself in the volcanic environs of the bay of Naples.

—Sotto ai quali chi sarà mai che creda che e populi e ville e città nobilissime siano sepolte? Come veramente vi sono, non solo quelle che da le arse pomici e da la ruina del monte furon coperte, ma questa che dinanzi ne vedemo, la quale senza alcun dubbio celebre città un tempo nei tuoi paesi, chiamata Pompei, et irrigata da le onde del freddissimo Sarno, fu per sùbito terremoto inghiottita da la terra, mancandoli credo sotto ai piedi il firmamento ove fundata era. Strana per certo et orrenda maniera di morte, le gente vivi vedersi in un punto tòrre dal numero de' vivi! Se non che finalmente sempre si arriva ad un termino, né più in là che a la morte si puote andare.—

E già in queste parole eramo ben presso a la città che lei dicea, de la quale e le torri e le case e i teatri e i templi si poteano quasi integri discernere.

["Beneath which who would ever believe that peoples and villas and most noble cities are buried? As, in truth, there are, not only those which were covered by the burnt pumice and the collapse of the mountain, but this which we see before us, which was once without any doubt a famous city in your region called Pompeii, irrigated by the waters of the cold Sarno, was swallowed up into the earth by a sudden earthquake, the ground giving way upon which it was founded. Surely a strange horrible manner of death, living people seeing themselves in one instant removed from the ranks of the living! Were it not that ultimately one arrives at one destination, nor can one go any farther from there except to death."

And with these words we were now very near the city of which she spoke, whose towers, houses, theaters, and temples could be seen almost entirely preserved.]

The terrifying vision of Pompeii shows history as a process of dissolution which eventually buries everything human.[17] Man's existence is pure contingency, the "un punto" in which the earth opens up to swallow the city and its monuments. The only certainty is death, the common and inescapable endpoint.

Sincero soon discovers his personal implication in this nihilistic prospect of history. His underground journey culminates at the fountain of the Neapolitan river Sebeto—the national, patriotic source. There he finds the nymphs surrounding the river-god weeping and in disarray. Two nymphs lead him toward the stricken city and announce to him the death of his lady during his absence in Arcady. His private loss is conflated with, and made to stand for, the destruction of the public, political world under the impact of foreign invasion. He has nothing to come home to now that, in the words of the twelfth eclogue, "Napoli tua non è più Napoli" (117). Whatever sources of value, love, and community may have resided in the city have now disappeared.

Lettore, io ti giuro, se quella deità che in fin qui di scriver questo mi ha prestato grazia, conceda, qualunque elli si siano, immortalità agli scritti miei, che io mi trovai in tal punto sì desideroso di morire, che di qualsivoglia maniera di morte mi sarei contentato. Et essendo a me medesmo venuto in odio, maladissi l'ora che da Arcadia partito mi era, e qualche volta intrai in speranza che quello che io vedeva et udiva fusse pur sogno

63

[Reader, I swear to you, if that deity which up until now has lent me the grace to write concedes immortality to my writings, whatsoever sort they may be, that I found myself at that point so desirous of dying that I would have been contented with any manner of death whatsoever. And having come to hate myself, I cursed the hour that I had departed from Arcadia, and at times I entered into the hope that what I was seeing and hearing was only a dream.]

Sincero has seen Naples and wants to die—or at least to awaken from the bad dream of history. But the real dream-world is pastoral Arcady, free from history and immune to death. The pattern of Eclogue 10 has been repeated: a return to the historical city in crisis which reveals the inauthenticity of the pastoral fiction and brings it to an end. Yet the nostalgia for the pastoral remains. Like Caracciolo and the Virgilian prototype Gallus, Sincero, too, yearns to escape from history and desire to the self-contained world of the bower. Pastoral and history mutually criticize each other. If history relegates pastoral to the status of wishful thinking and dream, from the pastoral vantage point history is a nightmare.

Sincero swears by whatever literary immortality may be conceded to him that he wished for death on his return to Naples. The phrase here applied to his writings—"qualunque elli si siano"—rhetorically balances the "qualsivoglia maniera di morte" he would have welcomed. But whereas the pastoral fiction, exemplified by the apotheosis of Massilia in Ergasto's elegy in Eclogue 11, offers literary immortality as a consolation for death, Sincero, even as he holds out the prospect of eternal fame, portrays himself as inconsolable. The narrator's address to the reader begins a revision of Eclogue 11 that continues in Eclogue 12, the closing poem of the *Arcadia*. Here, as again was the case of Caracciolo in the tenth eclogue, the speakers Summonzio and Barcinio are identifiable members of the Neapolitan poetic circle of Sannazaro and Pontano. Summonzio is Pietro Summonte and Barcinio is the sonneteer il Cariteo (the Spaniard Benedetto Gareth). The two of them recite the verses of Meliseo, which they have overheard or found written upon the trees and bushes of Naples—verses that mourn the death of Meliseo's beloved Fillide. Meliseo is Pontano himself, and Eclogue 12 is modeled on the *Meliseus,* Pontano's superb Latin elegy to his dead wife Adriana.[18] Even more so than the conventional pastoral elegy, Sannazaro's final eclogue is a poem about poets talking about poetry. But the fact that these shepherds are real-life poets talking in Naples rather than Arcady signals the general movement of the *Arcadia* into the perspective of history, where the conventional consolation offered by the pastoral elegy can be measured against an authentic human experience of loss.

At first, however, Eclogue 12 seems to copy the elegiac formula of Eclogue 11. The shepherds begin by reading Meliseo's verses on the effect of Fillide's death on the Neapolitan scenery. In a passage which continues the imagery of Sincero's prose narrative, Meliseo addresses the Sebeto.

> Quanti pastor, Sebeto, e quanti populi
> morir vedrai di quei che in te s'annidano,
> pria che la riva tua si inolmi o impopuli!
> Lasso, già ti onorava il grande Eridano,
> e 'l Tebro al nome tuo lieto inchinavasi;
> or le tue Ninfe appena in te si fidano.
> Morta è colei che al tuo bel fonte ornavasi,
> e preponea il tuo fondo a tutt'i specoli;
> onde tua fama al ciel volando alzavasi. [103–11]

[How many shepherds, Sebeto, and how many peoples among those who take shelter beside you will you see perish before your banks flourish again with elms and poplars. Alas, once great Eridanus honored you and the Tiber happily bowed down before your name; now your own Nymphs scarcely have faith in you. Dead is she who once adorned your lovely source and preferred your depths to all mirrors; whence your fame rose flying to heaven.]

The national river has lost the prestige which Fillide and Meliseo's love poetry to her conferred upon its source. The Sebeto, however, may recover some of its preeminence among the rivers of Italy when Fillide again becomes the subject of Meliseo's verses, commemorated in his elegiac song. Barcinio promises to circulate Meliseo's laments far and wide—il Cariteo and Summonte were Pontano's editors in real life.

> tal che farò che'l gran Tesino et Atesi
> udendo Meliseo, per modo il cantino,
> che Filli il senta et a se stessa aggratesi;

> e che i pastor di Mincio poi gli piantino
> un bel lauro in memoria del suo scrivere,
> ancor che del gran Titiro si vantino.   [274–79]

[so I shall make the mighty Ticino and Adige, hearing Meliseus, sing of him in such a way that Phyllis may hear him and be pleased with herself; and the shepherds of the Mincio will plant a fair laurel in memory of his writing, even though they boast of great Tityrus.]

Meliseo's elegiac poetry will reach the Ticino, the Adige, and the Mincio; by the banks of the latter it will be eternized with laurel and be honored alongside the verse of Virgil ("gran Titiro") himself. Meanwhile Meliseo, like Ergasto, promises to cover with laurel the tomb of his loved one—making it so famous through his verses that shepherds from Tuscany and Liguria will come to visit it (251–65).

But while one kind of poetry about Fillide may be replaced by another, and Neopolitan poetry may continue to earn the tribute of the rest of Italy, the eclogue makes no pretense that Fillide herself may be made present. In contrast to the fiction of pastoral apotheosis in Eclogue 11, there is no attempt here to dress up literary immortality as the real thing. The separation of poetic convention and human experience in Eclogue 12 is at last made explicit, when Summonzio, tired of reciting Meliseo's verses, which have already acquired the status of literary artifacts, impatiently declares: "Io vorrei pur la viva voce intendere" (295; "I wish even to hear his living voice"), and the two shepherds strain to hear Meliseo himself, who is singing farther up the hillside. The eclogue switches from Meliseo's poetic texts to his living voice.

> I tuoi capelli, o Filli, in una cistula
> serbati tegno, e spesso, quand'io volgoli
> il cor mi passa una pungente aristula.
>   Spesso gli lego e spesso, oimè, disciolgoli,
> e lascio sopra lor quest'occhi piovere;
> poi con sospir gli asciugo, e inseme accolgoli.
>   Basse son queste rime, esili e povere;
> ma se 'l pianger in cielo ha qualche merito,
> dovrebbe tanta fé Morte commovere.
>   Io piango, o Filli, il tuo spietato interito,
> e 'l mondo del mio mal tutto rinverdesi.
> Deh pensa, prego, al bel viver preterito,
>   se nel passar di Lete amor non perdesi.   [313–25]

[I keep your locks, O Phyllis, preserved in a little basket, and often, when I turn them over in my hands, a sharp dart pierces my heart. Often I bind them and often, alas, I untie them; and I let these eyes rain upon them; then with sighs I dry them and gather them together. These rhymes are lowly, frail, and poor, but if weeping has some merit in heaven, so much faith should move death. I weep, O Phyllis, for your cruel death, and the world grows green again from my sorrow. Ah think, I pray you, on the fair life of our past, if at the crossing of Lethe love is not lost and forgotten.]

The third *terzina*, in which Meliseo hopes to move Death to pity, invokes the myth of Orpheus, and its combination of a disclaimer of poetic power with the wish to repeat Orpheus's successful example recalls and verbally echoes Ergasto's verses in Eclogue 11.

E se le rime mie non son si note
come quelle d'Orfeo, pur la pietade
dovrebbe farle in ciel dolci e devote.
[11, 73–75]

Basse son queste rime, esili e pov-
ere / ma se 'l pianger in cielo ha
qualche merito, / dovrebbe tanta fé
Morte commovere. [12, 319–21]

But the pastoral version of Orphic success has already given way to the failed Orpheus of the *Fourth Georgic* during Sincero's journey to the source. Barcinio's earlier description of Meliseo at his lyre imitates the triple repetition of Eurydice's name by the severed head of Virgil's Orpheus (*Georgics* 4.525–27).

La qual, mentre pur "Filli" alterna et itera,
e "Filli" i sassi, i pin "Filli" rispondono,
ogni altra melodia dal cor mi oblitera. [187–89]

[Which, while it still alternates and repeats "Phyllis," and "Phyllis" the rocks and "Phyllis" the pines give back in answer, blots every other melody from my heart.]

The negative implications of this repetition become clear when Meliseo attempts to braid together and reconstitute Fillide's hair—along with her name, all that is left of her—but then undoes his work with a fresh recognition of her absence. Like his wet tears and drying sighs, this pathetic alternation of retrieval and loss is an endless, unresolved cycle. The Orphic consolation of the pastoral elegy, which restores the dead once and forever to the bower in the poet's eternal song, cannot withstand close examination in the world of history. The momentary calling into being of the remembered dead points simultaneously to their loss, and the attempted recovery is repeated over and over again without outcome. Meliseo's tears water the earth, but while nature may renew itself through the course of time, Fillide will not be returned to him. Unlike Ergasto's Massilia, who is brought back into the pastoral world to shed her influence over its abiding present, Fillide is invited to think with the poet on their irrecoverable past— "preterito" suggests with special force an experience that is finished and unrepeatable—while the final verse removes her to the other side of death, where even memory and love may cease to link her to her former humanity.

The juxtaposition of Eclogues 11 and 12, with their mirroring but alternative versions of the pastoral elegy—and of its underlying Orpheus myth—allows the *Arcadia* to reexamine its intratextual bucolic fiction in the light of history. The consolation of the pastoral elegy now seems escapist and merely conventional. But the elegy's substitution of the poetic artifact for historical loss is emblematic of the larger pastoral strategy: the poet's inability to find any significance in history preconditions his retreat into a self-referential, purely literary realm of meaning. Pastoral thus makes itself a model for any timebound literary text—which must ultimately reduce itself to pastoral's self-declared intratextuality. The return to Naples in the final pages of the *Arcadia* discloses the book's historicity at the same time that it renounces any authority outside its own textual structures. The underground journey to the source reveals no source of meaning for poetry, and in the address to the reedpipe which concludes the *Arcadia* Sincero announces that Neapolitan poetry is no more.

> Le nostre Muse sono estinte; secchi sono i nostri lauri; ruinato è il nostro Parnaso; le selve son tutte mutole; le valli e i monti per doglia son divenuti sordi. Non si trovano più Ninfe o Satiri per li boschi; i pastori han perduto il cantare

> [Our Muses are extinct; our laurels are dried up, our Parnassus is ruined; the woods are all mute; the valleys and the mountains are grown deaf with sorrow. Nymphs or Satyrs are found no more in the woods; the shepherds have lost their songs.]

Having no place in historical Naples, the reedpipe is sent back to Arcady.

> Per la qual cosa io ti prego, e quanto posso ti ammonisco, che de la tua selvatichezza contentandoti, tra queste solitudini ti rimanghi.

> [for which reason I pray you, and admonish you as much as I can, that, making yourself content with your rusticity you remain among these solitary regions.]

The consignment of the reedpipe to a suitable home in the bower derives from a literary tradition of false modesty of which Petrarch's envois at the end of the two canzoni 125 and 126 of the *Canzoniere* are a good example. Petrarch debates whether his poems are elegant enough to leave the woods and circulate among the sophisticates of the city. Sannazaro invests the rhetorical convention with new thematic meaning.[19] The banishment of the reedpipe to the bower reflects less an aesthetic judgment on the lack of polish of pastoral poetry than the meditation of the *Arcadia* on the possibilities of literary meaning. Its poetry belongs in the autonomous, literary realm of the bower because it can find no source of intelligibility in the historical world of the city. That world requires the authority of epic poetry, which Carino, at the end of Prosa 7, had predicted that Sincero would one day come to write.

> tra sonore trombe di poeti chiarissimi del tuo secolo, non senza speranza di eterna fama trapasserai.

> [you will spend (your youth) among sonorous trumpets of the most famous poets of your age, not without hope of eternal fame.]

But by the address to the reedpipe, Sincero's poetic expectations seem drastically reduced, and there is more than a merely stylistic discomfort felt in his injunction to the instrument to stay away from the epic arena.

> Il tuo umile suono mal si sentirebbe tra quello de le spaventevoli buccine o de le reali trombe.

> [Your lowly sound would be heard amiss among fearful horns of battle or royal trumpets.]

Epic claims to provide an authoritative interpretation of history— usually national history—but the *Arcadia* perceives Naples only in terms of destruction and death. Its poetry is enjoined once more to turn away from the history it will not explain—from the real battles ravaging Sannazaro's Italy—and to resume its humble, unaspiring song. Seen now from the perspective of history, however, that song no longer expresses a fictional pastoral contentment, but a real human grief.

> Non ti rimane altro omai, sampogna mia, se non dolerti, e notte e giorno con ostinata perseveranza attristarti.

[Nothing remains to you now, my reedpipe, except to grieve, and to sadden yourself with stubborn perseverance, night and day.]

This is the final vision of the pastoral song in Orphic terms. Obsessive repetition may give the song an internal coherence and a lasting existence across time. Yet its constant refrain tells of the sense of temporal loss its poetry cannot console.

The *Arcadia* ends by revealing the dark world outside the pastoral bower, whose happily ordered interior is maintained only by excluding as surd elements the most compelling and ultimately tragic aspects of human experience: desire, history, death. The pastoral evasion indicts with itself the literary language for which its closed code serves as a model. The renunciation of the city for the bower reduces to an autonomous system the text which cannot transcend its historical moment. Carino's prediction of an epic Sannazaro must await the merging of poetic and scriptural language in the *De partu Virginis*. Like the weeping reedpipe, exiled in Arcady from a source which has been replaced by death, the pastoral poet Sannazaro's language can only be the sign of bereavement and loss.

THE *DE PARTU VIRGINIS*

Antonio Altamura notes that both the *Arcadia* and the *De partu Virginis* end with the appearance of a river-god: the Sebeto in the former work, the Jordan in the latter.[20] His remark points to a carefully developed parallel between the two episodes—both, in fact, imitations of the *Fourth Georgic* epyllion. The encounter with the Jordan at the end of book 3 of the *De partu Virginis* (281–504), moreover, follows directly upon the apparition of the angels to the shepherds of Bethlehem (126–280), a pastoral episode which also looks back upon the *Arcadia*. The bulk of book 3 contains a palinodial rewriting of the earlier work, particularly of the last three eclogues and prose sections. Sannazaro reinvests his epic with a transcendent source of literary authority which his pastoral fiction had renounced. This source is located at the Jordan and is revealed by the oracular words of Proteus.

After the good tidings are brought to them by the angels and a personified figure of Joy, two of the shepherds of Bethlehem, with the conventional pastoral names of Lycidas and Aegon, recite the song of "noster Tityrus," applying his prediction of a messianic child to the newborn Christ. Tityrus is Virgil and his song is the *Fourth Eclogue,* which Sannazaro quotes almost verbatim (196–232). The shepherds' performance is immediately followed by the response of nature.

70

> Talia dum referunt pastores, avia longe
> responsant nemora et voces ad sidera iactant
> intonsi montes; ipsae per confraga rupes
> ipsa sonant arbusta: deus, deus ille, Menalca.[21]   [233–36]

[While the shepherds were saying these things, the lonely forests echoed from afar and the leafy mountains threw their voices to the stars; the cliffs resounded through the thickets, and the groves re-echoed: "a God, He is a God, Menalcas."]

The last three lines are lifted from the *Fifth Eclogue* (63–64) where Menalcas's song announces the apotheosis of Daphnis. The coupling of the two Virgilian passages makes clear the direction which Sannazaro's palinode will take. While the Christianizing of the *Fourth Eclogue* is a commonplace, it here comments retrospectively upon Caracciolo's anti–*Fourth Eclogue* in the tenth eclogue of the *Arcadia.* His satirical view of a history emptied of meaning demonstrated the absolute discontinuity between human history and the literary world of pastoral. The *De partu Virginis,* however, announces the one true pastoral-in-history, the Golden Age brought into being by the Incarnation. Similarly, whereas the *Arcadia* disclosed the inauthenticity of the pastoral apotheosis, the *De partu Virginis,* by applying the words of the *Fifth Eclogue* to Christ, points to an immortality that is not merely literary, the Resurrection. Pastoral fictions, born of wishful thinking and temporal evasion, suddenly come true in the context of the Nativity.

Meanwhile the god of the Jordan contemplates a scene depicted upon the urn from which the waters of his river flow. What he sees, and begins to understand only now is the future Baptism of Christ.

> Hic iuvenis, fulvis velatus corpora setis,
> stans celso in scopulo, regem dominuque deorum
> vorticibus rapidis medioque in fonte lavabat.
> At viridi in ripa lecti de more ministri
> subcincti exspectant, pronisque in flumina palmis
> protendunt niveas, caelestia lintea, vestes.
> Ipse pater caelo late manifesta sereno
> signa dabat natoque levem per inane columbam
> insignem radiis mittebat et igne corusco:

adtonitae circum venerantur numina nymphae
et fluvius refugas ad fontem convocat undas.   [307–17]

[Here a youth, his body covered with a tawny and bristly hide, standing
on top of a steep rock, was washing in the rapid eddies and in the middle
of the font the King and Lord of the gods. And on the green bank, his
elected ministers, garbed according to custom, waited and in their open
palms proffered snow-white garments, heavenly linens, toward the
river. The Father, Himself, in the serene heavens was giving a manifest
sign far and wide, and was sending through the empty air a fleet dove,
marked by rays and gleaming fire; the astonished nymphs gather about
and worship the deity, and the river recalls his fleeing waves to their
source.]

By His immersion in its stream, Christ will sanctify the Jordan. The
river-god receives a token of the future event, as his waters take on a
new power and "saporem" (318–22). He recalls a prophecy of Proteus
which had promised the Jordan preeminence over the other rivers of
the earth.

qui te olim Nili supra septemplicis ortus,
supra Indum et Gangen fontemque binominis Istri
adtollet fama, qui te Tiberique Padoque
praeferet atque tuos astris aequabit honores.   [341–44]

[who one day will raise your fame above the sevenfold source of the Nile,
above the Indus and Ganges and the source of the double-named Ister,
who will make you greater than the Tiber and Po, and will place your
fame among the stars.]

This promise of eternal fame, raising the Jordan to the stars, directly
inverts Meliseo's lament in the *Arcadia* over the loss of Fillide, which
deprives the Sebeto of its former superiority to the Tiber and Po. But
whereas the source of the Sebeto's prestige was mortal poetry, the
Jordan is glorified by a metaphysical event. Sannazaro invokes, moreover, a tradition of patristic texts that describe the Jordan as the
greatest of rivers, the source from which all other rivers flow.

In a treatise on baptism, Gregory of Nyssa exalts the sanctified
Jordan: "Alone among all rivers, the Jordan received the first-fruits of
sanctification and blessing, and has shed the grace of baptism over the
whole world, as from a source."[22] The Jordan here symbolizes all
baptismal water. Christ, himself pure, did not need to be baptized. His
baptism institutes the rite and purifies its waters. Ambrose puts the
case succinctly: "Baptizare est ergo Dominus non mundari volens, sed

mundare aquas. . . ."[23] Conversely, all baptismal water carrying the sanctified properties of the Jordan may be considered to *be* the Jordan, an idea which is present in the Greek and Roman liturgies. This spiritual Jordan ceases to be limited to a specific geographical location, as is demonstrated in another Ambrosian text.

> We must therefore, brothers, be baptized in that same stream as our Saviour; but in order that we may be immersed in that fountain, we need not seek out the kingdom of the east nor the river of the land of the Jews: for now Christ is everywhere, the Jordan is everywhere.[24]

The ubiquity of the Jordan is also commented upon by Gregory of Nyssa.

> For indeed the river of grace flows everywhere. It does not rise in Palestine to disappear in some nearby sea: it spreads over the whole earth and flows into Paradise, flowing in the opposite direction to those four rivers which come from Paradise, and bringing in things far more precious than those which come forth. Those rivers carry perfumes, the fruit of culture and germination of the earth: this river brings in men, begotten of the Holy Spirit.[25]

Jean Daniélou shows that Gregory has fused the idea of the Jordan's universality with the Greek myth of the Oceanus, the river which circles the earth. Daniélou cites an earlier patristic passage, Hippolytus commenting on the preaching of the Naasenes.

> The Ocean is the birth-place of the gods and of men: ever flowing backwards and forwards, now upwards, now downwards. When the Ocean flows downwards, then are men born; when it flows upwards, then are the gods born. . . . All that is born below is mortal: all that is born above is immortal, for it is begotten spiritual, of water and the spirit. . . . This is said of the great Jordan, whose current, which when it flowed downwards, prevented the children of Israel when they left the land of Egypt from entering, was arrested and made by Jesus-Joshua to flow the other way.[26]

In this specific linking of the Jordan and the Oceanus, the flux and reflux of the holy river, which flowed back upon itself to allow Joshua and the Israelites to cross into the Promised Land (Joshua 3:15–16), corresponds to the circular flow of the Oceanus. The Oceanus already has eschatological significance in the *Phaedo*, where it is linked with the purgatorial rivers of Hades. The crossing of the Jordan under

Joshua—commemorated in the third verse of Psalm 114 (Vulgate 113): "Iordanis conversus est retrorsum"—became a figure for the salvation conferred by baptism, as the waters of the river flow upward and men are reborn as gods. In the traditional iconography of the baptism of Christ which institutes the sacrament, the Jordan, personified as a river-god, was often depicted as fleeing from the scene of the Baptism.[27] The description of the baptism depicted on the urn of Sannazaro's Jordan concludes with the image of the river's waters flowing back upon their source: "et fluvius refugas ad fontem convocat undas."

If the Jordan flowing upstream symbolizes the spiritual ascent of man toward God, the downward flow of the river becomes a figure for the Incarnation, the descent of God into humanity. Origen comments on the traditional etymology of "Jordan" as "their descent."

> This current flowing in a descending stream makes glad, as we find in the Psalms, the city of God, not the visible Jerusalem—for it has no river beside it—but the spotless Church of God, built on the foundation of the Apostles and Prophets, Christ Jesus our Lord being the chief cornerstone. By the Jordan, then, we have to understand the Word of God who became flesh and tabernacled among us. . . .[28]

Origen's identification of the Jordan with the incarnate Word depends on the Johannine portrait of Christ as a spring of living water, the rivers of living water which flow from His side at the Crucifixion (John 7:38).[29] The evangelist appropriates the symbolism of the Logos philosophy of Philo of Alexandria—the Logos is a fountain of life-giving streams.[30] Philo's Logos, in turn, takes on the attributes of the Old Testament Wisdom, who in a famous passage in Ecclesiasticus (24:19–34) compares herself to the Jordan and the four rivers of Eden. The same passage narrowly defines Wisdom as Torah. It is against this water of the Torah that Jesus, the Johannine Logos, contrasts his own superior dispensation, the water of eternal life, in the episodes of the Marriage at Cana (John 2:1 ff.) and the Samaritan Woman at the Well (John 4:5 ff.).[31] John associates the waters of life with the Spirit, which flows from Christ, the Word. Origen cites the Johannine passages in a meditation upon the Word as river.

> And I know another river whose stream makes glad the city of God, according to the word of the Psalmist: *There is a river the stream wherof shall make glad the city of God* (Ps. 46, 5). Do you wish to hear who is this river whose stream makes glad the city of God? Jesus Christ our Lord is the

river whose stream makes glad the city of God. He is the one who speaks through Isaiah: *Behold I descend among you as a river of peace* (Isaiah 66, 12). I know those promised rivers which flow from this river. *Whosoever drinketh of the water that I shall give him shall never thirst; but the water that I shall give him shall be in him a well of water springing up into everlasting life.* (John 4, 14) and *Out of his belly shall flow rivers of living water.* (John 7, 38).[32]

The Word descends as a river, so that men, drinking in the Spirit, may ascend as tributary rivers into eternal life. Origen's commentary, which makes Christ both river and source, shifts the sacramental interpretation of "living water" from baptism to the eucharist. Paul had invoked the fountain which sprang from the rock in the desert during the Exodus (Numbers 20:8–13) as a figure of the eucharistic meal (1 Corinthians 10:4). In a passage in which Christ alternates as river and source, Ambrose exhorts the readers of his commentary on the Psalms:

> Drink in Christ, for he is the rock which poured forth water, drink in Christ for he is the fountain of life, drink in Christ for he is the river whose stream makes glad the city of God, drink in Christ for he is peace, drink in Christ for *out of his belly shall flow rivers of living water.*[33]

Jerome identifies the river which makes glad the city of God in Psalm 46:4, a river whose waters are not "gathered here and there from the rain, but flow from a living and perpetual fountain," with the river of the Messianic Jerusalem in Ezekiel 47, a river which is clearly presented as a superior type of the Jordan.[34] Ezekiel's river, in turn, is associated with the Johannine river of life which streams through the heavenly Jerusalem in Revelation 22:2.

Ferdinand Ohrt has defined two distinct, if overlapping, medieval traditions of the Jordan, the circular river which is also the source of rivers. The first, based on the identification of the Jordan with the Oceanus, makes the Jordan the center of a world river system. All rivers and streams may be considered to be branches of the Jordan. The second conceives of the Jordan as a heavenly river, flowing out of Paradise. Its nonterrestrial waters are the waters of eternal life. The two Jordans intersect at the moment of Christ's baptism, where, according to one iconographic tradition, the waters with which Christ is baptized descend with the Spirit from above.[35] The heavenly Jordan flows into and transforms the nature of the earthly Jordan.

The baptism of Christ is the central event celebrated in the Epiphany liturgy of the Eastern church. The Orthodox rite features a blessing of the waters in commemoration of the consecration of the Jordan. Although the Latin church shifted the emphasis of the festival to commemorate the visit of the Magi, its liturgy continues to celebrate the two sacramental miracles of the waters, the purification of the Jordan by Christ's baptism and the transformation of water into eucharistic wine at the Marriage of Cana, the first miracle of Christ's ministry—which Sannazaro's poem describes at vv. 447–55. There is a sense in which the Jordan episode, which takes up almost half of book 3, changes the subject of the *De partu Virginis* from the Nativity to the Epiphany, from the Incarnation of the Word to its revelation and manifestation throughout creation.

Sannazaro's Jordan represents a Christianized version of the oceanic source myth of the *Fourth Georgic*. Virgil posited a divine intelligibility operating through the processes of creation which originate in Cyrene's cave. The significance which resides at the cave of the Jordan, the source of the world's rivers, is constituted by the Word that dwells within nature and history. The presence of the prophetic urn at the headwaters of the Jordan indicates, moreover, that the Word has been present from the beginning. The Judaeo-Christian god created by the Word and its intelligibility is built into the cosmos. The Jordan exclaims:

> O maris, o terrae, divûmque hominumque repertor,
> quis tua vel magno decreta incognita caelo
> detulit huc audax mediisque abscondit in undis?   [331–33]

["Who, O Creator of the sea, of the land, of gods and of men, has boldly taken Your decrees, unknown even to great heaven, and hidden them here in the midst of the waves?"]

Sannazaro follows a traditional reading of the opening verse of the Gospel of John where the Word "in mundo erat, et mundus per ipsum factus est et mundus eum non cognovit" (John 1 : 10). God has abided in His creation all along but His presence seemed hidden, awaiting the revelation of Christ to make itself known.[36] The spokesman for that revelation is Proteus, who in Virgil's fiction had stood for the totality of natural creation. In the *De partu Virginis*, we learn that Proteus had once delivered his oracle in the cave of the Jordan, a prophecy which the river-god now remembers and recites, much as the shepherds of Bethlehem recall the messianic eclogue of Tityrus. The episode is balanced in the structure of the larger *De partu Virginis* with the ending of book 1, where David, dwelling in Limbo among the other patriarchs of the Old Testament, prophesies the Passion and the Harrowing of Hell. Christianity traces the lineage of Jesus back through the house of David (Matthew I : 1–17, Romans 1 : 3) and sees an allegorical relationship between David's Psalms, together with all of Old Testament scripture, and Christian revelation. Proteus is paired with David to suggest that the Incarnation discloses the presence of God working in nature just as it fulfills His providential plan in biblical history.

The nature of Proteus's prophetic inspiration is taken up by Badius Ascensius in his Renaissance commentary on the *Fourth Georgic* (1501). The need to bind Proteus signifies

> that the *vates* do not speak the truth as masters of themselves, but are compelled by the divine spirit, as the sacred scriptures attest with regard to Balaam, and our Maro concerning the Sibyl in *Aeneid* VI. And indeed the history of Kings witnesses Saul rapt among the prophets against his will.[37]

Badius connects Proteus with biblical prophecy. But his examples, Balaam and Saul, are the non-Israelite and the rebel against God who nevertheless become the instruments of divine prophecy. Balaam and the sibylline prophecies became figures in medieval and Renaissance thought for the divine inspiration of profane letters which may possess a Christian meaning independent of their authors' intentions. Sannazaro's Mary is in fact discovered by Gabriel as she reads over the vatic songs of the Sibyls (1.91–95). Traditionally grouped with Balaam and the Sibyl as pagan prophets of Christ was the Virgil of the *Fourth Eclogue*.[38] The identification of Proteus as a prophet in spite of himself may comment on the very inclusion of Proteus and the other elements of the *Fourth Georgic*, as well as the verses of the *Fourth* and *Fifth Eclogue*, in Book 3 of Sannazaro's epic. Proteus stands for the process by which these Virgilian works are allegorized by the *De partu Virginis* in order to produce a Christian significance.[39]

Virgil's Proteus is a figure not only for the changing forms of nature but also for a poetry capable of speaking the truth. He is appropriately paired by Sannazaro with David, the divinely inspired poet of the Psalms. His appearance in the source cave of the Jordan, moreover, completes the palinodial reading which the *De partu Virginis* makes of the *Arcadia*. The descent to the source in the *Arcadia* revealed only the story of Orpheus and the failure of poetry before the forces of history and death. The *De partu Virginis*, by featuring the oracular Proteus whom Virgil had opposed to the human poet

Orpheus in the *Fourth Georgic*, announces the claim of *its* poetry to an epic, transcendent authority.

But the truthfulness of Proteus's song is confined to its Gospel subject matter. His prophecy of Christ is for him a "novo . . . cantu" (485), something strange and unaccustomed. For according to the Jordan, Proteus is telling the truth for the first and only time.[40]

> mendax si cetera Proteus,
> non tamen hoc vanas effudit carmine voces.   [336–37]

[even if Proteus is in other respects a liar, nonetheless in this song he has not poured out empty words.]

Moreover, Proteus, whose shape-changing was infinite in the *Fourth Georgic*, here finds himself at a loss for words.

> non si Parnasia Musae
> antra mihi sacrosque aditus atque aurea pandant
> limina, sufficiam; non si mihi ferrea centum
> ora sonent centumque aerato e gutture linguae
> vocibus exspument agitantem pectora Phoebum,
> laudatos valeam venturi principis actus
> enumerare novoque amplecti singula cantu.   [479–85]

[I would not be able, even if the Muses were to open to me the caves of Parnassus and its holy entrances and its golden thresholds; even if I had a hundred mouths of iron resounding and a hundred tongues from a bronze throat madly frothing out in words the presence of Phoebus which shakes my breast, I would not be able to number the deeds of this future prince and grasp each one with this unaccustomed song.]

Proteus's disclaimer is modeled ultimately on verses 488–92 of book 2 of the *Iliad* where the Homeric poet despairs of his own powers and invokes the aid of the Muses in order to catalogue the Greek fleet. Even with the Muses' assistance, however, Proteus could not describe all the miracles of Christ. Sannazaro is evidently using the epic formula to rewrite the final words of the Gospel of John.

> Sunt autem et alia multa quae fecit Iesus; quae si scribantur per singula, nec ipsum arbitror mundum capere posse eos, qui scribendi sunt, libros.

But even taking account of the scriptural precedent, the exhaustion of Proteus's oracle reflects the limitations which the *De partu Virginis* places upon its epic language. However the polyvalent figure of Proteus is read—whether as the collective voice of nature, allegorized pagan letters, or now as the poetry of truth—his prophecy depends upon the revelation of the gospels. When Proteus stops talking after having catalogued the miracles of Christ, the reader should conclude that Sannazaro has run out of scriptural testimony.

The scriptural subject matter of the *De partu Virginis* is, then, not so much a choice as a necessity which closes off all other poetic options. The plenitude of Proteus's language, unique in its newfound truthfulness, is coterminous with the evangelists' witness of Christ. The poet Sannazaro, like Proteus, becomes the mere vessel of divine meaning; coming too close to the source may involve the sacrifice of his individual identity as a writer. The task which is left to him is essentially one of style, of decoration and embellishment, and it has been argued that the true subject of the *De partu Virginis* is its attempted fusion of scripture and classical form. Yet Sannazaro's Virgilianism itself dutifully conforms to the stylistic norms laid down by Pietro Bembo and the Ciceronian movement in the first decades of the sixteenth century, and the *De partu Virginis* was attacked by Erasmus's anti-Ciceronian spokesman Bulephorus precisely for its excessively golden-age diction and its overlay of classical mythology.

> Why does he depict the Virgin intent above all on the Sibylline verses, or inappropriately introduce Proteus prophesying Christ, or make every place full of nymphs, Hamadryads, and Nereids?[41]

> How may [a pious subject] be treated in a pious way, if you never take your eyes away from Virgils, Horaces, and Ovids?[42]

If, in fact, Sannazaro's epic follows both the dictates of scriptural fundamentalism and the prevailing rules of literary style, there is little room left for his individual poetic voice to be heard. The palinodial dimensions of book 3—the Proteus whose presence Erasmus could not account for—may be one of the few means which the poet has to interject his own personality into the text of his poem. Significantly, this introduction of the poet's history can only take place in negative terms, as a rejection of earlier deviations from the true source.

Yet the *Arcadia* itself gave the poet little occasion for self-expression or originality.[43] There, too, his subject was defined by convention—the particularly conservative, closed convention of pastoral. There, too, Sannazaro regularized his language, taking pains to bring his meridional Italian into accordance with the Tuscan classics.[44] Both the *Arcadia* and the *De partu Virginis* can be understood as attempts to find a fixed meaning—whether the purely artificial meaning of pastoral or a sacred scriptural truth—that escapes the contingency of history. They may both, perhaps, represent an evasive response to the crisis which overcame Italian politics and culture at the end of the fifteenth century with the French and Spanish invasions of the peninsula—that frightening view of contemporary history which emerges briefly at the end of the *Arcadia*.[45] But to the extent that Sannazaro turns away from the history which defines his human individuality, he risks a loss of poetic identity.

Sannazaro's literary career, divided between the *Arcadia* and the *De partu Virginis*, fits neatly into an opposition between the ways in which historicist and allegorical modes of reading could define the nature of the Renaissance literary text. The neatness is the more complete because of the extreme positions taken by both works. In the face of history, the *Arcadia* reduces literary meaning to the kind of autonomous system which the pastoral fiction self-consciously declares itself to be. The *De partu Virginis* makes its meaning absolutely dependent upon the Word of God, to the point where the identity of the human writer all but disappears. The alternative ways in which the two works ask that they themselves be read are displayed in the double reading which they offer of Virgil. The *Arcadia* undertakes an imitation which is also a skillful historical reconstruction of the meaning of the *Eclogues* and the *Fourth Georgic*; the *De partu Virginis* allegorizes those works—and, in the figure of Proteus the reluctant pagan *vates*, points to its mode of allegory—in order to produce a Christian meaning from Virgil's poetry.

Partly because of the purity of their respective styles, partly because their subject matter *is* so conventional, the *Arcadia* and the *De partu Virginis* enjoyed a canonical status and immense popularity in the sixteenth century—and a subsequent decline in readership and reputation. They became instant classics because their author tried so little to assert his individual divergence from prevailing classical standards; they now seem brilliantly finished but one-dimensional and rather academic exercises.[46] Such academicism was a common enough pitfall for humanist authors intent upon the imitation of classical models. In the case of Sannazaro, a poet of genuine talent, the charge of empty formalism results from a retreat from history, away from vital human problems which resist conventional explanation. Perhaps when his two major works are read together, as the third book of the *De partu Virginis* suggests they should be, they may question each other's generic assumptions and gain a measure of human depth and complexity. The contrast between their pastoral and epic aspirations points to Sannazaro's divided attitude toward his vocation, as well as to his awareness of the limits of literary convention itself.

Tasso

ANTITYPE: ASTOLFO'S VOYAGE TO THE MOON

> In principio era il Verbo a presso a Dio,
> Ed era Iddio il Verbo e 'l Verbo lui;
> Questo era nel principio, al parer mio,
> E nulla si può far sanza costui[1]

[In the beginning the Word was with God, and God was the Word and the Word Him; this was in the beginning, according to my opinion, and nothing can be done without him.]

The solution to the problem of literary authority reached by Sannazaro in the *De partu Virginis*, where the poet's word became a paraphrase of scriptural testimony to the Word of God, left little, if any, autonomy to the individual human author. With the words, *al parer mio*, the opening lines of Luigi Pulci's *Morgante* (1483), with their direct quotation of the beginning of the gospel of John, reverse the poet's position of dependency upon the Word and assert his creative freedom. The Christian Word is now authorized by Pulci's "parere," which is both an assertion of faith and of poetic control, and it is unclear whether the "costui" of the fourth line, upon which all things are said to depend, refers to the divine Word or again to that human "parere," the poet's word, which is about to generate twenty-eight cantos of burlesque epic. Whereas Sannazaro finds himself limited to scripture, Pulci will write what he pleases.[2] As a creative instrument, his word, authoritative or not, is made coequal to the authorized Word. But if this equation is reversed, the Incarnate Word is reduced to just another literary word. Such a reduction, in fact, takes place in the masterpiece of the next generation of Italian letters, when Ludovico Ariosto affirms the autonomy of his poetic fiction in the *Orlando furioso* (1516).

81

The allegory of human futility and loss which appears on the moon in cantos 34 and 35 of the *Orlando furioso* has generally been regarded as an interpretative key to the larger epic, a summation of Ariosto's thematic concerns.[3] The lunar episode concludes with the poem's only explicit meditation on literature, a satirical discourse which equates writers and liars. Relatively little critical attention has been paid to this juxtaposition, yet it controls the episode's overall design. The absence of meaning in the universe of the *Furioso* is thereby linked to a critique of the literary text which is the source of meaning. Conversely, the *Furioso* implicates all texts in its own refusal to open onto true significance. The nexus of thematics and poetics, moreover, provides a focus for a close reading of the lunar allegory itself, a reading which attempts to map out the complicated interplay between meaning and structure in Ariosto's text.

The location of the absurdist allegory on the moon inverts the literary tradition from which the lunar episode derives. In those Platonic ascents through the stars which served as models for Ariosto's fiction—the *Somnium Scipionis,* the *Paradiso,* even the burlesque *Icaromenippus*—the moon is the first way station above the flux and mutability of elemental creation and human history. As Astolfo leaves behind the sublunary world in the company of Saint John the Evangelist, the reader may anticipate entering into a "higher" timeless sphere of meaning. But the shifting, multiple perspective which defines the poetics of the *Furioso* rules out the privileging of any one viewpoint, even of a superterrestrial Archimedean point.[4] The moon turns out to be the repository not of meaning, but of unmeaning. The vertical dimension characteristic of epic fiction, transcending the world of human action and lending it intelligibility, has been effectively collapsed and eliminated from the *Furioso.*

The first indication that Ariosto's moon is not privileged, that it does not operate on a plane of meaning superior to the rest of the poem, appears in the initial description of the lunar landscape.

> Altri fiumi, altri laghi, altre campagne
> sono là su, che non son qui tra noi;
> altri piani, altri valli, altre montagne,
> c'han le cittadi, hanno i castelli suoi,
> con case de le quai mai le più magne
> non vide il paladin prima né poi:
> e vi sono ample e solitarie selve,
> ove le ninfe ognor cacciano belve.[5]   [34.72]

[Other rivers, other lakes, other fields are up there which are not here in our world, other plains, other valleys, other mountains, which have their cities, and castles, and houses—the knight never saw larger houses than these before or afterwards; and there are broad and lovely forests, where nymphs still hunt wild beasts.]

Here, as was the case in Sannazaro's Eclogue 5, the anaphora *altri* plays a peculiar rhetorical trick. The passage may appear to indicate a kind of Platonic doubling, as if the moon's geographical features represented "higher" forms of their earthly counterparts. But, despite the additional grandeur of the lunar mansions, this is not the case. The moon and the earth are mirror images of each other, a fact borne out by the earlier statement (70) that the moon is in size "uguale, o minor poco" to the earth. As an attempt to escape from the terrestrial, the trip to the moon is a short circuit.

A similar circularity is contained in the lunar allegory. Saint John tells Astolfo:

> Tu dèi saper che non si muove fronda
> là giù, che segno qui non se ne faccia.
> Ogni effetto convien che corrisponda
> in terra e in ciel, ma con diversa faccia.   [35.18, 1–4]

[You should know that not a leaf moves down there (on earth) which does not make a sign up here. Every event has corresponding outcomes on earth and in heaven, but in different guises.]

Now at first this statement seems to posit a traditional allegorical relationship. Human events, unreadable as they are unfolding on earth, create a series of signs, a gloss to the earthly book, upon the moon. It rapidly becomes apparent, however, that the gloss itself is unreadable. Astolfo sees a succession of junk piles containing such items as swollen bladders, golden fishhooks, burst cicadas, spilled soup, and bird-lime. At their face value, these are nothing but junk, and it is difficult for Astolfo or the reader to know that they represent, respectively, vanished empires, gifts to princely patrons, laudatory verses, bequeathed alms, and feminine beauty. The poem insists upon the necessary presence of Saint John, who is the walking glossator of its allegory.

> Passando il paladin per quelle biche,
> or di questo or di quel chiede alla guida.   [34.76.1–2]

> Vede in ghirlande ascosi lacci; e chiede,
> et ode che son tutte adulazioni. [34.77.5–6]
>
> Domanda, e sa che son trattati . . . [34.79.3]
>
> Di versate minestre una gran massa
> vede, e domanda al suo dottor ch'importe. [34.80.1–2]
>
> che se non era interprete con lui,
> non discernea le forme lor diverse. [34.82.3–4]

[Passing among those heaps, the knight asks his guide now about this one, now about that one.]

[He sees hidden snares in garlands, and asks, and hears that they are all flatteries.]

[He asks, and learns that they are treaties . . .]

[He sees a great quantity of spilled soup, and asks his teacher what it means.]

[for if there were no interpreter with him, he would not be able to make out their different meanings.]

Saint John is meant to recall Dante's Virgil, and the lunar episode caps the extended Dantesque parody of canto 34. But Ariosto has, in fact, reversed the allegorical principles which structure the *Commedia*. In Dante's allegory, earthly events constitute signs pointing to a higher, anterior set of signs—a typology which rests ultimately upon the absolutely anterior significance of the Incarnation. But Ariosto's fiction, as it seems to collapse hierarchical distinction between a physically identical earth and moon, assigns anteriority to neither the earthly nor the lunar signs. The two sets of signs are interchangeable—one is the "diversa faccia" of the other—and mutually interdependent as well; neither can be read without the other. The play of reference, where earthly sign A points to lunar sign B, which merely points back to A, is a closed circle which never opens onto any authoritative meaning beyond itself. Moreover, the interplay of the two sign systems is governed by Ariosto's text: the text, in the person of the Evangelist, must spell out their relationship.

The lunar allegory has thus been constructed according to intratextual principles, a system of signs which are interpretable only within the context of that system. But the system of meaning over which Ariosto's text exerts its authority is not its own invention: much of the bric-a-brac found on the moon and its allegorical meaning derive from the *Somnium*, one of the *Intercoenales* of Leon Battista Alberti.[6] In fact, provided one has Alberti's book in hand, one could dispense with Saint John and still understand most of the significance of the lunar junkyard. The poetics of the episode thus alternate between a model of allegory as a self-authorized, intratextual system and a more customary allegorical practice, the allegory of a Dante or a Boiardo, which presupposes an earlier text or history of texts which authorize and guarantee the readability of its figures. Dante's Virgil is not needed to explain the meanings of allegorical figures whose component parts derive from long iconographic and literary usage. Ariosto, on the island of Alcina, has himself used this traditional allegory, composed from that great storehouse which is the common cultural inheritance of Western writers.[7]

But the *Furioso* now proceeds at its *thematic* level to charge all literary texts with mendacity and bad faith; by doing so, it reduces that time-honored storehouse back into a junkyard which the text—on its own authority—turns into allegorical meaning.

Astolfo passes into a palace where the Fates sit spinning out threads from fleeces ("velli"), which, each equipped with a separate nametag, represent the lives of human beings. One such fleece, stored for the future, is of exceptional splendor and beauty. It is identified as the life of Ippolito d'Este and occasions a brief encomium on the poet's patron. After the threads of life have run their course, a fleet-footed old man, Time, carries off the nametags and dumps them into the river Lethe. There the tags sink except for those few which are retrieved by a pair of swans and deposited in a temple of Immortality. The swans are poets, whose verses preserve human fame from the oblivion of Time and Death.

The theme of fame is the second line of Ariosto's mock "defense of poetry." Failing to arrive at timeless significance, the text falls back upon its ability to survive time. As does the pastoral fiction, Ariosto's poem extols the endurance of the literary artifact, quite apart from its truth or falsehood. Indeed, the poet wryly comments, the fame conferred by literature has its origin not in historical fact but in patronage and self-interest: the poet will twist the truth and lie, provided he is well paid. Of those lords and great men who failed to cultivate the adulation of writers, Saint John remarks:

> Credi che Dio questi ignoranti ha privi
> de lo 'ntelletto, e loro offusca i lumi;

che de la poesia gli ha fatto schivi,
acciò che morte il tutto ne consumi.
Oltre che del sepolcro uscirian vivi,
ancor ch'avesser tutti i rei costumi,
pur che sapesson farsi amica Cirra,
più grato odore avrian che nardo o mirra.

Non sì pietoso Enea, né forte Achille
fu, come è fama, né sì fiero Ettorre;
e ne son stati e mille e mille e mille
che lor si puon con verità anteporre:
ma i donati palazzi e le gran ville
dai descendenti lor, gli ha fatto porre
in questi senza fin sublimi onori
da l'onorate man degli scrittori.   [35.24–25]

[Believe that God has deprived these ignoramuses of their intellect, and
blinded their sight; for he has made them averse to poetry in order that
death may totally consume them. For they would issue from the tomb
alive, and even if they possessed all the worst vices, they would be more
sweet-smelling than nard or myrrh, so long as they knew how to make
friends with Apollo (Cirrha).

Aeneas was not so pious, nor was Achilles so strong as fame reports
them, nor was Hector so brave; and there have been thousands and
thousands and thousands who could truthfully be held up as their
betters: but gifts of palaces and great villas on the part of their descendants has caused them to be set in their places of highest eternal honor by
the honored hands of writers.]

The play of Ariostesque irony has become wonderfully complex.
Stanza 24 irreverently substitutes a resurrection into poetic immortality for the mystery of the Passion. The myrrh which turned out to be
superfluous when Christ rose from His tomb has here turned into a
kind of poetic embalming fluid, preserving a counterfeit memory of
the deceased. Ariosto takes aim at his ever-present target, Dante. The
nonpatrons, "privi de lo 'ntelletto," recall the damned of the *Inferno*
"c'hanno perduto il ben de l'intelletto."[8] The equation of the two
revives a common Dantesque theme: that fame is the only consolation
of the damned. Now fame is the sole consolation for all the dead—
their only form of salvation. The equation furthermore raises a fundamental and disturbing question, which must occur even to the naive
reader of the *Commedia:* on just what basis does Dante consign his
contemporaries to heaven and hell, eternizing them for posterity?
Ariosto hangs a halo of bad faith above the *poema sacro.*

Stanza 25 impugns the authority of Homer and Virgil, the found-
ers of epic, an attack which continues in stanza 27, where Saint John
asserts that the events represented in the *Iliad* and the *Odyssey* exactly
reverse the true facts.

> che i Greci rotti, e che Troia vittrice,
> e che Penelopea fu meretrice.   [35.27.7–8]

[that the Greeks were routed, that Troy was victorious, and that Penelope
was a whore.]

And in stanza 28 we learn that Dido was actually chaste and that her
shady reputation is due solely to Virgilian malice.[9] The argument has a
direct bearing upon Ariosto's own epic, whose central hero, Ruggiero,
modeled on Aeneas and supposedly descended from Hector, is the
ancestor of the poet's patron.

Finally, the Evangelist implicates himself in the general mistrust
of writers and texts.

> Gli scrittori amo, e fo il debito mio;
> ch'al vostro mondo fui scrittore anch'io.
>
> E sopra tutti gli altri io feci acquisto
> che non mi può levar tempo né morte:
> e ben convenne al mio lodato Cristo
> rendermi guidardon di sì gran sorte.   [35.28.7–8; 29.1–4]

[I love writers, and I am obligated to love them, for in your world I, too,
was a writer. And above all others I acquired a reward which neither time
nor death can take away from me: and it was right for my Christ whom I
praised to give me happy lot in recompense.]

How seriously is one to take this joke, which climaxes the entire lunar
episode? The nontemporal reward which the much-praised Christ has
conferred upon Saint John may refer to his eternal domicile in Eden or
to the "immortality" which any famous literary character bestows
upon its author. The depiction of the Gospel as the product of a
patron–writer relationship reduces its testimony to the status of a
literary fiction. This was the view gleefully taken by Voltaire, who
declared to Casanova that these lines were his favorite moment in the
Furioso.[10]

Among modern critics, Robert Durling argues for a more balanced reading. After a careful examination of Ariosto's measured and
not uncritical praise of his patrons elsewhere in the poem, he reminds
us that a joke is a joke, and suggests that after the comic discussion of

poets and patrons, Saint John's wisecrack is the final ironic coun-
tertwist: "For to suppose that Ariosto meant that he was lying about
his patrons is tantamount to thinking that he meant to suggest that the
Evangelist lied about Christ."[11] For Durling, then, Ariosto's remarks
about the status of scripture would be inseparable from his sincerity
about his patrons. This hypothesis can be tested by reexamining the
encomium to Ippolito d'Este earlier in the same canto in light of its
allegorical sources.

The Fates and their splendid fleece representing the future illus-
trious life of Ippolito d'Este have their model in the *Apocolocyntosis* of
Seneca. This mock-apotheosis of the Emperor Claudius had wide
currency in learned Renaissance circles of the second decade of the
sixteenth century; first published in 1513, it also served as a model for
the *Julius Exclusus* (1518), a satire about the unsuccessful efforts of
Julius II to enter heaven which has been attributed to Erasmus.[12]
Seneca's satire on apotheosis tries to have it both ways, denigrating
the dead Claudius while slavishly celebrating the virtues of his imperial successor. As Clotho cuts the thread of Claudius's life, Lachesis
unfolds a fleece ("vellus") of unparalleled brilliance.

> Mutatur vilis pretioso lana metallo;
> Aurea formoso descendunt saecula filo.[13]

[The lowly wool is changed into precious metal; the golden ages unfold
in a beautiful thread.]

This golden fleece promising a new golden age is clearly recalled by
Ariosto's description of the fleece of Ippolito d'Este.

> e scorse un vello che più che d'or fino
> splender parea; né sarian gemme trite
> s'in filo si tirassero con arte,
> da comparargli alla millesma parte. [35.3.5–8]

[and he saw a fleece which seemed to shine more than fine gold; nor
could beaten and artfully threaded gems compare with it even in a
thousandth part.]

Seneca makes Apollo himself deliver a prophecy on the wondrous
creature promised by the threads of fate.

> Ne demite, Parcae,
> Phoebus ait, vincat mortalis tempora vitae
> Ille mihi similis vultu similis decore,

Nec cantu nec voce minor. Felicia lassis
Saecula praestabit legumque silentia rumpet.
Qualis discutiens fugientia Lucifer astra
Aut qualis surgit redeuntibus Hesperus astris,
Qualis, cum primum tenebris Aurora solutis
Induxit rubicunda diem, Sol aspicit orbem
Lucidus et primos a carcere concitat axes,
Talis Caesar adest, talem iam Roma Neronem
Aspiciet. Flagrat nitidus fulgore remisso
Vultus et adfuso cervix formosa capillo.[14]

["Do not curtail your spinning, O Fates," says Phoebus, "let him surpass the span of mortal life, he who resembles me both in countenance and beauty, nor is he inferior in voice and song. To weary mortals he will usher in happy centuries, and put an end to the silence of the laws. Just as Lucifer, chasing away the fleeing stars, or Hesperus rising with the returning stars, just as, when blushing Aurora, dissolving the shadows, brings in the dawn, the radiant Sun contemplates the earth and begins to drive his chariot from its station, so does this Caesar appear, on such a Nero does Rome now gaze. His shining face blazes with a mild splendor, as does his shapely neck beneath his flowing locks.]

Nero is the subject of this extravagant, abject flattery. The praise of the new emperor's musicianship is one particularly salient detail in a document permeated by historical irony. This selfsame Nero destroyed his former tutor, Seneca, as well as other writers of the imperial circle, such as Petronius and Lucan. Lucan, like Seneca, died leaving behind his earlier adulatory verses. In a clue to his literary model, Ariosto comments on the emperor's mistaken policy.

Nessun sapria se Neron fosse ingiusto,
né sua fama saria forse men buona,
avesse avuto e terra e ciel nimici,
se gli scrittor sapea tenersi amici.   [35.26.5–8]

[No one would know that Nero was unjust, nor would his fame perhaps be less good, even if he had made enemies of both earth and heaven, had he known how to keep writers his friends.]

Had he not murdered his poets, Nero might be remembered in the glowing terms of Seneca's encomium, the same terms which Ariosto has applied to his patron. The poet has paid Ippolito the most backhanded of compliments, implicating his own fiction in the charge that literary "truth" is a function of the author's wage scale.

The strategy of Ariosto's poetics may now be assessed. The allegorical text may point to a history of meaning outside itself, but that meaning remains a sheerly literary property, produced by another text. In the case of the palace of the Fates, the principal source text of the allegory is Seneca's Nero-worship, a monument of literary error and untruth. Meanwhile the thematic argument of canto 35 has relegated all texts to more or less the same lack of authority, a sweeping blow which discredits any typology from which allegorical fictions might derive their meaning. At this point the difference disappears between an intratextual model of allegory (the poem's character, Saint John, explaining the poem's meanings) and the allegory which depends upon a previous text, when that previous text is itself revealed as an intratextual system of meaning, disjunct from and even contrary to historical "truth." This perception of Western poetic tradition as a pack of lies—based on the idea that literary meaning, when traced back to its source, will turn out to be counterfeit and inauthentic—can be understood as a reflection and reductio ad absurdum of the historicist and philological ideas of Renaissance humanism. To insist that all texts tell lies out of the self-interest of their authors is an extreme way of placing the text in a specific historical context which delimits its claim to truth. No text can pose as that anterior point of origin and truth upon which a subsequent allegorical system can be based; instead, any such text discloses its historicity and *originality*, a closed and self-created code of meaning. With the elimination of its necessary first term, the allegorical mechanism falls apart.

Saint John's quip about Christ's "patronage" comes as the final, logical step in Ariosto's argument. It is, of course, John's Gospel which announces the doctrine of the Logos, the "verbo Incarnato" which organizes history in octave 4. The allegorical misfunction caused by the inauthenticity of literary texts would disappear before the Word of God, toward which all human discourse, whatever its intentionality or factual truth, may point: witness the treatment in the *De partu Virginis* of Virgil's *Fourth Eclogue,* a text whose "misreading" is also responsible for the conversion of Dante's Statius (*Purgatorio* 22.70–72). As the source of all intelligibility, the presence of the Word prevents any text from closing off its system of meaning: further allegorization will always be possible. But it is precisely to effect such a closure that Ariosto dismisses the Logos with a joke, wittily reducing the status of the scriptural Word to the level of the words of his poem.

The episode of the moon in effect repeats the argument of the first two-thirds of *The Praise of Folly*—which reduces from the perspective of history all human meaning to self-gratifying fictions—while it self-consciously blocks off the recovery of meaning through Christian allegory which takes up the last section of Erasmus's work. On the moon, Astolfo arrives at the vantage point of Folly's Olympian gods, and they look down on an earth full of madness as Lucian's Menippus had looked down from the moon—the *Icaromenippus* is imitated by both works. Ariosto's "pazzia," the one item of human experience which is immune to Fortune and does not appear in the moon's depository of loss (34.81.7–8), seems very close to Erasmian folly. The crucial difference between the two is that "pazzia" is an inescapable result in a world where signs do not point to a higher meaning but to the human desire which has generated them, while folly is produced by a willful transformation of preexisting allegorical signs into a mirror of desire and self, a transformation which stops the sign from pointing beyond itself to the original significance of the Christian Logos. Thus the deconstructive movement of Folly's oration exposes an abusive misappropriation of signs in order to reveal the allegorical meaning which has been present in them all along. But a similar deconstruction in the world of the *Furioso*, from which the Logos has been removed and in which signification is entirely man-made, reveals only non-sense and madness.

The self-contained lunar allegory provides a model for the much discussed autonomy of the larger fictional universe of the *Furioso*.[15] Unlike the autonomy of the pastoral *Arcadia*, this autonomy is not a flight into fixed poetic convention or art-for-art's-sake away from the "real" human world. Rather, it is inextricably joined to the poem's thematic representation of our world, a world in which true meaning is impossible precisely because the instrument of meaning, the text, is shown to be autonomous, a set of signs which point ultimately to their identity as signs. That poets lie is a Renaissance commonplace, but the defenders of poetry justify its lies in the name of a higher truth. But the "higher" truth delivered from Ariosto's moon is merely that poets lie.

Ariosto's singular achievement is to have sustained a forty-six-canto epic fiction while inverting the conventional premises of epic. The transcendent meaning which epic customarily claims to incorporate from an authoritative source outside its text is shown in the *Orlando furioso* to have been the product of the text all along. The Providence which governs the action of the epic is a transparent disguise for the poet who arbitrates its meaning. In his hands, the real

92 dynamics of the *Furioso*'s narrative are shown to spring from the experience of a purely human temporality, generated by a desire which cannot be fulfilled and terminated by a meaningless death.[16] And, even in the absence of an organizing transcendent intelligibility, the machinery of this epic world functions perfectly.

THE MAGUS OF ASCALON AND THE WISDOM OF JOB

In terms of plot, the voyage to the moon in the *Orlando furioso* is paralleled in the *Gerusalemme liberata* by the visit to the Magus of Ascalon in canto 14. Each episode forms an essential part of a pattern which Tasso calls in his letters a *soluzione per machina*: a resolution of the epic plot through the agency of the supernatural.[17] Following the model of the *Iliad*, the outcome of both epics hinges upon the return to battle of an absent hero: the mad Orlando, the errant Rinaldo. In both poems the search for the missing paladin begins with a providential detour into a realm of the marvelous presided over by a divinely inspired agent or guide. The searcher is instructed in the nature of his quest and receives some object necessary for its successful conclusion: Astolfo obtains the wits of Orlando from the moon, the Magus gives the knights Carlo and Ubaldo the diamond shield which will bring the enamored Rinaldo back to his senses.

The parallel between the two epic plots was made even clearer in a series of octaves which Tasso canceled from canto 17. There, the Magus takes the sleeping Rinaldo and immerses him seven times in the ocean—"sette volte il tuffò ne l'onde salse."[18] This purgation recalls and verbally echoes the scene in the *Furioso* where Astolfo washes Orlando seven times before restoring his wits to him—"e sette volte sotto acqua l'attuffa" (39.56.2). Although Tasso preferred to discuss the expedition to retrieve Rinaldo in terms of the Philoctetes story, he was, in fact, consciously rewriting the work of his great predecessor poet in Ferrara.[19] The descent to the cavern of the Magus of Ascalon takes the place in the epic plot of Astolfo's voyage to the moon, and the episode of the Magus, together with Goffredo's dream at the beginning of canto 14, constitutes a revision of the meaning—with all that it implies for a poetic epistemology—of Ariosto's lunar episode.

Following the instructions of Peter the Hermit, Carlo and Ubaldo seek out the coastline near Ascalon where a river empties into the sea.

Here the Magus appears to them, walking miraculously upon the stream (14.33–34). The waters part at his command, in verses which directly echo the entrance of Aristaeus into the cave of Cyrene in the **93** *Fourth Georgic* (36). The Magus invites the two knights to accompany him into his underwater realm, murky with shadowy light.

> ma pur gravide d'acque ampie caverne
> veggiono, onde tra noi sorge ogni vena
> la qual rampilli in fonte, o in fiume vago
> discorra, o stagni o si dilati in lago.
>
>   E veder ponno, onde il Po nasca ed onde
> Idaspe, Gange, Eufrate, Istro derivi,
> ond'esca pria la Tana; e non asconde
> gli occulti suoi princìpi il Nilo quivi.
> Trovano un rio più sotto, il qual diffonde
> vivaci zolfi e vaghi argenti e vivi:
> questi il sol poi raffina, e 'l licor molle
> stringe in candide masse e in auree zolle.[20]   [14.37.5–8; 38]

[yet even so they see vast caverns pregnant with water, from which springs up every vein that here on earth gushes forth as a fountain, or flows as a wandering river, or stands in pools, or widens into a lake.

    And they can see whence the Po is born, and whence the Hydaspes, the Ganges, the Euphrates, and the Ister are derived; and there the Nile does not conceal his secret beginnings. They find a river farther down which pours out living sulfur and quicksilver: these the sun subsequently refines, and presses together the soft liquid into gleaming masses of silver and lumps of gold.]

The *Fourth Georgic* is again the principal literary source, though octave 37 also recalls the description of Oceanus in the *Phaedo* (9112c). In addition, following an opinion widely held in contemporary geological speculation, Tasso depicts the common origin of all metals and minerals in the liquid insides of the earth.[21] In a kind of natural alchemical laboratory, sulfur and quicksilver "grow" and are combined into silver and gold. Like Cyrene's cave, the realm of the Magus is located at the source of natural creation; the Magus tells Ubaldo:

> Sete voi nel grembo immenso
> de la terra, che tutto in sé produce   [14.41.1–2]

[You are in the vast womb of the earth, which produces all things inside itself.]

From his unique vantage point at the source, the Magus investigates the earth's hidden secrets. His magical powers, carefully distinguished from those of the demonic necromancer, are the result of his knowledge of the inner workings of nature.

> Né in virtù fatte son d'angioli stigi
> l'opere mie meravigliose e conte
> (tolga Dio ch'usi note o suffumigi
> per isforzar Cocito e Flegetonte),
> ma spiando me 'n vo da' lor vestigi
> qual in sé virtù celi o l'erba o 'l fonte,
> e gli altri arcani di natura ignoti
> contemplo, e de le stelle i vari moti.   [14.42]

[Nor are my marvelous and manifest works performed through the powers of the angels of Hell (God forbid that I employ charms or smoky spells to coerce Cocytus and Phlegeton), but I go searching from the traces which they leave behind the properties which the herb or fountain conceals within itself, and I contemplate the other unknown secrets of nature and the varying motions of the stars.]

The Magus has no demonic agent up his sleeve, no spirit hovering at his beck and call. His marvels are accomplished by natural means. In an epigrammatic phrase, he tells the two knights that everything in his splendid underground palace is "non fatto, ma nato" (48). He seems to perform the kind of white, natural Renaissance magic which Eugenio Garin, in two classic essays, has shown to have been interrelated with the rise of modern science: if magic seemed at times to compete with "pure" scientific research, the two were nonetheless complementary.[22] The Magus's observations of the innate forces ("virtù") and processes of nature are a kind of data collection and his magic a type of applied science. But the status of the Magus's science of nature in relationship to the divine intelligibility which guides the action of the *Liberata* is problematic. As opposed to its Virgilian model, the natural source cave in which the Magus resides is *not* also the source of a primal truth and wisdom.

In his thumbnail sketch of the allegory of his epic, Tasso explains that the Magus of Ascalon ("il Saggio") is a figure for human understanding unaided by Revelation, particularly for pagan philosophy. Revelation is figured by Peter the Hermit, and the two stand roughly in the same relationship as do Virgil and Beatrice in the *Commedia*.[23]

Ma l'Heremita, che per la liberatione di Rinaldo indirizza i due Messagieri al Saggio, figura la cognitione sopranaturale, ricevuta per divina gratia, si come il Saggio la humana sapienza; imperoche dall'humana sapienza, & dalla cognitione dell'opere della natura, & de magisteri suoi, si genera, & si conferma ne gli anima nostri la giustitia, la temperanza, il disprezzo della morte, & e delle cose mortali, la magnanimità, & ogn' altra virtù morale, grande aiuto può ricever l'huomo civile in ciascuna sua operatione dalla contemplatione; Si finge, che questo Saggio fosse nel suo nascimento Pagano; ma che dall'Heremita convertito alla vera fede si sia renduto cristiano, & c'havendo deposta la sua prima arroganza, non molto presume del suo sapere; ma s'acqueti al giuditio del Maestro, peroche la Filosofia nacque, & si nutrì tra Gentili nell'Egitto, e nella Grecia, & di là a noi trapassò, presontuosa di se stessa, & miscredente, & audace, e superba fuor di misura; Ma da san Tomaso, & da gli altri santi Dottori è stata fatta discepola, & ministra della teologia, & divenuta per opera loro modesta, e più religiosa, nessun cosa ardisce temerariamente affermare contra quello, che alla sua Maestra è rivelato.[24]

95

[But the hermit, who directs the two messengers to the Sage for the liberation of Rinaldo, figures supernatural cognition, received by divine grace, just as the Sage figures human wisdom; for since human wisdom, from the knowledge of the works of nature and of her ministers, creates and confirms in our souls justice, temperance, contempt for death and for mortal things, magnanimity, and every other moral virtue, civic man can receive great assistance in all his activities from such wisdom; the fiction goes that this Sage was Pagan by birth, but that, having been converted to the true faith and made a Christian, and having put aside his former arrogance, he did not presume much on account of his wisdom, but was contented with the judgment of his Master, because Philosophy was born and nurtured among the Gentiles in Egypt and in Greece, and from there came to us, presumptuous, unbelieving, bold, and proud beyond all measure: But by Saint Thomas and other holy doctors it has been made a disciple and servant of theology, and, through their efforts, it has become modest, and more religious, and dares to assert nothing boldly against that which has been revealed to its Mistress.]

The conversion of the Magus, symbolizing the submission of philosophy to the revealed truth of Christianity, parallels Tasso's own spiritual autobiography. In the well-known letter to Scipione Gonzaga of April 15, 1579, written during the first months of his imprisonment in Sant'Anna, the poet looks back upon his own flirtation with pagan philosophy. Under its influence, he had come to doubt some of the central tenets of Christian doctrine. Eventually, he recognized his error and returned to his earlier faith.

E se del nascimento di Cristo e de la sua eterna generazione non so render cagione, non la so anche rendere de la generazione de' tuoni e de' lampi e de le grandini e de le tempeste e de' venti, se non molto fallace e incerta; né so, se non molto dubbiosamente, come l'aria si dipinga di tanta varietà di colori in quel suo arco, che arco del patto è nominato; né come ne la regione del fuoco o ne la vicina ci appaiano le comete e la strada di latte e tante altre apparenze ora spaventose ora vaghe, ma sempre maravigliose; né so come ne le viscere de la terra si generi l'oro e l'argento e gli altri metalli, e nel letto del mare le perle e i coralli si producano; né saprei de la generazione de gli animali abbastanza ragionare. . . .

E se pure di sì fatte cose un non so che simile al vero dicono i filosofi, quante altre ce ne sono ne le quali confessano di non conoscere l'ambizioso artificio de la natura, e a quelle loro proprietà occulte si riducono, come sotto lo scudo d'Aiace era solito Teucro di ripararsi? Questi erano i miei pensieri e i ragionamenti che fra me stesso faceva, per li quali sempre più mi andava accorgendo de l'incertitudine de le scienze mondane e sempre meno di credenza prestando a tutto ciò che da' filosofi contra la nostra religione può essere addotto, sì che ormai nulla, o molto poco, da quelle mie prime molestie era agitato.[25]

[And if I don't know how to explain the birth of Christ and His eternal generation, nor do I know how to explain the generation of thunder and lightning and of hail and of storms, and of the winds, unless very unsoundly and uncertainly; nor do I know, except very doubtfully, how the air depicts itself in such a variety of colors in that bow which is called the bow of the covenant; nor how in the region of fire or in its neighbor (of ether) there appear to us comets, and the milky way, and so many other apparitions, now frightening, now lovely, but always wondrous; nor do I know how in the bowels of the earth gold and silver and the other metals are generated, and how in the bed of the sea pearls and corals are produced; nor do I know enough to explain the generation of animals. . . .

And if philosophers say something similar to the truth about such things, how many others are there in which they confess not to understand the complicated workings of nature, and where they are obliged to stop and posit hidden properties, as Teucer was accustomed to take shelter beneath the shield of Ajax? These were the thoughts and reasoning which I made to myself, for which I came ever increasingly to realize

the uncertainty of our worldly sciences and ever less to lend faith to all
which the philosophers say that can be used against our religion, so that,
at length, I was troubled by none, or very few, of my former anxieties.]   **97**

Tasso's doubts were transformed into a *docta ignorantia*. Before an
unknowable godhead, the Christian must cling to revelation and faith:
"io conosceva che tu eri inconoscibile e ch'era follia il pensar di
raccoglier te, che sei infinito, dentro a' piccioli confini del nostro
umano intelletto." ("I knew that You were unknowable and that it was
folly to think of containing You, who are infinite, within the little
confines of our human intellect.")[26] But even before this meditation on
the immensity of the Creator, Tasso had arrived at an awareness of the
limitations of the human intellect from the demonstrated inability of
philosophy to understand the phenomena of the natural world,
"l'ambizioso artificio de la natura." The argument against intellectual
pride which uses nature as a test case—for if the mind cannot attain
natural truths, how can it hope to grasp the supernatural?—derives
from scriptural tradition. But in the episode of the Magus of Ascalon,
who allegorically figures the effort of philosophy to master a "cognitione dell'opere della natura, & de magisteri suoi," Tasso has given this
argument and its biblical precedents an ingenious reworking.

In the wisdom literature of the Old Testament, which regularly
disparages the very idea of human wisdom, few passages are so
uncompromisingly bleak as the voice that issues from the whirlwind
in the thirty-eighth chapter of the book of Job. To Job's suffering there
is no answer, but rather a barrage of questions. The voice of God
sarcastically inquires whether Job was present at the Creation and
then subjects him to a cosmological quiz. Job cannot answer. Knowledge of the secrets of nature, equated with the power to control its
elemental forces, is an attribute of the deity alone, a token of the
immeasurable distance separating God and man. Humbled, Job recognizes the presumption of questioning the ways of his creator.

Job is asked (vv. 8–11) if he can explain how the sea is kept within its
bounds, referring back to the separation of the waters from dry land in
Genesis 1:9–10 and, in a related question, whether he has walked in
the abysmal depths of the sea (v. 16). Some other questions: Has Job
seen the shadowy underworld (v. 17)? Does he understand the course
of rainstorms and thunder (v. 25), or the origin of the rain and the dew
(v. 28)? Can he explain the order of the heavens (v. 33)?

To these selected questions Tasso's Magus of Ascalon could answer yes, and he might achieve a passing grade on the examination in natural history which Job had failed. He separates the waters at the entrance of his underwater cave.

> e quinci e quindi di montagna in guisa
> curvata pende e 'n mezzo appar divisa   [14.36,7–8]

[and on this side and that (the water) hangs arched in the guise of a mountain and seems to be divided down the middle.]

These lines, it has been noted above, echo the *Fourth Georgic*.

> at illum
> curuata in montis faciem circumstetit unda
> accepitque sinu uasto misitque sub amnem.   [360–62]

[and the wave, arched in the guise of a mountain, stood about and welcomed him into the vast hollows and sent him beneath the river.]

But the scene also suggests the parting of the Red Sea waters. Lactantius had in fact used the Virgilian passage to describe the crossing of the Red Sea,[27] and the biblical analogy was noted by Renaissance commentators on the *Georgics*.[28] In turn, according to Wisdom 19:7, in a passage where the events of the Exodus are seen to recapitulate those of the Creation, the parting of the Red Sea is analogous to the separation of the waters from dry land. Equipped with his divinatory staff (*verga*), the Magus in his Mosaic guise assumes powers similar to those of the Cosmocrator. The Magus, moreover, makes his home in the abyss, at the source of the earth's rivers. In Job 38:8, these are said to spring up "quasi de vulva procedens"; the Magus's cavern is described as the womb (*grembo*) of nature. It is not readily apparent that this watery abyss is also a kind of underworld. But it should be remembered that the *Phaedo* locates the oceanic source in Tartarus, and, in the same series of octaves canceled from Canto 17 which have been referred to above, the Magus's realm is identified with Plato's Tartarean river system.[29] In the expanded version of the episode in the *Gerusalemme conquistata* (12.27–30), examined in the next section, the streams that originate in the recesses of the Magus's cave include the rivers of hell in which the damned are immersed and tortured.

The Magus satisfies other conditions imposed upon Job by the exigent voice of the whirlwind. God asks Job who it is that gives a track (*cursum*) to the stormcloud and a path (*viam*) to the thunderbolt (25).

From his observatory on Mount Carmel, the Magus observes the progress of thunderstorms.

> come il vento obliquo spiri,
> come il folgor s'infiammi e *per quai strade*
> tortuose in giù rispinto ei si raggiri;   [14.44,4–6]
> (my italics)

[how the wind blows aslant, how the lightning is kindled, and by what twisting paths it travels when it is driven down to earth.]

God asks Job: "quis est pluviae pater vel quis genuit stilla roris?" (Job 38:28). Tasso's echo is clear: the Magus tells Carlo and Ubaldo "e generar le pioggie e le rugiade/risguardo" (14. 44, 3–4; "and I observe the rains and the dews being born"). Job is further asked (33) whether he understands the arrangement of the heavens and their effects upon the earth. ("Numquid nosti ordinem caeli et pones rationem eius in terra?"). Tasso's Magus is a first-rate astrologer.

> ivi spiegansi a me senza alcun velo
> Venere e Marte in ogni lor sembianza,
> e veggio come ogn'altra o presto o tardi
> roti, o benigna o minaccievol guardi.   [14. 43, 5–8]

[there Venus and Mars in all their aspects are spread out unveiled before me, and I see how every other planet circles quickly or slowly or regards the earth with a favorable or threatening influence.]

Tasso has gone the argument of Job 38 one better while arriving at the same conclusion. In the Job chapter, the unexplained processes of nature are the measure of a human intellect unable to fathom the ways of God. But the Magus of Ascalon has succeeded in mastering the innermost secrets of creation: he has the answers to some of the cosmological riddles proposed by Job's whirlwind. Yet the Magus comes to realize how insignificant is his understanding of nature before the greater mystery which is God.

> Di me medesmo fui pago cotanto
> ch'io stimai già che 'l mio saper misura
> certa fosse e infallibile di quanto
> può far l'alto Fattor de la natura;
> ma quando il vostro Piero al fiume santo
> m'asperse il crine e lavò l'alma impura,
> drizzò più su il mio guardo, e 'l fece accorto
> ch'ei per se stesso è tenebroso e corto.

> Conobbi allor ch'augel notturno al sole
> è nostra mente a i rai del primo Vero,
> e di me stesso risi e de le fole
> che già cotanto insuperbir mi fero;
> ma pur sèguito ancor, come egli vole,
> le solite arti e l'uso mio primiero.
> Ben son in parte altr'uom da quel ch'io fui
> ch'or da lui pendo e mi rivolgo a lui,

> e in lui m'acqueto.   [14.45–46; 47, 1]

[I was so satisfied with myself that I once thought that my knowledge was a certain and infallible measure of all that the Holy Maker of nature can do; but when your Piero sprinkled water on my hair beside the holy river and cleansed my impure soul, he directed my gaze farther upwards, and made it aware that by itself it is limited and full of shadows. I knew then that our human mind before the rays of primal Truth is like a nocturnal bird dazzled by the sun, and I laughed at myself and at those silly fables of mine which once made me swell with so much pride; yet I still pursue, as he desired, my accustomed arts and former practice. I am truly in part another man than the one I was, now that I depend on him, refer myself to him,

and find my peace in his words.]

Converted at the Jordan by Peter the Hermit, the Magus recognizes the folly of his own earlier intellectual pride. The gap between the natural and the supernatural is absolute, a difference that is qualitative rather than quantitative. The Magus's natural philosophy, *scientia*, will not lead him to the spiritual wisdom, *sapientia*, that is only available through revelation.[30] The Magus avoids the fate of Doctor Faustus, and his conversion allows him to place his powers at the disposition of the Crusader cause. He becomes the agent of Peter the Hermit,[31] in accordance with Tasso's poetic allegory where philosophy is the "ministra della teologia."

Tasso did not need to venture outside the Book of Job to authorize this revision of Job 38. The earlier wisdom poem in chapter 28 anticipates and serves as a corrective to the voice of the whirlwind ten chapters later. Here, too, knowledge of the hidden places of the earth is a divine attribute. These include underground sources and natural refineries of precious metals.

> Habet argentum venarum suarum principia
> et auro locus est, in quo conflatur.   [28:1]

> Locus sapphyri lapides eius,
> et glebae illius aurum. [28:6]

These verses apparently inspire the description of the Magus's alchemical cave, and "glebae . . . aurum" may be directly translated by
Tasso's "auree zolle" (14.38.8). But after describing God's power to
scrutinize these subterranean wonders and the "profunda . . . flu-
viorum" (11), Job 28 shifts its argument and removes divine wisdom
from the natural world altogether.

> Sapientia vero ubi invenitur?
> et quis est locus intelligentiae?
> Nescit homo pretium eius,
> nec invenitur in terra suaviter viventium.
> Abyssus dicit: Non est in me,
> et mare loquitur: Non est mecum. [Job 28 : 12–14]

The home of Tasso's Magus in the primordial abyss cannot be regarded
as the true locus of wisdom.

Carlo and Ubaldo descend into the earth to the source of material
creation and find that the source of truth resides not below but above,
in the mind of God, which lies outside His creation and beyond the
ken of the unaided intellect. Their descent is, in fact, balanced against
the ascent through the stars which takes place at the beginning of
canto 14 in the dream of Goffredo, the only other character in the poem
who shares with the Hermit the grace of divine revelation. To Goffredo, too, are opened "i secreti del Cielo e de le stelle" (14.4.4; "the
secrets of Heaven and the stars"). In an imitation of Cicero's *Somnium
Scipionis*, Goffredo finds himself transported into the heavens, where
he meets the blessed spirit of his dead companion, Ugone. He learns
that the divine will dictates the recall of Rinaldo to the crusader cause
and that the fall of Jerusalem is at hand. But, aside from a brief glimpse
of heaven—described in the most abstract terms: "L'ampiezza, i moti, i
lumi e l'armonia" ("the spaciousness, the motions, the lights, and the
harmony")—Goffredo is introduced into no further theological doctrines or divine mysteries. Instead, on Ugone's instructions, his gaze
reverts to the earth, and the real emphasis of the episode is on the
immense distance which separates the human and the divine. Earthly
events seem vain and unimportant from his higher perspective.

> in giuso i lumi
> volse, quasi sdegnando, e ne sorrise,
> ché vide un punto sol, mar, terre e fiumi,

che qui paion distinti in tante guise,
ed ammirò che pur a l'ombre, a i fumi

la nostra folle umanità s'affise,
servo imperio cercando e muta fama
né miri il ciel ch'a sé n'invita e chiama. [14.11]

[(Goffredo) cast his eyes downward, almost with disdain, and smiled at the sight, for he saw as one single point the sea, the earth, and the rivers which here seem separated into so many different shapes, and he marveled that our foolish humanity is attached only to earthly shadows and smoke, seeking slavish empire and mute fame, and fails to gaze at the heavens which call and invite us up to them.]

This God's-eye view—Tasso's God also sees the earth as "un sol punto" (1. 7)—brings on a moment of *contemptus mundi*. Goffredo, like Cicero's Scipio, recognizes the relative insignificance of the world in which he nevertheless must continue to sweat and bleed and do his duty.[32] Goffredo's virtuous pursuits are their own reward, untainted by the worldliness which blinds man to the heavenly invitation beckoning him to a higher reality. Yet even the Crusade is diminished beside that greater, exalted reality.

Goffredo's dream recalls not only the *Somnium Scipionis* but the recent imitation of the Ciceronian text in the lunar voyage of the *Orlando furioso* as well. Astolfo, too, gazes downward upon the earth, just able to make out the seas and earth which for Goffredo are indistinguishable.

e ch'aguzzar conviengli ambe le ciglia,
s'indi la terra e 'l mar ch'intorno spande
discerner vuol [*Orlando furioso* 34.71.5–7]

[and he had to squint with both eyes, if he wanted to discern from up there the land and the sea which flows around it.]

Ariosto's moon is the literary model which *both* the composite episodes of canto 14, the celestial vision of Goffredo and the terrestrial source-cave of the Magus of Ascalon, attempt to rewrite. Together, they constitute Tasso's answer to the skepticism of his poetic predecessor and his attempt to renew an epic formula which the *Furioso* had subjected to a rigorous, if playful, deconstruction. That this crucial canto of the *Liberata*, which constitutes its *peripateia* two-thirds of the way through the epic, should be so obsessed with Ariosto's episode suggests how seriously Tasso took it as a challenge to his own poetics, and, perhaps, to what extent its nonsense structure has delimited the possibilities of meaning in the *Liberata*. The Magus locates divine wisdom *outside* his earthly domain, while Goffredo sees the vanity of human activity. Tasso seems to accept one-half of the Ariostesque formula—sublunary experience in itself has no source of meaning. But Ariosto's formula was an equation: the nonmeaning of the lower world was matched by the nonmeaning of a "higher" one to which it points. Tasso's God, however, reveals to the dreaming Goffredo the splendors of heaven and, with them, the assurance of a divine intelligibility guiding the action of the poem from above. But just how the human world of events may point to this divine realm of meaning remains unclear, for Tasso's division has made the two impossibly remote from one another. Human apprehension can only bridge the gap as the passive recipient of revelation, which, as in Goffredo's dream, invariably takes the language of a Platonic contemplative ascent and of a negative theology. Goffredo gazes up at the stars, which summon man back to his celestial homeland. The description closely echoes Sophronia's earlier exhortation to the lovestruck Olindo to redirect his misplaced attentions.

> Mira 'l ciel com'è bello, e mira il sole
> ch'a sé par che n'inviti e ne console.   [2.36, 7–8]

[Look at the sky, how beautiful it is, and look at the sun which seems to invite us to him and console us.]

The theme of this celebrated couplet is taken up again with a similar renunciation of the erotic in the predawn repentance and conversion of Rinaldo in canto 18.

> Fra se stesso pensava: "Oh quante belle
> luci il tempio celeste in sé raguna!
> Ha il suo gran carro il dí, l'aurate stelle
> spiega la notte e l'argentata luna;
> ma non é chi vagheggi o questa o quelle,
> e miriam noi torbida luce e bruna
> ch'un girar d'occhi, un balenar di riso,
> scopre in breve confin di fragil viso."   [18. 13]

[He thought to himself: "O how many beautiful lights the heavenly temple gathers inside it. The day has its great solar chariot, the night displays the golden stars and the silvery moon; but there is nobody who looks lovingly at either one, and we gaze at the dim and dark light that a quick turn of the eyes or the flash of a smile reveals in the small confines of a frail countenance.]

The Platonic injunction to look up at the heavens does not here suggest a flight of the unaided intellect. Rinaldo ascends the Mount of Olives as the final step of a penitential program guided by that orthodox "ministro del Cielo," Peter the Hermit. His contemplation precedes a prayer for grace which descends to him in the form of the morning dew. Nonetheless, Rinaldo's either/or describes a radically Platonic universe. The stars and the incorruptible heavens point toward the true Light, but man, imprisoned in the world of matter, gazes only at the evanescent light in the face of his beloved. Rinaldo repudiates his dalliance with Armida and a whole theory and aesthetic of Platonic love as well. Embroidering upon the teaching of the *Symposium*, Renaissance Neoplatonists saw the erotic as a springboard to heavenly contemplation; the lover sees traces of the divine in his beloved and embarks upon a mystical ascent.[33] But Rinaldo appears to out-Platonize the Platonists, pointedly separating earthly love from divine contemplation, insisting upon the dichotomy between the immutable heavens, where contemplation properly begins, and the sublunary material world of human experience.

By locating divine meaning above and outside the world of matter and history, the Platonism of the *Liberata*, no less than the self-ironizing Saint John in the *Furioso*, has removed the practical episte-mological consequences of the Incarnation from its epic universe. Whereas the source-river Jordan in the *De partu Virginis* testified to the presence of the Word in nature, the source-cave of the Magus of Ascalon separates the Creator from His creation: Tasso has accommo-dated the pessimism of Job to his own Platonic distrust of matter. Unlike Milton's portrait of the godhead, there is no mediating Son, no Word made flesh in the epic heaven of the *Liberata:* Christ's presence in this Christian epic is marked almost solely by His sepulchre, the goal of its action. Tasso's God, introduced in a description which elevates Him as far above the stars as the stars themselves lie above the earth (1.7), who dazzles the sight of even the highest angels (9.57), is described by negation, in terms of His remoteness and unknowability. There is a divinity which shapes the end of the epic, but it lies beyond human understanding: "ove senso o ragion non si conduce" (9.56, 4; "where sense or reason do not lead").[34]

This Platonized divinity, operating from without upon the human world of the poem, provides a model for a poetics which claims a source of intelligibility and authority outside the text, a source which lies, however, beyond the text's representation. This poetics has several obvious advantages. For one thing, it avoids the trap set by the circular nonsense poetics of the *Furioso*, where the text created its source of meaning in the act of representing it, and where the source became simply one more product of the text. Its nonrepresentational source allows the *Liberata* to bypass external authority; and here again, Tasso evades the *Furioso*'s skeptical attack upon the bad faith of writers and of the literary tradition on which they depend. Moreover, by removing his source of authority to the periphery of his poem, Tasso opens up a realm for his own poetic imagination.

Tasso seeks a middle ground between the total autonomy of the *Orlando furioso* and the kind of subordination of the poet to external authority which had been Sannazaro's lot in the *De partu Virginis*. In the *Discorsi dell'arte poetica*, the treatise he wrote in preparation for the *Liberata*, Tasso objects to basing his epic upon scriptural subject matter.

> perché in esse il fingere non è lecito; e chi nessuna cosa fingesse, chi in somma s'obligasse a que' particolari ch'ivi son contenuti, poeta non sarebbe, ma istorico.[35]

> [because in them (sacred histories) the making of fictions is not permissible; and he who feigns nothing, who, in brief, is obliged to follow the particulars which are contained there, would not be a poet, but a historian.]

Because the biblical text is inviolable—its record of true events admits no alteration—it leaves no room for the poet's fiction. Tasso's quest for an independent poetic voice similarly causes him to exclude the presentation of theological doctrine in his poem. Through a letter to Scipione Gonzaga, Tasso asks his friend Flaminio Nobili for advice on the allegorical significance of the *Liberata*.

> Avvertisca però di mescolare fra i miei concetti manco concetti teologici che sia possibile; perchè io desidero che si possa credere che sia mia fattura: e da l'altra parte non voglio fingere di saper teologia, non ne sapendo;[36]

> [Advise him, however, to mix among my ideas as few theological ideas as possible; because I want one to be able to think that (the poem) is my work: and, on the other hand, I don't want to pretend to know theology, since I don't know it.]

Tasso insists that the poem should be thought to be his own creation ("fattura"); theology thus becomes competition for his fiction. So does history, despite the importance history plays in Tasso's defense of the truth of his poem.

In the *Discorsi*, Tasso directly attacks Ariosto's claim that Homer and other poets have played havoc with the historical facts. Quoting from Saint John's speech on writers in the *Furioso*, he concludes that it is Ariosto who is lying, not the poets he accuses.[37] Following Aristotle's dictum that poetry is more philosophical than history, Tasso states that the epic poet has the liberty to embroider and expand upon historical events so long as he does not change their outcome. But it is apparent in Tasso's theoretical writings and within the *Liberata* as well that his interest and sympathy are commanded by the fictional elements of his epic—the invented heroes in both the crusader and pagan armies, the love affairs, the battle scenes, and, above all, the marvelous—rather than by the facts. The objection which Tasso voiced to rewriting the sacred history of the Bible is applied by the *Discorsi* to secular history as well: Lucan is dismissed from the ranks of epic poets for being too factual.[38] The episode of the Magus is included among other marvels of the *Liberata* which Tasso in his letters at one time or another considers removing because of possible irreligiosity. He defends the episode with a historical source: some unspecified "istorie gotice" in which he had recently found "cosa che a questa mia invenzione s'assomiglia: dico cosa naturale, non fatta per arte diabolica" ("something which resembles this invention of mine, I mean something natural, not made by diabolical art").[39] But this source, in which history is found to imitate poetry, is adduced after the fact: the episode had already been written. In another letter, Tasso writes of the desirability of finding in his poem "una certa similitudine e quasi imagine de la storia, in quello che non guasta la poesia" ("a certain resemblance and almost an image of history, so long as it doesn't spoil the poetry").[40] Poetry is Tasso's first consideration, to which theological and historical authorities take second place.[41]

The allegory that Tasso outlined for the *Liberata* may also be understood as a defense of the poet's autonomy. He declares the subject of his epic to be a "felicitá civile," a happiness available in the life of human action to which Renaissance humanism assigned an independent dignity alongside the life of religious contemplation. The moral truths the humanists sought to derive from the contingency and variety of the active life constituted a kind of situation ethics, necessarily relativistic and of a different order from the eternal truths of contemplation.[42] In the body politic of the crusader army, the commander-in-chief Goffredo is a figure "di quell'intelletto, che considera non le cose necessarie ma le mutabili, & che possono variamente avvenire" ("of that intellect, which considers not necessary things but contingent ones, those which can happen in a variety of ways").[43] This definition of his subject matter allows Tasso to turn the events of his poem, its marvels in particular, into figures for subjective and psychological human processes which the poet may analyze without recourse to transcendent authority.[44] This impulse toward internalizing the meanings of the *Liberata* (which would not be lost on Milton, whose Heaven and Hell are as much spiritual states as physical realities) is checked, however, by Tasso's insistence in his account of his allegory upon the necessity of divine inspiration and grace for the perfection of human wisdom. Like any other prudent Renaissance man, Goffredo may try to lead his army on the basis of his understanding of contingent events, but the crucial decision to recall Rinaldo comes from above, from God.[45] Tasso's moral allegory is clearly an insufficient description of his crusade subject matter which, with an eye to Lepanto and the contemporary struggle against the Turks, represents an episode in providential history. Renewing the epic formula which Ariosto's celestial machinery had burlesqued, the *Liberata* strives to describe a divine plan working through human action. But it is here that Tasso's Platonizing epistemology militates against a convincing depiction of the link between a Christian source of meaning and a virtually autonomous world of action. For Goffredo, and later for Rinaldo, grace and divine guidance take the form of a contemplative ascent above and beyond that world of action.

The removal of a source of intelligibility from the sensible confines of its fictive universe, beyond the language of the poem itself, is reflected in the confused experience of the *Liberata*'s protagonists and accounts in no small part for its tremendous imaginative power and complexity. There is a genuine pathos in the moral error which drives Tasso's heroes away from their headquarters outside Jerusalem, the stage of civic action, and toward the peripheries of the poem, when truth, too, is placed outside the epic world. The siren who bewitches Rinaldo in canto 14 (63) by inviting him to give up his soldierly responsibilities echoes the *contemptus mundi* theme expressed by Ugone in Tasso's Platonized heaven fifty octaves earlier. The moral center of the poem becomes that much tougher and hard-earned because it is so difficult to find.

Rinaldo complains at the moment of his conversion that human beings cut themselves off from the true light; they are left in the dark. Indeed, perhaps more than any other epic, the *Liberata* is a nocturnal poem, its tone set by the celebrated description of Argante traveling toward Jerusalem at nightfall at the end of the second canto. Episode after episode takes place in a night which corresponds to the confusion, deception, and error of the protagonists. Enamored of Armida, Eustazio and other paladins sneak out of the crusader camp under the cover of darkness, "ove ne 'l mena/per le tenebre cieche un cieco duce" (5.80, 3–4; "where a blind leader leads them through blind darkness"). Similarly, the lovestruck Erminia abandons Jerusalem at night (6.103), only to be chased into a wood of error. Tancredi mistakes her for Clorinda and follows her into the wood; on the succeeding night (7.28 ff.) he is brought to the castle of Armida on the Dead Sea where, in one of Tasso's finest effects (44), the lights suddenly go out, plunging him into darkness and captivity. Solimano launches two surprise attacks by night, first on the troops of Sveno in canto 8, and then on the entire Crusader army in canto 9. During the second battle, the night becomes literally diabolical (9.15), as the Powers of Darkness take to the air. Again, Tancredi fights and mortally wounds his beloved Clorinda at night in canto 12, only to discover his mistake in the first light of dawn. The poem's darkness finally breaks on the day of the last battle and the taking of the Holy City.

> Non fu mai l'aria sì serena e bella
> come a l'uscir del memorabil giorno:
> l'alba lieta rideva, e parea ch'ella
> tutti i raggi del sole avesse intorno;
> e 'l lume usato accrebbe, e senza velo
> volse mirar l'opere grandi il cielo.   [20.5.3–8]

[The sky had never been so clear and fair as it was at the opening of that memorable day: the happy dawn laughed and it seemed that she had gathered about her all the rays of the sun; and the customary light increased, and heaven wished to see the great deeds without a veil.]

Only after twenty cantos do human action and God's providential plan merge, resulting in clarity and revelation.

Closely related to this thematic darkness is the *Liberata*'s insistence upon the hidden. *Nascosto, ascoso, celato, occulto, secreto* are adjectives that crop up repeatedly throughout its pages. An atmosphere of concealment and mystery pervades the poem, particularly associated with the marvelous. The Magus of Ascalon invites Carlo and Ubaldo into "le nascose/ spelonche ov'ho la mia secreta sede" (14.36; "the hidden caves where I have my secret dwelling"), to where the Nile "non asconde/gli occulti suoi principi" (38; "does not conceal his hidden beginnings"); he studies (42) the powers hidden in plants and springs. But the result of the Magus's research is that the secrets of nature are *not* equivalent to the knowledge of a God who truly remains hidden, outside of His creation. The withdrawal of Tasso's deity from the natural world leaves a vacuum which demons rush in to fill. The language of concealment is transferred to the marvels wrought by black magic, to the devils lurking in the enchanted wood of cantos 13 and 18, to the dangers latent in Armida's island paradise. The fountain of laughter at its entrance is apparently guileless:

> trasparente sí che non asconde
> de l'imo letto suo vaghezza alcuna   [15.56.5–6]

[so transparent that it does not hide any of the beauties of its deepest bed.]

The bottom is visible and clear, but the peril, as the Magus of Ascalon has forewarned Carlo and Ubaldo, is contained in the fountain's water itself.

> ma dentro a i freddi suoi cristalli asconde
> di tosco estran malvagità secreta   [14.74.3–4]

[but inside its cold crystals is hidden the secret evil of strange poison].

Inside the fountain, two splashing nymphs continue this play of disclosure and concealment, tempting the knights with intermittent glimpses of their naked bodies.

> Si tuffano talor, e 'l capo e 'l dorso
> scoprono alfin dopo il celato corso.   [15.58.7–8]

[now and then they dived and revealed their heads and backs after a hidden underwater swim.]

> Così da l'acque e da' capelli ascosa
> a lor si volse lieta e vergognosa.   [15.61, 7–8]

[thus hidden by the waters and their own hair they turned happily and bashfully toward them.]

These nymphs are alluring precisely because they are half-hidden in the water. Tasso's erotic psychology perceives the quality of unknowability and concealment as a prime source of the desired object's fascination. Armida's artfully careless décolletage in canto 4 is the occasion for a meditation on "l'amoroso pensier."

110

> ché non ben pago di bellezza esterna
> ne gli occulti secreti anco s'interna.

> Come per acqua o per cristallo intero
> trapassa il raggio, e no 'l divide o parte,
> per entro il chiuso manto osa il pensiero
> sì penetrar ne la vietata parte.   [4.31. 7–8; 32. 1–4]

[which not content with external beauty also enters into hidden secrets.

Just as a ray of light passes through water or a perfect crystal, and does not divide or separate it, so thought dares to penetrate beneath her closed dress into her forbidden parts.]

The simile of the transparent water anticipates the scene at the fountain of laughter. Armida, in her turn, falls in love with Rinaldo. His eyes, the source of the erotic *spiritus,* are closed in sleep. Tasso underlines the paradox of "sopiti ardori/d'occhi nascosi" (14.67; "the dormant fires of hidden eyes"). The attraction of the hidden is made explicit in the song of Armida's parrot in praise of the blushing rose.

> che mezzo aperta ancora e mezzo ascosa
> quanto si mostra men, tanto è più bella.   [16. 14.3–4]

[which, half open and half hidden, is most beautiful when it shows itself least.]

The impulse to uncover the hidden arises in a universe whose virtually undecipherable surfaces seem to coalesce. The description of nightfall in canto 17 could characterize the general physiognomy of Tasso's epic.

> Sorgea la notte intanto, e de le cose
> confondea i vari aspetti un solo aspetto.   [17.56,3–4]

[night meanwhile arose, and one single aspect confused the various aspects of things.]

This confusion is reinforced by the number of parallel and mirror episodes whose mutual reflections become a structural device of the *Liberata.* Actions and characters on one side of the battle often have their counterparts on the other: the experience of the Crusaders is not so different from that of their Saracen foe. Armida appears in the

Christian camp in canto 4 with a false story of invented injuries and causes dissension in the ranks among the knights who would flock to her revenge; in canto 17, she arrives at the army of the king of Egypt with a tale of true injuries received from Rinaldo and again becomes the cause of discord. In canto 10, Ismeno comes to the aid of the downfallen Solimano, much as the hermits had succored Carlo after Solimano's victory in canto 8. Ismeno predicts that Solimano's lineage will produce Saladin, while at the end of the same canto 10, Peter the Hermit is rapt by the vision of Rinaldo's Estense descendents. Ismeno leads Solimano into a cavern that anticipates the descent into the cavern of the Magus of Ascalon. The career of the pagan magician Ismeno parallels that of the Magus, but in reverse. Whereas the Magus was born pagan and converted to Christianity, Ismeno is a renegade Christian. Ismeno embodies precisely that confusion between true and false, Christian and pagan, which exists throughout Tasso's epic.

> Questi or Macone adora, e fu cristiano,
> ma i primi riti anco lasciar non pote;
> anzi sovente in uso empio e profano
> confonde le due leggi a sé mal note.   [2.2,1–4]

[He worships the god of Islam now and he had been a Christian, but he is still unable to leave behind his former rites; rather, he often, in impious and profane practice, confuses the two religions, both faultily known by him.]

Even the divine machinery of the poem is open to demonic parody. Argillano in canto 8 has a false, diabolically inspired dream that anticipates Goffredo's dream-vision of heaven. In the mutiny which follows, Argillano is demonically possessed by the "stupor ch'Aletto al cor gl'infuse" (8. 59; "stupor which Allecto infuses in his heart"), while Goffredo "dal Cielo infuso ir fra le vene/sentissi un novo inusitato caldo" (8. 77; "felt a strange, unwonted heat, infused from Heaven, course through his veins"). While Raimondo is protected by his invisible guardian angel during the duel of canto 7, his opponent Argante is shielded by Beelzebub. In canto 9, Alecto appears to Solimano, recalling the descent of Gabriel to Goffredo in the first canto and triggering the counterintervention of Michael forty octaves later.

This confusion of Christian truth and its pagan-demonic alternatives—which leads the erring heroes of the *Liberata* into what Tasso's allegory calls "false credenze"[46]—seems to be the inevitable result of the dichotomy described in canto 14 between the world of history and matter and the divine intelligibility which lies outside that world. There is, however, one moment in this same crucial section of his epic where Tasso is able to overcome that dichotomy and portray a divine presence working *through* the processes of nature. This is the providential rainfall that comes at the end of the thirteenth canto, and whose aftereffects are described in the dew-laden night which opens canto 14, immediately preceding Goffredo's dream and the initiation of the poem's *soluzione per macchina:* this is the precise turning point of the poem.

> Usciva omai dal molle e fresco grembo
> de la gran madre sua la notte oscura,
> aure lievi portando e largo nembo
> di sua rugiada preziosa e pura   [14. 1.1–4]

[Now dark night was leaving the damp, cool womb of her mother Earth, bearing gentle breezes and a thick cloud of her pure and precious dew.]

Dew is a familiar Old Testament figure, associated in Hosea 14:6 and Isaiah 26:19 with the eschatological blessing that will befall Israel. The words of Isaiah's God—"Rorate, caeli desuper, et nubes pluant iustum; aperiatur terra et germinet Salvatorem" (Isaiah 45:8)—became part of the Latin advent liturgy: the dew now refers to the Incarnation. In the *De partu Virginis*, Sannazaro describes the moment of the birth of Christ with a beautiful simile of dewfall (2.360–65). Hrabanus Maurus provides a succinct gloss.

> Dew signifies the Word of God: for it waters the hearts of earthly men in order to bring forth fruit, as it is written in the Psalm: *Sicut ros Hermon quod descendit in montem Sion* (Psal. cxxxii).[47]

Dew also becomes a symbol of Christian grace through its association with the manna that fell to the children of Israel in the wilderness (Exodus 16:13 ff.). Christ presents himself as the eucharistic bread of life, the superior type of the manna, in John 6:49–51. Goffredo invokes this typology of grace when he prays for rain to end the drought in canto 13.

> devotamente al Re del mondo chiede
> che gli apra omai de la sua grazia i fonti   [13.70.5–6]

[he devotedly implores the King of the universe to open the springs of His grace to him]

> 'Padre e Signor, s'al popolo tuo piovesti
> già le dolci rugiade entro al deserto'   [13.71.1–2]

["Father and Lord, if you once rained sweet dews to your people in the desert . . ."].

The figure will be picked up again in canto 18, when the penitent Rinaldo implores heaven: "In me tua grazia piovi" (14; "Rain your grace upon me"); his prayer is answered by the fall of the morning dew.

> e ventillar nel petto e ne la fronte
> sentia gli spirti di piacevol ora,
> che sovra il capo suo scotea dal grembo
> de la bell'alba un rugiadoso nembo.
>
> La rugiada del ciel su le sue spoglie
> cade, che parean cenere al colore,
> e sì l'asperge che 'l pallor ne toglie
> e induce in esse un lucido candore:
> tal rabbellisce le smarrite foglie
> a i matutini geli arido fiore,
> e tal di vaga gioventù ritorna
> lieto il serpente e di novo or s'adorna.   [18.15.5–8; 16]

[and he felt the breath of a pleasant breeze fan his breast and brow, and it shook above his head a cloud of dew from the lap of the lovely dawn.

The dew of heaven falls upon his garments which seemed to be the color of ashes, and so sprinkled them that it took away their pallor and gave them a shining whiteness; so does a dry flower rebeautify its wilted petals in the chill morning dew, and so does a serpent happily return to its pleasing youth and adorn itself with new golden scales.]

Rinaldo's conversion recalls the opening of the *Purgatorio*, where Virgil bathes Dante in the morning dew (1.121–29). The episode is to be seen as a personal version of the larger collective intervention of God's grace in the form of the vivifying rain to the crusader army. The analogy between the two events is spelled out by the echo of the rhyme words *grembo* and *nembo*.

But this typological pattern is no sooner established than the demonic parodists go to work. The newly converted Rinaldo enters the enchanted woods which have so far resisted the Crusaders' attempts to cut them down. The woods now assume a false Edenic amenity reminiscent of the seductive charms of Armida's garden. The language of regeneration and renewal, however, seems to have been appropriated from the conversion scene seven octaves earlier.[48]

> e sovra e intorno a lui la selva annosa
> tutte parea ringiovenir le foglie;

s'ammoliscon le scorze e si rinverde
più lietamente in ogni pianta il verde.

Rugiadosa di manna era ogni fronda   [18.23.5–8; 24.1]

[and above and about him the aged forest seemed to rejuvenate all its leaves; the tree barks grow softer and every plant more happily grows green again.
Every branch was dewy with manna].

The old forest that puts out new leaves looks back to the two similes that describe the washing of Rinaldo's armor by the dew of grace: the revived flower and the rejuvenated serpent (18.16). The serpent is recalled through a buried metaphor. *Scorza*, which here means the bark of the trees, can also signify the rough skin a snake sloughs off in summertime. The dewy manna completes the parody and the reader's sense of déjà vu. Even the manifestation of divine grace can be replicated through the devil's art. The scene of natural regeneration is intended to tempt the regenerate Rinaldo to lapse back into his old error.

The language of Rinaldo's conversion is also anticipated by the metaphor in canto 4 which describes Armida bathed in her own crocodile tears.

Le guancie asperse di que' vivi umori
che giù cadean sin de la veste al lembo,
parean vermigli insieme e bianchi fiori,
se pur gli irriga un rugiadoso nembo,
quando su l'apparir de' primi albori
spiegano a l'aure liete il chiuso grembo   [4.75.1–6]

[Her cheeks, sprinkled with those running tears which fell down onto the hem of her dress, seemed to be red and white flowers watered by a cloud of dew when, at the appearance of the first dawn, they unfold their closed inner petals to the happy breeze.]

The rhymes "grembo" and "rugiadoso nembo" appear here, too. But the typological meaning of the dew metaphor—the grace necessary for spiritual renewal—is inverted. Literally, the metaphor tells us how beautiful Armida is when she is angry: her tears only make her cheeks more lovely. It further suggests her self-absorption, for her own self-renewing tears generate her beauty. She is described as a natural system complete in itself, a self-sufficiency corresponding to what we know about Armida's pride (4.27) and her cold-hearted, virginal resistance to love until she encounters Rinaldo (14.67). Even her love for him, as critics have pointed out, is described in terms of narcissism, culminating in the emblematic tableau in canto 16.20, where the two lovers are both shown to be absorbed by their mirror images.[49]

This chain of related metaphors comes to an end in Canto 20. After Rinaldo prevents Armida from committing the ultimate narcissistic act of suicide, *he* feels pity and weeps.

> e 'l bel volto e 'l bel seno a la meschina
> bagnò d'alcuna lagrima pietosa.
> Qual a pioggia d'argento e matutina
> si rabbellisce scolorita rosa,
> tal ella rivenendo alzò la china
> faccia, del non suo pianto or lagrimosa.   [20.129.1–6]

[and he bathed the lovely face and the lovely breast of the unhappy woman with some tears of pity. Just as, at the silvery rain of morning, a faded rose rebeautifies itself, so she, coming to, raised her bowed face, teary with weeping which was not her own.]

Now, Tasso explicitly states, it is not Armida's tears that bring back the rosiness to her cheeks but the tears of Rinaldo, genuine tears and the sign of a new mutuality in their love. Armida's position has changed from self-sufficiency to dependency, and the final scene of the two lovers ends with her declaration of submission to Rinaldo. Mediating her change of heart is the dew metaphor which points to the actual dewfall during the conversion of Rinaldo and draws an analogy between the two episodes. Rinaldo's own return to the fold involves a double surrender of autonomy. At the spiritual level, he acknowledges his need for divine guidance and grace. In the political scheme of the poem, he opens canto 18 by placing himself at the command of Goffredo, whose authority has been challenged ever since his acclamation as sole leader of the crusader army in the first canto.

> Imponga a i vinti legge egli a suo senno,
> porti la guerra e quando vole e a cui;
> gli altri, già pari, ubidienti al cenno
> siano or ministri de gl'imperii sui.   [1.33.3–6]

[let him give laws to the conquered according to his judgment, let him wage war when and against whom he wishes; let the others, once his equals, now obey his orders and be the ministers of his commands.]

Tasso's criticism of knight errantry calls for his hero to renounce its individualistic code and to submit to the will of the community. In her closing words, Armida speaks to Rinaldo in language which makes him both her God and her commander.

> "Ecco l'ancilla tua: d'essa a tuo senno
> dispon," gli disse "e le fia legge il cenno."   [20.136.7–8]

["Here is your handmaiden: dispose of her according to your judgment," she said to him, "and your order will be law to her."]

The echo of Mary's response to Gabriel (Luke 1 : 38) is joined to the echo from within the poem describing Goffredo's sovereignty. The echo of the Annunciation, furthermore, completes the action of a poem which began with the descent of the angel Gabriel to Goffredo (1.11–17), and joins Armida to the hierarchy: God-Gabriel-Goffredo-Rinaldo-Armida.[50] The transformation of Armida, turning outward from herself to another, is presented as analogous to the conversion of Rinaldo, who submits to his captain Goffredo, who, in turn, is following God's orders. By taking the first step, Armida is on her way to salvation.

The language describing the movement of Tasso's characters from autonomy to external authority is itself authorized by a recourse, not to some vague Platonic source of meaning beyond representation, but rather to a tradition of sacred texts. The *Liberata* can distinguish between a true and false appropriation of the figure of dew, and thereby organize the several appearances of that figure into a conceit, only because there already exists a scriptural typology which privileges one meaning of the figure as the true one; otherwise there would be no way of telling the demonic counterfeit from the Christian original. But if this example of typological language offers a bridge between the poet's fiction and Christian meaning, it remains virtually the only example of such language in the *Liberata*. For Christian allegory depends upon the Incarnation, with which the Platonizing epistemology of Tasso's epic cannot come to terms.

The Incarnation interprets and guarantees the meaning of the historical language of scripture: the dew, in fact, is a figure of the Christ-event itself. When Ariosto wished to prevent an allegorical reading of the *Orlando furioso*, he had perforce to dismiss the originary significance of the divine Word, and he was able to do so precisely because the Incarnation is revealed through scriptural texts which, as texts, could be subjected to a skeptical historical criticism. Consciously reacting against the *Furioso*'s model, Tasso's Platonism avoids history altogether—including a history of texts. While he may be defending his fiction from Ariosto's corrosive historicism, the practical result of Tasso's poetics is a virtual autonomy from external textual authority which seems to preclude an allegory based on typological language. Yet that language does surface in the *Liberata*, significantly enough at its most crucial moment. In Tasso's later revision of his epic, the *Gerusalemme conquistata*, when the poet sought to bolster his fiction with a series of outside authorities, he turned increasingly to scriptural typology. Yet, as the following section will suggest, the typological patterns of the *Conquistata* preserve those very Platonic dichotomies of the *Liberata* which they should normally resolve.

THE WATERS ABOVE THE FIRMAMENT

The revisions of the *Gerusalemme conquistata*, published in 1593, are so extensive that it should be considered a separate poem from the *Liberata*. The twelve years which intervened from the publication of the *Liberata* saw the host of polemics for and against Tasso's epic, *the* great literary debate of the late Italian Renaissance, and it has been generally affirmed that in the changes wrought in the *Conquistata* the poet hoped to placate and silence his critics.[51] The revisions are characterized by a retreat from Tasso's earlier defense of his poetic autonomy. Reflecting what seems to be a loss of confidence in his own creation, Tasso turns to a series of outside authorities—literary, historical, religious—to bolster the epic fiction.

The most remarkable new feature of the *Conquistata* is its imitation of the *Iliad*. Episode after episode is lifted from before the wall of Troy and set down in front of the ramparts of Jerusalem. Rinaldo, his name changed to Ricardo, becomes a second Achilles, equipped with a Patroclus-companion, Ruperto, and a Thetis-mother, Lucia. Argante, in a more spectacular transformation, now has a wife and infant son who play Andromache and Astyanax to his Hector. And so on. Whereas the classical imitations of the *Liberata* had seemed, in the best tradition of Renaissance poetry, to be a vehicle for self-expression, the reader of the *Conquistata* senses the sacrifice of Tasso's poetic personality as he subordinates his own inventions to the Homeric model. A second line of defense in the *Conquistata* is a further insistence upon historical fact and erudite detail, witnessed in set pieces such as Ducalto's tour of the historical sites of the Holy Land (II, 15 ff.) or the chronicle of the Crusade up to its arrival before Jerusalem depicted on Goffredo's tent (3. ff.).

The *Conquistata* has also acquired a new and dogmatic religiosity. One of its symptoms is the downplaying of what had been a central thematic pattern in the *Liberata*, the conversion of pagan heroines by crusader knights. Although Clorinda's death and baptism are retained, Armida, now the daughter of one of the diabolic sirens of Babylon (5.24), is an unredeemable witch who leaves the poem in chains after the destruction of her garden at the end of canto 13. Erminia, renamed Nicea, turns up in canto 23 in Jerusalem in time to join in the general lament for Argante; the celebrated scene of the *Liberata* in which she cuts off her hair in order to bind Tancredi's wounds has been omitted. Conversion, holding out an interpretative middle ground where the evident misdirection of paganism can be read in terms of its eventual reconciliation with Christianity, complemented and even seemed to grow out of the epistemological uncertainty of the *Liberata*'s universe, where surface distinction and outline seemed constantly about to fade into a gray ambiguity. The reverse is true in the *Conquistata*, where the absence of conversion reflects black and white spiritual and moral polarities. The symbolic and allegorical episodes of the *Conquistata* spell out their significance, carefully supported by the best theological authorities. To clear up any doubtful passages, Tasso published a further interpretative key to his poem, the *Del giudizio sovra la Gerusalemme*. Significantly, the *Conquistata* has reshaped those passages in the *Liberata* which emphasized the gap between human experience and an inaccessible divinity: Goffredo's dream, the conversion of Rinaldo, and the episode of the Magus of Ascalon. These episodes are all linked together by the figure of the source, which has now become the single most important allegorical figure of the *Conquistata*.

The *Conquistata*'s treatment of the cave of the Magus in canto 12 considerably expands the episode of the *Liberata*. The revisions are typical of the didacticism and the greater attention to learned detail of the later poem. The catalogue of rivers that have their origin in the cave, taking up four verses of the *Liberata*, now requires three octaves (14–16). In addition there is a list of the seas fed from the underground source (25–26), and a description of the rivers of Hell which is indebted to the *Phaedo* and the *Inferno*.[52] The Oceanus myth of the *Phaedo* and the *Fourth Georgic* is now made explicit for Tasso's reader.

Ma se degna di fede è fama antica,
l'Oceàn de le cose è il vecchio padre.
L'Oceàn chiuse in sé la terra aprica,
e 'n grembo siede a lui chi detta è madre.[53] [12.21.1-4]

[But if ancient fame deserves to be believed, Ocean is the aged father of things. Ocean encloses the sunny land, and in his lap sits she who is called mother (earth).]

In the *Giudizio*, Tasso explains that he is going back to the doctrine of Thales of Miletus: moisture is the source of material creation.[54] The Magus spells it out for his knightly visitors.

ed ecco i fonti a voi del mar dimostro
da cui deriva la materia oscura: [12.24.5-6]

[and here I show you the sources of the sea, from which lowly matter is derived.]

The meaning of the episode remains the same, and the *Conquistata* can here be used as a more discursive gloss to the *Liberata*. This holds true in spite of one very striking change in the fiction of the *Conquistata*, the transfer of the Magus's cave to the source of the Jordan (5–6). Tasso appropriates the traditional identification of the Jordan and the river Oceanus. But this earthly Jordan does *not* become here, as it did in the *De partu Virginis*, a figure of the Incarnation, of the diffusion of divine meaning and grace throughout natural creation. The earlier Platonism of the *Liberata* remains too strong for the poet to assign any intelligibility to matter. Instead, Tasso has recourse to the tradition of the two Jordans, the earthly and the heavenly rivers. The Magus explains:

Altri forse sará ch'a voi racconte
d'altre acque sovra il cielo in suon piú sacro,
d'altro vero Oceàno, e d'altro fonte
di luce, e d'altro puro ampio lavacro:
e le cinque fontane a voi fian conte,
non pur la somma, a cui purgo e consacro
il torbido pensiero e l'alma immonda,
e ber vi fia concesso in lucid'onda. [12.23]

[others, perhaps, will tell you in more sacred sound of other waters above the heavens, of another true Ocean, and of another fountain of light, and of another pure spacious font; and the five fountains will be

made known to you, not just the highest one, in which I cleanse and
consecrate my turbid thought and impure soul, and you will be allowed
to drink of the waters of light.]

Once again the same "altro" anaphora appears which was found in the
fifth eclogue of the *Arcadia* and in the description of the moon in the
Orlando furioso. But the postulation of another, higher realm of being,
understood by Sannazaro and Ariosto to be, in fact, identical with the
worlds described by their intratextual fictions, is meant to be taken at
face value here. As the Magus suggests, Tasso elsewhere in the
Conquistata will portray these higher waters as a matter of theological
fact. Behind his fiction are hexameral commentaries on the separation
of the waters by the interposition of the firmament in Genesis 1 : 6–7.
In his *Homilies on Genesis,* Origen sees the two waters as, respectively,
the spiritual and corporeal worlds, which are both contained and
contest one another within the microcosm, man.

> Let each of you take to heart the task of
> separating 'the water above from that which
> is below,' in order to understand and to
> assimilate this spiritual water 'which is
> Jn. 7 : 38   above the firmament' in order to draw from
> 4 : 14   'its belly streams of living water' 'springing
> up into everlasting life,' far removed, very
> far from the water below, that is, the water
> of the abyss where Scripture places the
> Rev. 12 : 7   shadows and where 'the prince of this world'
> dwells and the enemy 'dragon' 'with his angels,'
> as it is said above.[55]

The waters below the firmament, Origen later remarks, are "the sins
and vices of our bodies," and they are further identified with the abyss
where Satan dwells.[56] Tasso's fiction depicts the watery underworld of
Tartarus situated alongside the source of materiality. Origen's refer-
ences to the Johannine waters of life, moreover, link the supracelestial
waters to his figure of the Jordan, the river which makes glad the city
of God. Other commentators preferred to interpret the division of the
waters by the firmament in terms of a hierarchy of being, though here,
too, they did not escape the Platonism which informs Origen's dichotomy between body and spirit. In the unfinished *De Genesi ad litteram,*
Augustine calls the firmament an "aethereum caelum," which is
probably to be associated with the fire of the *Epinomis* and the

Aristotelian ether or "quintessence," a stable element that does not participate in the mutability of the elemental bodies beneath it. Those dissoluble bodies are designated by the waters below the firmament. The waters above the firmament are purely intellectual beings: these are angels, though Augustine may also have in mind Plato's description of a realm of pure forms beyond the heavens (*Phaedrus*, 274c).[57] In the *Heptaplus*, one of the several interpretations which Pico della Mirandola gives to the separation of the waters distinguishes between the intelligible forms enjoyed by the angels and the sensible forms of the lower elemental world.[58]

The Magus promises the two knights and the reader that the description of the "altro vero Oceano, e d'altro fonte / di luce" will be entrusted to another character of the poem. He appears to refer to the revised version of Goffredo's dream in canto 20. The dream is now structured between visions of Jerusalem, the earthly city (9–25), and the heavenly New Jerusalem, following the Augustinian division in the *City of God*. But despite a roll call of popes and champions of the Faith culminating in encomia to Charles V, Philip II, and the princely commanders at Lepanto (101 ff.), Tasso's emphasis does not lie upon the horizontal dimension of history, where the two cities have a common meeting ground, but upon the vertical distance which separates them.[59] Augustine's spiritual polarities become virtually subsumed in a general Platonic disdain for all things earthly, and the poet gives Goffredo's expression of *contemptus mundi* in the *Liberata* a contemporary application.

> Che gioverá, ch'al suo valore estenda
> l'angusto spazio Carlo, o 'l gran Filippo
> oltra le mète, e sia chi i nomi intenda,
> e nel marmo gl'intagli, altro Lisippo?   [20.147.1–4]

[What does it avail, if by their valor Charles or great Philip extend narrow space beyond their goals, and if he who hears their names and carves them in marble is another Lysippus?]

In place of the vague, indescribable Platonic heaven of the *Liberata*, the heavenly city has acquired a new concreteness, its details derived from the figural New Jerusalem of the Book of Revelation. Streaming from the throne of God is the River of Life.

> Poscia un fiume di lucide onde
> fender l'alta cittá quasi per mezzo,

piú bel del Nilo, ove il principio asconde,
o d'altro ch'al ciel mandi il fumo e 'l lezzo:
che dal seggio divin, tra fronde e fronde,
esce odorato, mormorando al rezzo:
fa il legno de la vita i frutti e l'ombre,
e par che quella sponda e questa ingombre.

   Quinci veder pareagli in riva a l'acque
d'angeli un nembo che lampeggia e vaga;
quindi l'umano stuol ch'infermo giacque,
e vi risana di vetusta piaga;
qual dove d'alta selva agli occhi piacque
fiorita vista, o d'un bel rio ch'allaga,
volano infra le foglie augei dipinti
e l'api tra narcisi e tra giacinti.   [20.37–38]

[Then a river with waters of light divides the holy city almost in half, fairer than the Nile where it hides its beginnings or than any other river that sends its vapor and earthly smells to heaven: for from the divine throne it emerges, fragrant among the branches and leaves, murmuring to the breeze: the tree of life produces fruit and shade and seems to cover both this and that side of the river.

He seemed to see on one side of the bank beside the waters a cloud of angels which flashed like lightning and wandered about; on the other a human throng that lay ill and was being cured of an ancient wound; just as where a flowery vista pleases the eye in a lofty forest or beside a lovely, overflowing river, painted birds fly among the leaves, and bees fly among narcissus and hyacinths.]

Dante had turned the river of Revelation 22 : 1 into a river of light, and Tasso appears to be dependent upon *Paradiso* 30 (61 ff.) for the idea of the river as a spiritual boundary—between the angels and a humanity healed of Original Sin—and hence a figure of the Jordan. The bee simile in octave 38 recalls the description of the celestial rose at the beginning of *Paradiso* 31. Dante's river flows "in circular figura," the typological circularity of the oceanic Jordan: it strikes the primum mobile and surrounds the universe with an ocean of light (*Par.* 30.100–08). But Dante's river is finally just a figure, disappearing the moment it is crossed. Beatrice tells the pilgrim:

Il fiume, e li topazii
Ch'entrano ed escono, e 'l rider de l'erbe
Son di lor vero umbriferi prefazii.[60]   [*Paradiso* 30.76–78]

[The river, and the topazes which enter and go forth, and the smiling of
the grasses are shadowy prefaces of their reality.]

What Dante and, quite probably, what the author of Revelation
himself understood as a figure pointing to a theological mystery, Tasso
represents as a heavenly reality. To understand this distinction, there
is no need to leave the text of the *Conquistata*. Goffredo's vision can be
compared to Clorinda's prophetic dream in canto 15.

In her dream, based upon the poem *De Pascha* of Saint Cyprian,
Clorinda sees a great plant growing up above the clouds (15.41). This
Tasso identifies in the *Giudizio* as the cross, traditionally assimilated
with the tree of life.[61] The tree's height, recalling the trees which
represent the anticommunities of Babylon (Daniel 4 : 7 ff.) and Egypt
(Ezekiel 31 : 3 ff.), suggests that it may stand for the Church as well, a
reading supported by the crowd rushing beneath its shade. Clorinda
next sees a flowing fountain.

> Chiara fontana ancor sorgea d'un monte,
> mormorando con acqua dolce e fresca,
> e parea quasi tomba il vivo fonte
> ov'uom si tuffi immondo e puro n'esca:
> ed a chi si bagna in lei l'umida fronte
> par ch'onore e virtute indi s'accresca;
> quivi correano, al dolce suon conversi,
> Greci, Latini, Assiri, ed Indi, e Persi. [15.44]

[A clear fountain rose from a mountain, murmuring with sweet and cool
water, and almost like a tomb appeared the living fountain in which man
is immersed unclean and emerges pure: and whoever bathes his wet
brow in it seems to augment his honor and virtue; thither, turned toward
its sweet sound, rush Greeks, Latins, Syrians, Indians, and Persians.]

The *Giudizio* states that this fountain is the figure of baptism, extended
to all the nations of the earth.[62]Within the poem's fiction, it is a
premonition of Clorinda's own imminent baptism and conversion-in-
death on the battlefield. But together the tree of life and the living
waters ("vivo fonte") form an important typological complex that goes
back to their coupling in Eden (Genesis 2 : 9–10) and to the description
of the just man in the first of the Psalms.

> Et erit tanquam lignum, quod plantatum
>   est secus decursus aquarum,
>   quod fructum suum dabit in tempore suo,
>   et folium eius non defluet,
>   et omnia quaecumque faciet prosperabuntur. [Psalms 1 : 3]

The just men of Israel are the never-withering fruit trees which grow along the banks of the eschatological river of Ezekiel 47:12. In Christian exegesis, the trees are the saved, watered by the sacrament of baptism. They have become *like* Christ, the tree of life.[63] Christ, from whose belly flow streams of living water, is also the fountain of life. A pictorial tradition portrays the Holy Sepulchre as a fountain of life, often surrounded by trees.[64] Clorinda's fountain, "quasi tomba," may recall this iconography. The author of Revelation has placed tree and waters together in the New Jerusalem at 22:1–2, and Goffredo sees the river of light in the heavenly city shaded by "il legno de la vita."

Clorinda and Goffredo thus gaze upon the *same* typological figure. But for Clorinda the tree and waters are pure figures, signs pointing to her own salvation history. By contrast, they have become eternal fixtures in the topography of Goffredo's heavenly city, which is placed above and outside of human history. The projection of the figure into the eschatological future is built into biblical typology, and the New Jerusalem of Revelation is to be regarded as the fulfillment of history at the end of time. But it is history which unites the meanings of typology, a history organized around the Christ-event which retrospectively glosses the biblical history of the Old Testament, which gives significance to the present-day sacraments of the church and the moral life of the Christian (the figure has a personal application for Clorinda), and which is fully revealed in the apocalyptic end of history: this is the fourfold structure of Christian allegory. But Tasso, by depicting the heavenly city as disjunct from the historical process, effectively removes the mediating significance of the Incarnation from the figure. The tree, waters, and the rest of the celestial landscape which Goffredo beholds merge into heavenly archetypes, a confusion of typological figures and Platonic *eide*, the timeless higher forms of which earthly reality is merely the reflection. The "other" waters and fountains mentioned by the Magus seem to refer to both scriptural and Platonic types.

This confusion is also present in the allegory of the five fountains, Tasso's most extensive addition to the marvels of the *Conquistata*. Though they are first mentioned at the end of the sixth canto, Tancredi comes across the series of fountains in canto 8, shortly before he arrives at the castle of armida on the Dead Sea.

> Giunse dove perpetue e rapide onde
> con larga vena uscian d'un vivo sasso,
> e facean cinque fonti ampie e profonde,

da l'imo al sommo, o pur da l'alto al basso.
Fêa la prima due rivi: e l'un s'asconde,
nel suo principio ritorcendo il passo:
l'altro queto scendea con l'acque chiare,
sin ch'egli si moria nel morto mare.   [8.12]

    L'aurora intanto candida e vermiglia
lieta apparia nel lucido orizzonte:
e discopria l'antica maraviglia,
come si faccia l'un da l'altro fonte.
Il primo, che'l suo occulto e'l ver simiglia,
ha per sostegno un uom che pare un monte,
lo qual gli omeri incurva, e quasi stanco
china al peso lucente il capo e'l fianco.   [13]

    Paion quell'acque liquidi zaffiri,
non turbate da nembi o da procelle;
e luminosi raggi in lor rimiri
percossi lampeggiar de l'auree stelle.
E i torti lor viaggi, e i torti giri
da quelle a queste, o pur da queste a quelle,
e con ogni altra piú serena imago,
l'errante luna e'l sole errante e vago.   [14]

    Ma nel secondo pur, qual cervo o damma,
l'uom correria per ammorzar la sete,
bench'egli tutto al novo dí s'infiamma
co' rai che sembran quasi accese mète.
Il fonte è del color di viva fiamma,
in cui spiegano i crin varie comete;
e d'ardenti sembianze auree faville
or turbate vi scorgi ed or tranquille.   [15]

    Il terzo fonte par ch'al sol s'indori,
come suol ne le nubi arco dipinto;
e dispiega sue forme e suoi colori
onde fe' Delia la corona e'l cinto:
e verghe e spegli in luminosi orrori,
da cui lo stil d'Apelle ancora è vinto;
né formeria l'algente ed umid'ombra,
ch'a rai s'alluma, e'l lume in lei s'adombra.   [16]

    Quasi gran mar fremendo il quarto ondeggia
ne l'ampio vaso e'n su la molle arena,
e scopre la squamosa orrida greggia,
e come isola in mezzo orca o balena,

e'l corallo e la perla: e quel rosseggia,
questa è nel suo candor tutta serena:
e l'onda vaga co'l suo moto alterno
simiglia de la luna il corso eterno. [17]

La quinta fonte è del color de l'erba,
ma pur di gemme ella riluce e d'oro;
e di quanti metalli in sen riserba
l'antica madre, abbonda il bel tesoro:
e con fiorita vista e con superba
frondeggia intorno a lei palma ed alloro,
che, coronata di sue verdi selve,
nel grembo accoglie armenti e gregge e belve. [18]

[He arrived where perpetual and fast-flowing waters sprang with a wide stream from a living rock, and made five spacious and deep fountains, from bottommost to highest, or rather from the top to the bottom. The first produced two streams, and one conceals itself, twisting its path back to its source: the other one quietly descends with clear waters until it dies in the Dead Sea.

Meanwhile the white and vermilion dawn appeared in the clear horizon and disclosed the ancient marvel, how each fountain is produced from the other. The first, which resembles its hidden reality, has for support a man who seems to be a mountain, whose shoulders are bent and who, almost as if he were tired, bows his head and body beneath the shining weight.

Those waters seem to be liquid sapphires, undisturbed by clouds or storms; and they are seen to be struck and flashing with the luminous rays of the golden stars. And one sees their winding journeys and winding orbits, from this side to that (the stars), or from that to this (the planets), and together with every other most lovely heavenly body, the errant moon and the errant, wandering sun.

But to the second fountain, like a hind or hart, a man would run to quench his thirst, even though at the coming of day it is all aflame with rays that resemble burning piles of hay. The fountain is the color of living flame, in which various comets unfold their fiery tails, and there one sees golden sparks, now stirred up, now dormant, of what seem to be burning objects.

The third fountain seems to be gilded by the sun as a rainbow is wont to appear among the clouds; and it unfolds its forms and colors from which Delia made her crown and girdle: and streaks and reflections in gleaming darkness which outdo even the effects of Apelles' painting; nor could he fashion the cold and moist shade which is illuminated by the rays of sunlight, while that light is lost in its shadows.

The fourth undulates almost like a roaring sea in its large basin and on the soft sandy shore; and discloses a dreadful herd of scaly creatures, and in the middle an orc or whale like an island, and coral and pearls: the former gleams red and the latter is all serene in its whiteness: and the wandering wave with its alternating motion resembles the eternal course of the moon.

The fifth fountain is the color of grass, and yet it glistens with gems and gold; its lovely treasure abounds with all the metals which the ancient mother stores in her breast; and with proud and flowery countenance, leafy palms and laurels flourish around the fountain which, circled with green woods, gathers in its lap herds, flocks, and wild beasts.]

The inspiration for this allegory, Tasso affirms in the *Giudizio*, is to be found in the *De dilectione Christi et proximi* of Thomas Aquinas.[65] Thomas posits five descending fountains, the higher fountains feeding into the lower ones, which signify the unfolding of elemental creation. Tasso explains that his fountains "possono significare i cinque generi della sostanza sensibile" ("may signify the five kinds of sensible substance"),[66] the five Aristotelian elements, from the quintessence (octaves 13–14) through fire (15), air (16), water (17), and earth (18). Tasso gives each fountain its appropriate iconography. The quintessence is represented by the heavens supported on the shoulders of Atlas. Through its undisturbed medium move the stars, planets, sun, and moon. The second fountain, corresponding to the sphere of fire, contains flaming comets. The third displays a rainbow, the visible manifestation of air; the fourth the ocean and its marine creatures; the fifth the minerals, plants, and beasts of the "antica madre," the earth. The soul, according to Thomas, cannot be satisfied by the material elements and rushes to the fountain of life, Christ.

In his treatise, Thomas goes on to suggest that there are five *other* fountains, signifying the five types of substances—mixed, vegetative, sensible, rational, and intellectual or angelic—which correspond to five stages in the soul's ascent to God, an ascent which is largely cognitive and whose participants include the pagan philosophers.

In the *Giudizio*, Tasso makes it clear that he has fused *both* of Thomas's systems of fountains into one; the five fountains can be read in two ways, "da l'imo al sommo, o pur da l'alto al basso." The first fountain, the quintessence, consequently corresponds to "ogni sostanza metafisica, o soprannaturale, che vogliam dirla, dalla quale derivano gli accidenti, come cagioni da loro effetti, ed alle superficie di questo primo fonte vennero i filosofi . . ." ("every metaphysical substance, or supernatural one, whatever we wish to call it, from which accidents are derived, as causes from their effects, and the philosophies arrived at the surface of this first fountain . . .").[67] But, Tasso continues, even this fountain must be bypassed.

> Ma benchè tutto questo fonte fosse sparso nell'aride fauci dell'anima assetata, la cui sete è il desiderio di conoscer Dio, non potrebbe, se non come una minuta stilla mitigar la sua sete; quanto meno potrebbono estinguerla gli altri quattro fonti della sostanza variabile e corrutibile, ne' quali bevvero i filosofi naturali, i medici, i meccanici, e gli alchimisti. . . .[68]

> [But even were this fountain sprinkled into the dry throat of the thirsty soul, whose thirst is the desire to know God, it could not, except as a minute droplet, allay its thirst; how much less could it be extinguished by those other four fountains of variable and corruptible substance, which were drunk by natural philosophers, doctors, practical scientists, and alchemists. . . .]

The allegory of the five fountains repeats the significance of the Magus's cave: the human sciences and philosophy, based on the contemplation of material creation, even the incorruptible matter of the quintessence, are far inferior to the knowledge of God, the true source. Man must turn from these corporeal waters to the spiritual waters above the quintessence, above the firmament, waters whose source is indicated in the division of the first fountain in octave 12.

> Fêa la prima due rivi: e l'un s'asconde,
> nel suo principio ritorcendo il passo:
> l'altro queto scendea con l'acque chiare,
> sin ch'egli si moria nel morto mare.

The *Giudizio* gives a moral interpretation to these two streams. The one that empties into the Dead Sea is "il piacer della contemplazione perversamente derivato, e distorto al diletto sensuale" ("the pleasure of contemplation perversely diverted and distorted to sensual pleasure"), and is located appropriately beside the witch Armida's castle. The stream that returns to its source is "la cognizione riflessa," an intellectual self-consciousness which ultimately leads the contemplative man to a knowledge of his Creator.[69]

But it is easy to see in these two rivers the types of the earthly and heavenly Jordans, the first flowing into the Dead Sea, the second flowing back on itself toward a heavenly source. "Ritorcendo" echoes Psalm 114: "Iordanis conversus est retrorsum." Gregory of Nyssa had described the cosmic Jordan: "It does not rise in Palestine to disappear in some nearby sea: it spreads over the whole earth and flows into Paradise." But whereas for Gregory the Jordan is one great system of grace, joining heaven and earth as a figure of the Incarnation, Tasso carefully distinguishes between two Jordans: the material, earthly river that has its origin in the Magus's cave, and the incorporeal river whose source is the Fountain of Life: "Il fonte della vita è Dio medesimo" ("The fountain of life is God Himself").[70]

The Jordan typology of this heavenly stream is indicated again in its final appearance in the poem, during the conversion of Riccardo in canto 21. Like his *Liberata* prototype Rinaldo, Riccardo is bathed in the morning dew after contemplating the beauty of the incorruptible stars. In the following stanza (99), he repeats his contemplation allegorically by drinking from the first of the five fountains. This marvelous fountain has been described to Riccardo a few stanzas earlier by Peter the Hermit.

> Sacra fama ed occulta a me rivela
> la maraviglia ove condurti io penso:
> questo al ciel volge un rio lucente e vago,
> né si vanta di lui marina o lago.
>
> Primo é di cinque, a cui talor ricorre
> turba gentil ch'alto desire accenda   [21.90.5–8; 91.1–2]

[Sacred and hidden fame reveals to me the wonder to which I plan to guide you: it sends a lovely river of light toward heaven, nor does any sea or lake boast over it.

It is the first of five, to which a noble band resorts, kindled by high desire].

The important literary echo here is from *Inferno* 2.108, where Lucia asks Beatrice whether she perceives the plight of the pilgrim Dante: "su la fiumana ove 'l mar non ha vanto?" ("on the river over which the sea does not boast?"). This verse is the focal point for a study by John Freccero, who demonstrates that Dante's reference is to the typological Jordan, which, identified with the river Oceanus, is greater than any sea.[71] Freccero suggests that Lucia's speech to Beatrice may recall Arethusa's calling to Cyrene in the *Fourth Georgic*. The sixteenth-century commentator on Dante, Daniello da Lucca, also found an echo of the Virgilian passage in the verse, in an edition of the *Commedia* owned by Tasso and bearing marginal notes in his hand.[72]

As the convert Riccardo drinks in "sapere eterno" (99) from the stream of this celestial Jordan, he completes the chain of river-source symbolism in the *Conquistata*. The Jordan, the fountain of life, the river which streams through the New Jerusalem—all versions of the same typological figure—unify the poem's several depictions of metaphysical reality. Tasso turns to typology in the *Conquistata* in an attempt to flesh out the Christianity which had been suffused in a larger Platonism in the *Liberata*. But though the figures of scripture endow the New Jerusalem of Goffredo's vision with a splendid substantiality that is absent from the vague, ineffable heaven of the *Liberata*, and though the contemplative heights which Rinaldo scales in the *Liberata* are now dramatized by Riccardo's drinking of the spiritual waters above the fifth fountain, the Platonic dualities of the earlier poem remain intact in the *Conquistata*. The earthly Jerusalem and the Jordan find doubles in the celestial city and heavenly river: there is little or no meeting place between the physical and metaphysical levels of the epic universe. Paired with his baptismal immersion in the dew, Riccardo's drinking from the waters of life is probably intended to suggest the sacrament of the eucharist. But the eucharist, above all other sacraments, is based on the mystery of the Incarnation, the Word made flesh. Riccardo drinks from the incorporeal waters above the quintessence—firmament—the Word without the flesh. Even as he strives for Christian significance, Tasso is unable to reconcile the source of natural, material creation with the divine source of meaning set outside that creation.

This inability accounts for the paradox that the *Conquistata*, with its accretion of theological symbolism and authority, has actually reduced the significance of the action of its human characters. The balance that is maintained in the *Liberata*, where a divine reality that cannot be represented only now and then threatens to devalue and belittle the events on the battlefield, is upset when the *Conquistata* frequently depicts a metaphysical plane of being above and beyond the world of history. The taking of Jerusalem, the allegory of civic felicity in the *Liberata*, is in the penultimate stanza of the *Conquistata* only a token of a higher, spiritual bliss.

> Cosí gli accoglie la cittá terrena,
> la cittá che lor serba e pace e regno
> regno e pace ch'il cielo ha più serena   [24.136.1–3]

[Thus the earthly city receives them, the city which holds in store for them peace and a kingdom, a peace and kingdom which heaven possesses in a happier form.]

Jerusalem is only the terrestrial city. It pales, even in the Crusaders' hour of triumph, before its heavenly archetype.

But the conquest of Jerusalem is the subject matter of Tasso's fiction. It is at the expense of his personal poetic property that the *Conquistata* imports outside authority, whether the Homeric model that turns Jerusalem into an imitation Troy or the enlarged framework of Christian typological symbolism that deprives rather than gives meaning to the epic action. The revisions of the later epic—which diminish and devalue the inventions of the *Liberata*—raise again the question of the autonomy of the poet's fiction vis-à-vis an authoritative divine Word with which this chapter began. The Platonism of the *Liberata* allows Tasso to have it both ways; he claims an extratextual source of meaning in Christian truth, yet preserves the distance between that source and his own fiction, which is, for practical purposes, autonomous. But this distance, no less than the self-conscious declarations of literary independence made by a Pulci or an Ariosto, keeps the individual poet's word separate and apart from the Word of God. In the *Conquistata,* a Christian truth supported by religious authorities and cloaked in typological language operates on a level unrelated and frequently antithetical to the poet's fictional world: whereas the *Liberata* manages to balance, if not reconcile, the conflicting claims of autonomy and authority, the later epic seems to pose a choice between the two. And the choice is made definitively in the final major work of Tasso's career, his hexameral epic, the *Mondo creato:* the poet surrenders his personality to scripture and exegetical tradition.[73] His decision is comparable to Sannazaro's turning from the conventional poetic autonomy of the pastoral to his Nativity poem. Ariosto with joking blasphemy chose autonomy—*and* a poetic world of madness and nonmeaning. Sannazaro and Tasso ultimately chose authority, though not without first experiencing, in the case of Sannazaro, the dissolution of the Neapolitan kingdom by the French invasions, and, in Tasso's case, the nightmare of a real and recurrent madness.

The difference between the scriptural subject matters of Sannazaro and Tasso is significant. For Sannazaro chose the moment of the Incarnation and the restoration of a fallen creation, while Tasso, in the *Mondo creato,* writes of a unity between the divine Creator and His creation that existed before the Fall, *outside* of his own human history. Tasso's inability throughout his career to find some mediation between his individual poetic imagination and the authority of Christian truth is reflected in a consistent downplaying of the historical dimen-

132

sion of the Incarnation. The location of a dichotomy between poetry and truth within a more fundamental division between matter and spirit is Tasso's clearest anticipation of the crisis of baroque poetics and thought.[74]

The Jordan Comes to England

Comme de l'Infiny de la Couronne ronde
Découle la Sagesse au sourgeon eternel,
Tout ainsi par rondeurs son ruisseau perennel
Es siecles retournez se retorne en ce Monde.
   En Luz Israel beut de sa source feconde,
   Moyse en arrousa le terroir solennel
   Qui est baigné du Nil, le grand Mercure isnel
   L'y puisa, & depuis Orfée encor l'y sonde:
Puis le divin Platon d'Egypte la derive
En la ville où Pallas feist naistre son Olive,
E d'Athenes Denis sur Seine la borna:
   Si que Paris san pair de la ville à Minerve,
   De Thrace, Egypte, & Luz fut faite la reserve,
   Ou le Rond accomply des Sciences torna.[1]

[As Wisdom flows from the round Crown of Infinity and its eternal source, just so by cycles does its timeless stream flow back in this world through the restoration of the ages. At Luz, Israel drank from its teeming fountain; with it Moses watered the solemn ground that is washed by the Nile; there the nimble great Hermes imbibed it and Orpheus too tasted it: then divine Plato derived it from Egypt to the city where Pallas caused her olive tree to sprout up, and from Athens Dionysius confined it along the Seine: so that Paris, without equal, greater than the city of Minerva, than Thrace, Egypt, and Luz, was made its reservoir, where the completed Cycle of the Sciences returned.]

In this dedicatory sonnet preceding the *Galliade* of Guy Lefebvre de la Boderie, the terms *Crown* and *Wisdom* derive from the Cabala, where they describe the first two emanations from Infinity. They were assimilated by Christian cabalists with God the Father and the Son.[2] The sonnet documents the geographical movement of the river Wisdom through a series of incarnations in human history. Moses brings to the Nile the mystical lore received at the Palestinian source of Luz, where Jacob (Israel) experienced his dream of the heavenly ladder (Genesis 28 : 12 ff.). From Egypt, where Hermes Trismegistus and Orpheus drank from the occult store, Plato "derives," in the sense of diverting a stream, his doctrine to Athens, from which it is finally brought, now figuratively embodied in the Seine, to Paris by Dionysius the Areopagite. The result, so satisfying to the nationalism of the author of the *Galliade,* is that Paris and her river have become the final stage in this historical process, the preeminent source.

La Boderie outlines a separate dispensation of theological wisdom which branches from its Jewish source through the pagan philosophy of Egypt and Greece, a dispensation that runs parallel to and is in syncretic harmony with Christian revelation: Dionysius fuses Neoplatonism and Christianity. The analogy between the two dispensations is underlined by the figure of the river rolling back upon itself, the traditional type of the Jordan as Logos. La Boderie's conception of the reemergence of the river Wisdom in different locations through history may be indebted to the idea of the Jordan's ubiquity: that all rivers of the earth, as tributaries and branches of a great circular system, are versions of the Jordan. The circular river is further used to describe a cyclical movement of history ("par rondeurs") which incorporates the related ideas of *translatio imperii* and *translatio studii,* the transfer of the center of empire, civilization, and the arts from one geographical and historical situation to another.[3] In the third book of the *Galliade,* France becomes the origin and final goal of a progressive historical scheme in which the cyclical rise and fall of civilizations is viewed as the completion of a single, larger cycle.

> Dont le petit ruisseau en sa fontaine né
> Apres s'estre en Itale et Grece pourmené
> Et s'estre enflé des eaux, et de richesse estrange
> De Tigris, et du Nil, et d'Eufrate, et du Gange
> En Gaule est retourné bruyant impetueux
> Se descharger au sein de Seine tortueux,
> Amenant avec luy des torrents de faconde,
> Et meint fleuve profond, meinte source feconde
> De doctrine et scavoir, despouillant Babilon,
> Ecbatane, et la Suse, et le grande Pavillon
> De la Terre et du Ciel, Jerusalem doublee,
> Athenes, et Memphis, et Romme toute emblee

Afin d'orner Paris la Cité des Citez
Et l'Université des Universitez.[4]

[The little stream born from its fountain, after having traveled through **135**
Italy and Greece, and having been swollen with the waters and the
foreign riches of the Tigris, the Nile, the Euphrates, and the Ganges, has
returned to Gaul with its rushing sound and empties itself into the bosom
of the winding Seine, bringing with it torrents of eloquence, and many
profound streams, many a teeming source of doctrine and knowledge,
despoiling Babylon, Ecbatana, Susa, and the great Pavilion of Heaven
and Earth, twofold Jerusalem, Memphis, and Rome completely pillaged
in order to adorn Paris, the City of Cities and the University of Universi-
ties.]

Succeeding all the earlier centers of world empire and human learning, the university town of Paris has become the universal city. In this
apocalyptic passage, Paris assumes the position of the messianic
Jerusalem described in Isaiah 66 : 12, receiving the spoils of the other
nations of the earth in an overflowing stream.

quia haec dicit Dominus
ecce ego declinabo super eam quasi fluvium pacis
et quasi torrentem inundantem gloriam gentium . . .

The descent of Isaiah's God in the form of a river, a passage cited by
Origen in his meditation on the Logos as river (see above, p. 74), links
these lines to La Boderie's sonnet and suggests the complementary
relationship between the history of human knowledge and civilization
and the progressive unfolding of divine revelation, both of which
reach their goal in France. In the former case, this goal is nothing less
than a return to the source, for the arts first sprang up as a "petit
ruisseau" in France. The absolutely originary status of French civilization and its present apocalyptic fulfillment in La Boderie's plan are
asserted by his depiction of the traditional four rivers of Eden—Tigris,
Nile, Euphrates, and Ganges—absorbed into the Seine, which is
punningly revealed to be the mother and nurse of the arts. France has
become a restored Eden.

The idea that human history moved progressively through a
series of geographical centers toward an eventual return to Eden was
not lost upon Renaissance explorers of the New World. Sailing west,
the traditional direction of the *translatio imperii* which followed the
course of the sun, Christopher Columbus thought he had come full

circle to the portals of the east when, on his third voyage of discovery, he reached the estuary of the Orinoco.

> There are great indications of this being the terrestrial paradise, for its site coincides with the opinions of the holy and wise theologians whom I have mentioned; and moreover, the other evidences agree with the supposition, for I have never either read or heard of fresh water coming in so large a quantity, in close conjunction with the water of the sea . . . .[5]

Columbus identifies the Orinoco with the river that flows out of Eden, dividing into the four rivers of paradise, in Genesis 2 : 10. But the basis for his claim, the size of the freshwater stream flowing out into the ocean—a river "over which the sea cannot boast"—appeals to the typology of the Jordan. This typology surfaces, perhaps even subconsciously, in Columbus's description of a marvelous lake which appears to be part of the Orinoco system, "which latter might more properly be called sea; for a lake is but a small expanse of water, which, when it becomes great, deserves the name of a sea, just as we speak of the Sea of Galilee and the Dead Sea."[6] The river which flows between and widens into the Sea of Galilee and the Dead Sea is, of course, the Jordan. Other Renaissance discoverers also saw the typological Jordan in great rivers that poured fresh water miles out into the sea. "Rio Jordan" was one of the early names given to the immense estuary of the River Plate.[7] A similar broad river mouth in the Solomon Islands, extending its current far into the Pacific, was christened "Jordan" by the evangelically minded Pedro Fernandes de Quiros. De Quiros, too, thought in terms of Eden, the restored Eden of the Apocalypse. He founded a settlement called New Jerusalem beside the banks of his Melanesian Jordan.[8]

Closer to Europe lies the estuary of the Thames, beginning as far inland as London. A tidal river, the Thames regularly flows backward upon its current.[9] Here Giordano Bruno and Edmund Spenser each sets an allegory which, exploiting the figure of the circular source-river, describes the source of allegorical meaning itself. Both fictions celebrate Elizabeth and the glory of her reign. Yet, for all their striking parallels and the historical proximity of the two authors—Spenser may well have known Bruno's text and imitated it after his own fashion— the versions of the Thames-as-source in the *Eroici furori* and the *Faerie Queene* define fundamentally opposed structures of allegorical thought. Whereas for Spenser the claim of the Thames to the status of source depends upon its location beside Elizabeth's royal city and

England's recent entry into the historical succession of empire, for Bruno the river loses its historical and geographical specificity once it is viewed as one manifestation of an eternally available, ubiquitous source. Bruno's poetic allegory is a kind of philosophical gnosis from which the dimension of history has been removed. By contrast, Spenser's fiction locates allegorical meaning in particular, historical circumstances, and the eventual removal of its basis in history will signal his allegory's end.

THE *EROICI FURORI*

Giordano Bruno's *De gli eroici furori* (1585) ends with an allegorical tale about nine young men who set out in search of a beauty higher than or equal to the lady with whom all nine are in love. On their way, they enter the palace of Circe, who stands for the changing shapes and forms of material generation. She casts water upon them and they become blind under her spell. After a ten-year quest, they reach the nymphs of the Thames, one of whom "like Diana among the nymphs" ("come la Diana tra le ninfe") opens a fatal urn given to the nine men by Circe. Sprinkled by the waters of this urn, the nine can see again and are spiritually enlightened as well. They sing the praises not merely of their illumination but of the quest itself, which, for all its difficulties and travails, has brought them to their present happiness.

Bruno's prefatory *Argomento* offers an explanation of this allegory.

> Significa ancora che son due sorte d'acqui:inferiori, sotto il firmamento che acciecano; e superiori, sopra il firmamento che illuminano: . . . Là s'intendeno illuminati da la vista de l'oggetto, in cui concorre il ternario delle perfezioni, che sono beltà, sapienza e verità, per l'aspersion de l'acqui, che negli sacri libri son dette acqui di sapienza, fiumi d'acqua di vita eterna. Queste non si trovano nel continente del mondo, ma *penitus toto divisim ab orbe*, nel seno de l'Oceano, dell'Anfitrite, della divinità, dove è quel fiume che apparve revelato procedente dalla sedia divina, che ave altro flusso che ordinario naturale.[10][P. 325]

> [It further signifies that there are two kinds of waters, the lower ones beneath the firmament that blind, the higher ones above the firmament that illuminate. . . . There they are understood to be illuminated by the sight of that object in which there come together the three perfections, which are beauty, wisdom, and truth, through the sprinkling of those

waters which in the sacred books are called waters of wisdom, rivers of the water of eternal life. These are not found on the continent of the earth, but *far off sundered from the whole world* [i.e., Britain; see Virgil *Eclogue* 1. 66] in the bosom of the Ocean, of Amphitrite, of divinity, where there is that river which appeared revealed to proceed from the throne of God, which has a different current than the ordinary natural one.]

Much like Tasso, Bruno uses the description in Genesis of the waters above and below the firmament to distinguish between spiritual and material reality. He assimilates the spiritual waters above the firmament with the Johannine waters of life and with the river of Revelation 22 : 1. But, unlike Tasso, who kept the lower and higher waters strictly apart in a vertical hierarchy of being, Bruno brings the heavenly river, with its Jordan-like supernatural current, down into the world of matter and sees it embodied in the Thames. One of the nine seekers describes England's river, which "Da basso in su rimonte / Riserpendo al suo fonte" (p. 514; "ascends backward from bottom to top, twisting back to its source"). The Thames flows back upon itself, like the oceanic Jordan, and it is here "nel seno de l'Oceano," that the source of spiritual wisdom is revealed.

It should be noted at the outset that Bruno employs this traditional Christian typology in a context which, in any ordinary sense, is *not* specifically Christian. For La Boderie, the separate dispensation to the pagan philosophers was ancillary to the primary truths of Christian revelation. Bruno, by contrast, accommodated Christianity to what was the primary basis of his metaphysical and religious thought: a highly personal syncretic philosophy which combined elements of Neoplatonism, Pythagoreanism, cabalism, and the doctrine of the Hermetic texts.[11] Bruno could regard his thought as Christian or in perfect harmony with Christianity, once Christianity itself was understood to be part of a larger religiophilosophical whole. Hence he could use the figure of the river which flows back upon itself, the traditional Christian type of the Incarnation, to describe his own broader concept of the relationship of spirit and matter.

The circularity of the river, with its flux and reflux, is assimilated by Bruno with a cyclical view of creation and history. He adapts the idea, which he ascribes to Origen, of an eternal series of spiritual cycles, treating the millennium not as an eschatological period at the end of a linear Christian history but as a model for the cyclical alternation between spirit and matter.

la revoluzione è vicissitudinale e sempiterna; e che tutto quel medesimo
che ascende, ha da ricalar a basso; come si vede in tutti gli elementi e cose
che sono nella superficie, grembo e ventre de la natura. [P. 324]

[the cycle is everchanging and eternal; and that everything which
ascends must also fall back down again; as one sees in all the elements
and things which are on the surface, in the womb, and insides of the
earth.]

The natural cycle of generation and corruption is not merely a metaphor for the interchange of matter and spirit along the ladder of being
but is itself part of that process. Natural change is perceived as the
means by which the divine presence inheres within the created
universe.

The belief in a constant oscillation between material and spiritual
poles leads Bruno logically to the doctrine of metempsychosis. The
orthodox tenet that the soul has only one body, he says, is a fiction for
the masses, whose morals can only be kept in line by the fear of eternal
punishments. But Bruno, as an enlightened philosopher, follows
Origen in believing in the soul's return into an infinite succession of
bodies. Most important, this cyclism is internalized for Bruno when
the soul of the philosopher attempts a gnosis whereby it reaches
upward to God. The gnosis is made possible by the eternal process at
the larger level of creation through which spirit enters matter and
matter fills itself with spirit: by exploring the various forms of the
sensible and the material, the soul may attain knowledge of the purely
intelligible and spiritual. This is the attainment of the nine men of
Bruno's allegory—although they are blinded by the Circean mutability
of matter, it is through that blinding that their quest eventually ends in
spiritual illumination. The process of material generation from which
the soul longs to escape is also the subject of praise.

l'alta e magnifica vicissitudine che agguaglia l'acqui inferiori alle supe-
riori, cangia la notte col giorno, ed il giorno con la notte, a fin che la
divinità sia in tutto, nel modo con cui tutto è capace di tutto, e l'infinita
bontà infinitamente si communiche secondo tutta la capacità de le cose.
[P. 326]

[the noble and magnificent vicissitude which makes the lower waters
equal to the higher ones, changes night with day, and day with night, so
that divinity may be in everything, in such a way that everything is

capable of containing everything, and infinite goodness can infinitely find communion in things to the fullest of their capacity.]

140

Just as, in spatial terms, his conception of the infinite nature of God leads to Bruno's well-known doctrine of an infinite universe and a plurality of worlds,[12] so that nature requires the infinite temporal expanse of eternity through which the universe may be diffused with divinity and rendered equal to its Creator: the material waters below the firmament made equal to the higher ones.

The final song of the nine enlightened men is constructed as a dialogue between Jove, the divine Creator, and Father Ocean, the created universe. The latter is the Homeric and Virgilian Ocean who is father of all things. He declares that he does not envy Jove his firmament and the wisdom which is earlier said to be hidden from the human mind in the purely intellectual forms above the firmament. Ocean boasts that he possesses within his realm the Thames and, beside its bank, the wondrous Diana-like nymph who in herself encompasses all of nature and the divinity which is in nature. What seems to be a series of three progressively smaller units, each containing the next within itself—Ocean, Thames, nymph—turns out, in fact, to be circular, since the innermost term (nymph) contains the outermost one (Ocean). The same paradox is described in the middle term, the Thames, which is both a local English river and the oceanic stream which encircles the earth, totality and source. Reminiscent of the Hermetic description of God as an infinite sphere whose center is everywhere and circumference nowhere, Bruno's allegory describes an immanent divinity permeating the universe.[13] Jove recognizes the validity of Ocean's arguments, just short of the other's claim to superiority.

> Giove responde: —O dio d'ondosi mari,
> Ch'altro si trove piú di me beato,
> Non lo permetta il fato;
> Ma miei tesori e tuoi corrano al pari.　　　　　[P. 518]

[Jove answers, "O god of the billowy seas, Fate does not permit that another should find himself more blessed than me: but my riches and yours are equal."]

God's creation is equal to its Creator insofar as it may be filled with His presence: "nel modo con cui tutto è capace di tutto." Every part of the universe becomes—*potentially*—the locus in which the infinite divine nature may become manifest.

Within this scheme, the choice of a specifically English setting and of Queen Elizabeth, in the figure of Diana, as the embodiment of divine revelation does not seem to be a necessary one. Frances Yates suggests that Bruno may have seen Elizabeth as the ruler under whose aegis he might promulgate his ideas and bring about a reform of religion.[14] In this case, the Jordan typology fitted to the Thames may refer to Giordano's own name, for it is his presence in England, as much as the queen's, which promises to reveal a source of divine wisdom there. But Elizabeth and the splendor of her reign lose their historical uniqueness when she is said to incarnate a divinity that is eternally and ubiquitously present in nature. As the monad gathering an infinite creation into herself, Diana-Elizabeth is a kind of Logos, and yet for Bruno the Christian Logos, too, is dehistoricized. The Incarnation loses its singularity as a historical event and is understood rather as the revelation of a gnosis which can be performed at any historical moment. The emphasis shifts to the mystical operator, for the divinity within nature is revealed only according to the capacity of the beholder, and the exaltation of this Diana into the container of infinity depends upon the infinite spiritual quest of the contemplating subject. Because this search is defined as infinite, it begins to replace or take the same shape as its desired object. For this reason, the nine illuminated men praise their travail and blindness, their experience of material vicissitude that has made possible their enlightenment. Their song, in which the opening line of each stanza repeats the closing line of the preceding one, describes a circle which ends where it began: with a catalogue of the natural landscape.

> De stagni, fiumi, mari,
> De rupi, fossi, spine, sterpi, sassi.   [P. 517]

[Of pools, rivers, and seas, of cliffs, ravines, thorns, stumps, and rocks.]

The mystical experience is itself cyclical or dialectical, an alternation between a blinding of matter and spiritual vision. The totality of this experience is an understanding of the presence of the divine throughout all of nature: the enlightenment which is figured in Diana.

The allegory at the end of the *Eroici furori* can also be understood as the culmination of the book's poetic progress: the admiration of the beautiful lady leads to a quest for divine beauty and truth, to a Diana worshipped not as Elizabeth or any other earthly woman but as the whole of natural creation. Bruno's *Argomento* begins with a violent attack on Petrarchism, all the more striking in that it is written to Sir Philip Sidney, the author of *Astrophil and Stella*. To be obsessed with the beauty of women, Bruno writes, is the act of a "basso, brutto, e sporco ingegno" (p. 309; "lowly, deformed, and dirty mind"), and that beauty itself is "un Circeo incantesimo ordinato al serviggio della generazione" (p. 311; "a Circean enchantment ordained to serve the purposes of procreation"). He carefully declares that he has nothing against procreation per se. His target is rather those writers who celebrate the physical beauty of women to the exclusion of all other concerns.

> ch'io mi stimarei molto vituperoso e bestialaccio, se con molto pensiero, studio e fatica mi fusse mai delettato o delettasse de imitar, come dicono, un Orfeo circa il culto d'una donna in vita, e dopo morte, se possibil fia, ricovrarla da l'inferno: se a pena la stimarei degna, senza arrossir il volto, d'amarla sul naturale di quell'istante del fiore della sua beltade e facultà di far figlioli alla natura e Dio. Tanto manca, che vorrei parer simile a certi poeti e versificanti in far trionfo d'una perpetua perseveranza di tale amore, come d'una cossí pertinace pazzia. . . . [Pp. 315–16]

> [for I would think of myself as very shameful and bestial, if with thought, study, and labor I were ever to have taken pleasure or to take pleasure in imitating, as they say, an Orpheus in worshipping a living woman, and after her death, if it were possible, in recovering her from Hell: since I hardly consider it an honest act, without blushing, to love her in a natural way in the moment of her beauty and capacity to make children for nature and for God. So much the less would I wish to appear similar to certain poets and versifiers in celebrating an endless perseverance of such a love, as if it were a persistent madness. . . .]

The Orpheus myth describes a kind of love poetry which is tied to contingency—the generation of children does have its place and moment—a contingency which the lover nevertheless attempts to mask by eternizing his desire in the poetic artifact. What is for Bruno an inferior love for the corporeal and temporal is transferred into a love for poetry for its own sake. He can only defend Petrarch's reputation by suggesting that the Tuscan poet chose to praise Laura much as other authors have chosen to write panegyrics to flies, monkeys, urinals, and other lowly objects: this is the Lucianic genre, a sheer rhetorical exercise, in which Erasmus's Folly claims to recite her own encomium. Petrarch's aim, then, would be not really to praise Laura but rather his own poetic skills ("celebrar non meno il proprio ingegno"). **143**

Against this cult of earthly love and of a poetry which is ultimately self-referential, Bruno opposes the love poetry of the *Eroici furori*. The book is constructed as a series of allegorical expositions of love sonnets. Four of the poems are by Bruno's fellow Neapolitan poet Luigi Tansillo (1510–68), the rest by Bruno himself. The tradition of providing a commentary to love poetry, which started with Dante's *Vita nuova*, was already well established by Bruno's time, but Bruno is taking no chances of being misunderstood.[15] His model, he says, is the *Song of Songs*, verses from which run throughout the pages of the *Eroici furori*. But although both works share the same philosophical subject matter ("quantunque medesimo misterio e sustanza d'anima sia compreso sotto l'ombra dell'una e l'altra"), the scriptural text is unmistakably allegorical rather than literal.

> ché ivi le figure sono aperta- e manifestamente figure, ed il senso metaforico è conosciuto di sorte che non può esser negato per metaforico [P. 314]

> [for there the figures are openly and manifestly figures, and the metaphoric sense is recognized in such a way that its metaphoric level cannot be denied.]

But Bruno's poetry looks just like the traditional conceits which love poets have written to "Citereida, o Licori, a Dori, a Cintia, a Lesbia, a Corinna, a Laura, ed altre simili," and the reader might be led to think that the sonnets of the *Eroici furori* are ordinary, garden-variety Petrarchism to which the allegorical interpretations have been tacked on.

> come è possibile di convertir qualsivoglia fola, romanzo, sogno e profetico enigma, e transferirle, in virtú di metafora e pretesto d'allegoria, a significar tutto quello che piace a chi piú commodamente è atto stiracchiar gli sentimenti, e far cossí tutto di tutto, come tutto essere in tutto disse il profondo Anaxagora. [P. 315]

> [as it is possible to convert any old fable, romance, dream, and prophetic enigma, and convey them, as metaphors and under the pretext of allegory, to signify all that pleases someone who is appropriately skilled at distorting meanings, and thus make everything out of everything, as the profound Anaxagoras said that everything is in everything.]

Bruno makes fun of outlandish interpretations that wrench the meaning of the text. Yet he describes what is, in fact, very close to his own allegorical method when he treats the poems of the *Eroici furori*. And his conclusion at the end of the book will be precisely to show how everything *is* in everything. For the time being, Bruno does not care whether the reader believes his claim that the poems were originally written with the meanings he attributes to them, so long as that reader follows the book's allegorical argument.

> Ma pensi chi vuol quel che gli pare e piace, ch'alfine, o voglia o non, per giustizia la deve ognuno intendere e definire come l'intendo e definisco io, non io come l'intende e definisce lui [P. 315]

> [But let him who wishes think what he wants and pleases, for finally, whether he likes it or not, it is only just that everyone must understand and define it [the meaning of the book] as I understand and define it, not I as he understands and defines it.]

Insisting that his poems point allegorically beyond themselves, Bruno carefully distinguishes his fiction from the self-referential verbal games of Petrarchan literature. He nonetheless appropriates to himself the key to his allegory: the analogy he makes is that just as the typology of the Song of Songs was best known to Solomon, so the figures of his own book are best known to him. In traditional Christian thought, however, Solomon's typology is part of a larger tradition of scripture whose meaning is revealed by the Incarnation. Bruno claims no such basis in sacred history for the figures of his allegory. His rejection of Petrarchan poetic autonomy leads him to an allegorical system which seems no less the autonomous creation of its human author. Any text or object—in the case of the emblem—*can* be allegorized, as Bruno somewhat sarcastically points out. But what is to guarantee that the allegory in fact points beyond its own textual structures toward a divine source of meaning?

Bruno is vague on specifics here, but some indication of his allegorical method and its relationship to his overall metaphysics is suggested by his treatment of the theme of praise in II.i.3. The passage comments upon an emblem of a phoenix, which, burning and consuming itself in the rays of the sun, creates so much smoke that the sun is obscured. Bruno's sonnet draws out the motto.

> Tal il mio spirto (ch'il divin splendore
> Accende e illustra) mentre va spiegando

Quel che tanto riluce nel pensiero,
  Manda da l'alto suo concetto fore
Rima, ch'il vago sol vad'oscurando,
Mentre mi struggo e liquefaccio intiero.
  Oimè! questo adro e nero
Nuvol di foco infosca col suo stile
Quel ch'aggrandir vorrebbe, e'l rend'umile.   [P. 437]

[So my spirit (which divine light kindles and illuminates), while it expresses what shines so greatly in its thought, sends forth from its lofty idea a poetry which darkens the lovely sun, while I entirely consume and melt myself away. Alas, this gloomy and black cloud of fire darkens with its style the object which it would elevate and makes it lowly.]

The subject of the emblem and the sonnet is the limitation of the poet who, in trying to exalt his beloved object, finds the object actually belittled by his inability to praise it according to its true worth and splendor. In a conventional Petrarchan scheme, the lady is too beautiful for the poet's words. Bruno takes the occasion to meditate on literary panegyric in general.

la lode è uno de gli piú gran sacrificii che possa far un affetto umano ad un oggetto . . . chi arebbe notizia di tanti grandi soldati, sapienti ed eroi de la terra, se non fussero stati messi alle stelle e deificati per il sacrificio de laude, che nell'altare del cor de illustri poeti ed altri recitatori ave acceso il fuoco, con questo che comunmente montasse al cielo il sacrificatore, la vittima ed il canonizato divo, per mano e voto di legitimo e degno sacerdote? [P. 438]

[praise is one of the greatest sacrifices which human love can make to an object . . . who would know about so many great soldiers, wise men, and heroes of the earth, had they not been sent to the stars and deified through the sacrifice of praise, which in the altars of the hearts of famous poets and other writers has kindled its fire, with the result that the sacrificer, the victim, and the canonized deity have risen to heaven together, through the actions and prayers of an authorized and worthy priest?]

In this positive valorization of poetic apotheosis, not only is the subject of praise ("canonizato divo") eternized, but the poet ("sacrificatore") and his poem ("vittima") as well. Unlike Ariosto's cynical view of literary immortality, conferred on good and bad men alike, Bruno distinguishes merited praise from hack encomiums on unworthy subjects. He labels the latter kind of literary flattery a kind of idolatry—"una statua di paglia . . . un tronco di legno . . . un pezzo di calcina" ("a statue of straw . . . a tree trunk . . . a piece of mortar cast")—which will not survive the onslaught of time (p. 438). In this category Bruno would presumably include the Petrarchan idolatry of the beautiful lady.

By contrast, the poet who praises a genuinely worthy object may, through the sacrificial act of praise, raise himself and his poetry to equality with that object. Such poetry will no longer be an idol, referential only to itself, but will point to the object it praises. However, Bruno now transfers this formula to his true object, the intellectual light of God, that "divino splendore" which instigates his laudatory verse. If his poetic sacrifice produces only smoke which obscures the spiritual source of illumination, it is because the sonnet presents a kind of negative theology. It depicts the inadequacy of any attempt to describe the infinite Godhead.

> Qualmente giamai possiamo non sol raggionare, ma e né men pensare di cose divine che non vengamo a detraergli più tosto che aggiongergli di gloria, di sorte che la maggior cosa che farsi possa al riguardo di quelle, è che l'uomo in presenza de gli altri uomini vegna più tosto a magnificer se stesso per il studio ed ardire, che donar splendore ed altro per qualche compita e perfetta azione. Atteso che cotale non può aspettarsi dove si fa progresso all'infinito, dove l'unità ed infinità son la medesima cosa. [P. 440]

> [So we can never speak, nor even think of divine things without coming to detract glory from them instead of adding it; wherefore the best action that can be taken with regard to them is that man in the presence of other men should magnify himself for his zeal and ardor, rather than [aspire to] bestow light and other gifts through some completed and perfect action. Seeing that the latter is not to be expected when one is progressing toward the infinite, where unity and infinity are the same thing.]

While the conclusion of this passage, proposing silence as a preferable mystical mode, seems to eliminate poetry altogether, Bruno does not criticize an allegorical language of praise as such, but rather praise that stops short of its infinite divine object by presenting itself as a finished act ("compita e perfetta azione"). The poem can never become equal to the God it tries to celebrate, and once the poem suggests that it has somehow completed its allegorical function—that it has made a definitive and finite statement about divinity—it merely obscures human understanding, casting smoke instead of light. True understanding of the divine derives from the allegorical act itself, the poem that points beyond its own letter in an act of signification which can never be completed. This refusal to stop the allegorical process authorizes Bruno's literary enterprise, for it defines knowledge of God in terms of the process by which the mind recognizes and refuses its limitations. If words and mental images cast darkness upon the understanding which searches beyond them toward the divine, allegory becomes analogous to the experience of the nine men who are blinded by matter while on their spiritual quest. In both cases the neverending mystical process itself is substituted for a final revelation. The zeal to keep the process going, what Bruno in his elevation of the will over the intellect calls "studio ed ardire," is the vital allegorical as well as contemplative principle. Bruno elsewhere (p. 500) cites the scriptural texts: "Qui quaerent me inveniunt me" (Matthew 7 : 7–8); "Qui sitit, veniat, et bibit" (John 7 : 37). The Johannine waters of life, Bruno's spiritual waters above the firmament, will be given only to the seeker, and Bruno repeatedly stresses his preference of the active quest for divine knowledge over passive reception.[16]

Bruno terms the active searcher after truth an "artefice" (p. 360). As a maker of philosophical knowledge, his philosopher begins to resemble the poet, just as his poet, through the creation of allegorical structures which defer an ultimate meaning, achieves a philosophical understanding. The ideal version of the philosopher as an individual creator may find an analogy in Bruno's defense of *poetic* originality with which the text of the *Eroici furori* (I.i) properly begins. Asserting that the rules found in treatises on the art of poetry are derived after the fact from poetic works, and that such rules serve insipid imitators rather than true inventors, Bruno claims that the latter are entitled to their own rules and their works are to be judged on their intrinsic capacities to please ("dilettare") and teach ("giovare"). This statement may be placed beside Bruno's insistence that his allegorical system be read according to its own terms.[17]

Yet, by Bruno's same allegorical method, the personal human identity of the poet-philosopher's creation is eventually to be transcended and consumed. Bruno as *poet* describes himself immolated on his sacrificial altar of praise ("mi struggo e liquefaccio intiero"), just as elsewhere, in an adaptation of a well-known Petrarchan image, the *philosopher* is described as Actaeon devoured by his dogs, which are the ideas of the beautiful he has conceived upon gazing at the naked, revealed Diana (p. 473).[18] The loss of an individual identity in the contemplation of divinity is an Averroistic problem which Ernst Cassirer, in his discussion of Bruno, has described in terms of a subject-object distinction which Renaissance thought was still in the process of making.[19] As an issue of poetics, the problem may be posed in the context of Bruno's negative concept of history.

By defining God as both transcendent and immanent in the universe, Bruno solves the epistemological question of the relationship of the human individual in time to an eternal divinity: the world in which the individual exists is given the divine attributes of eternity and infinity. By a gnosis that has been available from all time, the philosopher comes to understand the unending process of natural creation as a manifestation of the divine, and his understanding itself takes the form of process, a perpetual quest. The attempt to reproduce this gnosis forms the basis of Bruno's poetics and his conception of the open-ended allegorical text which points beyond itself without ever reaching an ultimate significance. Allegory becomes a model by which the mind may understand the shape of its own movement toward metaphysical enlightenment, the movement which is identical to the enlightenment itself. Since this poetic gnosis, too, is eternally present, it has no historically unique manifestation, and it is in this sense that Bruno's system of allegory may be as effective and authoritative as Solomon's. By the same token, in the absence of a linear concept of history, there exists no historical standard for literary excellence, and Bruno's radically modernist position on poetics follows as a logical consequence. But the inability to locate himself historically means that the poet-philosopher's own personal uniqueness is ultimately *undefinable* and of secondary importance: his subjective poetic voice is absorbed into its transcendent allegorical object.[20]

Like the other Renaissance writers in this study, Bruno faces the competing claims of literary individuality and of a literature of truth. But whereas those other writers understand this opposition in terms of a historicist versus an allegorical reading of the literary text, Bruno has eliminated the possibility of the first reading. The autonomy of poetic invention which Bruno celebrates is a prerequisite for his literary gnosis: through the process of creating meaning, the poet comes to understand meaning in terms of process. But the actual literary creation, the expression of his human personality, is relatively unimportant, the smoke which rises from what will be an eventual sacrifice of that personality before the divine object of praise. Human writing is deprived of a historical dimension that might isolate its specific components and allow for the reconstruction of the author's identity; and it becomes difficult, finally impossible, to separate out the individual human author from the divine meaning in which his allegorical language participates. Bruno's poet-philosopher is given the freedom to cultivate a literary individuality within an ahistorical, allegorical framework that devalues and finally annihilates individuality. The contradiction remains unresolved in the *Eroici furori*.

THE MARRIAGE OF THAMES AND MEDWAY

The eleventh canto of Book 4 of the *Faerie Queene*, published in 1597, eleven years after the *Eroici furori*, describes the wedding of the Thames to its tributary river, the Medway. This episode, in which Spenser takes up the figure of the oceanic source, both looks back at the landscape of Eden described in the first book of the poem, and will itself be commented upon in retrospect by the *Mutabilitie Cantos*, which give an ending to the poet's unfinished project. Spenser's depiction of the source occupies a central position both in the structure of the *Faerie Queene* and in the development of the poem's allegorical mode of thought.

The *Faerie Queen* begins with a review of the linear course of Christian history, following the adventures of the Redcrosse Knight in book I. Drawing heavily on the typology of the Book of Revelation, these adventures culminate in two specifically eschatological moments: the vision the convert Redcrosse receives of the New Jerusalem in canto 10 (55–57) and his battle with the dragon which restores Eden in cantos 11 and 12. Both passages repeat elements from Rinaldo's conversion experience in the *Gerusalemme liberata*. Redcrosse's ascent of the mountain near the House of Holinesse in the company of the old man, Contemplation, recalls the meditation of the penitent Rinaldo, confessed by Peter the Hermit, on the Mount of Olives, to which Spenser's mountain is compared (I.x.54). And Redcrosse, like Tasso's hero, is bathed and baptized in dew—the "holy water dew" of the Well of Life—between his bouts with the dragon in canto 11.

The dew figure, whose complex of typological meanings Tasso had explored in the *Liberata*, runs through the action of canto 11. The dew of the Well of Life regenerates the fortunately fallen Redcrosse and his "bright deaw-burning blade" (35). As in Clorinda's dream in the *Gerusalemme conquistata*,[21] the Well is coupled with the Tree of Life, whose balm revives Redcrosse after the second day of battle: this balm "ouerflowd all the fertill plaine, / As it had deawed bene with timely raine" (48). When he awakes after these two chrisms, Redcrosse is implicitly compared to the mythic descriptions of morning in stanzas 33 and 51. He rises from his sleep like the solar Titan who shows his "deawy face" as he emerges from the sea, and like Aurora leaving her "deawy bed."

The figure appears elsewhere in the *Faerie Queene*. Belphoebe's miraculous birth—"Her birth was of the wombe of Morning dew," (III.vi.3)—typologically resembles the birth of Christ, the dew in Mary's womb.[22] Belphoebe is one of the manifestations in the poem of Elizabeth, who is later celebrated as the dispenser of beauty to her court: "Dew'd with her drops of bountie Soueraine," (IV.viii.33). Elizabeth's association with the Incarnational figure of the dew is the punning sign that she is "due," the rightful and divinely sanctioned monarch. But, as in the *Liberata*, this dew figure is subject to demonic parody. The parodic perversion of Redcrosse's regenerative sleep in the Well of Life occurs at the end of canto 1, where the knight falls asleep beneath the "sweet slombring deaw" of Morpheus in the house of Archimago. The sorcerer summons forth erotic dreams, and meanwhile creates the false Una, "fram'd of liquid ayre," yet "borne without her dew" (I.i.46). This idolatrous counterfeit of the one Truth seems to signal the first appearance in the poem of Duessa, who, beginning as Whore of Babylon and the personification of the Roman church, will emerge in book V as Mary Stuart, the Catholic would-be usurper of Elizabeth's throne.[23] Her name complicates Spenser's pun. Duality has, in the act of parody, taken the place of dueness.

The presence of dew in Spenser's Well of Life apparently reflects two different translations of Genesis 2:6. Before the creation and fall of man, there was no rain to replenish the earth: "sed fons ascendebat e terra irrigans universam superficiem terrae." Jerome follows the Septuagint and calls this moisture a "fons"; this is the scriptural precedent for the Edenic fountain or Well of Life. But the Geneva Bible, closer to the Hebrew original, calls it "vapor," and in its English version "mist." Hexameral poets faced the task of harmonizing the two readings. In the *Mondo Creato*, Tasso rules out any "vapor terreno," and suggests that Eden was watered instead by the "rugiada del ciel."[24] Milton's scriptural paraphrase in *Paradise Lost* similarly identifies the mist of Genesis with the heavenly dew.

> though God had yet not rained
> Upon the Earth, and man to till the ground
> None was, but from the Earth a dewy Mist
> Went up and watered all the ground . . .[25] [7.331–34]

For Augustine, however, who had only Jerome's reading of "fons" before him, the problem in his *De Genesi ad litteram* was to explain how a single fountain could water the entire earth.

> Why should it therefore be incredible, if from one source in the abyss the earth were universally watered by an alternating flood, flowing out and flowing back? For if Scripture wished to call the great bulk of that same abyss—leaving aside that part which is called the sea and which, with its manifest breadth, surrounds the earth with its waves, rather that sole part which the earth contains in its hidden recesses, whence rivers are distributed as sources through different courses and veins, and which spring forth in their respective localities—a source (fontem) and not sources (fontes), because of the unity of their nature: they ascend, by innumerable paths through caverns and fissures, from inside the earth and everywhere water the entire face of the earth, almost like dispersed strands of hair, not in the all-covering way of a sea or a swamp, but rather as we see waters go through channels of rivers and bends of streams and overflow their surroundings with their excess—who would not accept this unless someone afflicted with a contentious spirit?[26]

Augustine's suggestion that the singular form has been used by scripture to express a plural meaning, and that the earth's rivers and springs have their common origin in the underground abyss, reads the "fons" of Genesis 2:6 in terms of the river Oceanus. The abyss is continuous with the sea which encircles the earth, and its waters appear to move in a circular flux and reflux. The transformation of the fountain into an oceanic underground current virtually identifies it with the river of Eden, mentioned four verses later at Genesis 2:10, which flowed through the garden and divided into four streams. Philo describes this river as flowing through subterranean veins, and, according to Josephus, it circles the globe.[27] Augustine probably has Philo in mind, when, later in the *De Genesi and litteram*, he examines the problem of the four rivers of Eden and their demonstrably separate sources.

> Shall we then be moved by that which is said of these rivers, some of whose sources are known, some absolutely unknown, and on that account be unable to accept literally that they are divided from one river

in paradise? Is it not rather to be believed, since the location of paradise is very remote from human knowledge, that the waters are divided thence in four parts as most faithful Scripture attests; but those rivers, whose sources are said to be known [may be believed] to have gone underground in one place, and after a course through extensive territories, to have sprung up above ground in other places where their sources are ascribed to be known. For who does not know that several waters are accustomed to do this?[28]

Later patristic writers, uncertain whether the "fons" of Genesis 2:6 was anterior to Eden and its river, generally concluded that the morphologically similar fountain and river were one and the same, part of an underground oceanic river that feeds the earth's other bodies of water.[29] This opinion is expressed by both Tasso and Milton in their hexameral poetry.

> Forse nel paradiso i primi fonti
> sorgono mormorando e chiari al cielo,
> e poi sommersi entro 'l profondo grembo
> de la caliginosa oscura terra
> van sotterra girando i ciechi regni,
> sin che di novo apparsi in chiara luce
> altri fonti di sé ne l'erte rupi
> fan de l'aspre montagne esposte a' sensi? [Mondo creato 7. 772–89]

[Perhaps in paradise the first sources rise murmuring and clear to heaven, and then submerged in the deep womb of the misty dark earth, they go underground circling the sightless realms, until appearing once again in the clear light, they form other fountainheads in the steep cliffs of high mountains where they can be observed by the human senses.]

> Southward through Eden went a river large,
> Nor changed his course, but through the shaggy hill
> Passed underneath ingulfed, for God had thrown
> That mountain as his garden mould high raised
> Upon the rapid current, which through veins
> Of porous earth with kindly thirst up drawn,
> Rose a fresh fountain, and with many a rill
> Watered the garden; thence united fell
> Down the steep glade, and met the nether flood,
> Which from his darksome passage now appears,
> And now divided into four main streams . . . [Paradise Lost 4. 223–33]

The "fons vitae" dividing into the four rivers of paradise beneath the Tree of Life became an iconographic commonplace, signifying the diffusion of Christ the Word through the four gospels.[30] In variant versions, the Tree, as the symbol of the cross, is replaced by the figure of the sacrificial Lamb of God, while in actual depictions of the Crucifixion, the four rivers are reflected in the four streams of Christ's blood which flow from the base of the cross.[31]

Exegetical tradition could, then, extend to the Edenic fountain the typology of an oceanic river system, the same typology which was associated with the Jordan. Inevitably the two were linked, and Columbus could identify the Jordan-like Orinoco with the river of Eden. Ohrt has adduced texts which place the source of the Jordan in Eden, a geographical belief reflected in one of the early traditions of medieval mapmaking.[32] Conversely, Tasso, in the episode of the Magus in the *Gerusalemme conquistata*, describes the four rivers of Eden flowing out of the oceanic source-cave of the Jordan. Coupled with the rivers of paradise in Ecclesiasticus 24 : 25–27, the Jordan is described by Gregory of Nyssa as flowing in an opposite direction to them back into Eden.[33] A tradition of mosaic decoration in Roman churches stretching from the sixth to the thirteenth century places the Jordan beside the four Edenic rivers.[34]

More commonly, the Jordan is identified with the River of Life in the New Jerusalem of the Book of Revelation. But that apocalyptic river is itself a typological manifestation of the "fons" in Eden. By calling his fountain a Well of Life, Spenser invokes the Johannine figure of the water of Life, while his Eden becomes part of a *restored*, eschatological landscape. John Hankins has commented on Spenser's scriptural conflation.

> John's vision of the New Jerusalem also furnishes two details for Spenser's description of Eden, the Well of Life and the Tree of Life (Rev. 22 : 1–2). The tree is the heavenly counterpart of the Tree that flourished in Eden, while the River of the Water of Life, is the same as the well of living water offered to the woman of Samari (John 4 : 14), the fountain of water which sprang up in Eden (Gen. 2 : 6), and the river which flowed from the fountain (2:10).[35]

Spenser's version of the divine source is placed in an Eden that is both prehistoric and apocalyptic. Book I offers an overview of the history of the church whose meaning has been disclosed once and for all time by the Bible. But, in spite of the apparent apocalyptic finality of

154

the first book, the *Faerie Queene* continues for five more books and was originally planned to include at least twelve. These remaining books are set in the historical space between Eden and the New Jerusalem, and occasion a shift in Spenser's allegory. His poem now seeks a counterpart for the holiness which exists eternally in the sacramental activities of the church in the secular virtues exercised exclusively within a world of contingency and time.[36] This assertion of continuity between an order of grace and an order of nature is given a particular location in the political history and royal house of England and reflects in large part the English religious settlement whereby church and state became one. The substitution of the historically specific for the eternal and sacramental as a source of allegorical meaning—a process by which history itself becomes sacramental—is underscored within the symmetries of the *Faerie Queene;* the chronicles of English political history in book II, canto 10, take the place of the House of Holinesse in the tenth canto of book I. In the proems preceding the individual books of the poem, Elizabeth, the Faerie Queene herself, becomes increasingly identified with the virtues they celebrate until she is praised in book VI as the historical source from which the poet derives the idea of Courtesy. His allegorizations of contemporary events allow Spenser to avoid the Platonic duality of Tasso's Jerusalem epics, in which the divine intelligibility that lies outside or at the end of history seems only rarely to be manifested within human experience; Tasso depicts a timeless, spiritual source that is disjunct from its temporal, material counterpart. In Spenser's Incarnational fiction, by contrast, the Edenic Well of Life of book I will reappear in the midst of historical process, conflated with its typological alter ego, the Jordan, in the waters of the Thames, England's oceanic river.

The reversion of the *Faerie Queene* from apocalyptic closure back into history is signaled at the end of book I by the deferral of Redcrosse's marriage to Una. The King of Eden invites the knight to settle down and live happily ever after.

> Let us deuize of ease and euerlasting rest.

> Ah dearest Lord, said then that doughty knight,
>> Of ease or rest I may not yet deuize;
>> For by the faith, which I to armes haue plight,
>> I bounden am streight after this emprize,
>> As that your daughter can ye well aduize,
>> Backe to returne to that great Faerie Queene,

> And her to serue six yeares in warlike wize,
> Gainst that proud Paynim king, that workes her teene:
> Therefore I ought craue pardon till I there haue beene.[37]
>
> [I.xii.17, 9; 18]

The "euerlasting rest" is that same eschatological "Sabaoth" yearned for at the end of the *Mutabilitie Cantos*. The passage seems analogous to the earlier episode on the mount of Contemplation (I.x.63), where it was Redcrosse who, like Tasso's Goffredo, sought to be released from history after his vision of the New Jerusalem, only to be reminded that he is still on active duty. Una comes to her wedding without her veil: the moment of Revelation which joins history to its meaning. But history has yet to run its course—the mention of the "Paynim king" reminds Spenser's reader of contemporary events, the struggle between England and Catholic Spain—and while Redcrosse and Una are betrothed, triumphing over the last-minute subterfuge of Duessa and Archimago, their marriage must be postponed.

This eschatological marriage has its counterpart within the unfolding of history. At one level of Spenser's biblical allegory, Redcrosse is Christ and Una is His Church. In exegetical tradition, Christ's love for His Church is the subject of the Song of Songs, and Spenser, in fact, provides Una with the typology of the bride of the Canticles.[38] Una's parents, rescued by Redcrosse in a version of the Harrowing of Hell, are Adam and Eve, the first wedded couple. Between their marriage and the union of Christ and the members of His Church in an apocalyptic Eden lies all of human history. Christian marriage in the historical world looks both backward and forward; according to the 1559 *Book of Common Prayer*, the marital rite was "instituted of God in paradise in the time of man's innocency, signifying unto us the mystical union, that is betwixt Christ and His Church."[39] Spenser's own *Epithalamion* ends by opening out to include an eschatological perspective, a vision of the wedding couple's posterity mounting up to inhabit the heavenly palaces of God's elect.

> So let vs rest, sweet loue, in hope of this,
> And cease till then our tymely ioyes to sing.   [424–25]

The nuptial repose waits "till then" to be assimilated with the "euerlasting rest" of apocalypse; the couple's "tymely ioyes" are a foretaste of a timeless bliss which is not yet. The *Faerie Queene*, too, presents a version of marriage as the historical incarnation of an Edenic and apocalyptic prototype. It does so at the same time that it demonstrates the participation of the divine, Edenic source in history. For Spenser describes not the wedding of two human protagonists, but a marriage of rivers.

In a letter to Gabriel Harvey published in 1580, Spenser declared his intention to write an *Epithalamion Thamesis:* "I shew his first beginning and offspring, and all the Countrey, that he passeth thorough, and also describe all the Riuers throughout Englande, whyche came to this Wedding, and their righte names, and right passage, etc."[40] Spenser apparently did not make good on this promise until he composed the marriage of Thames and Medway in canto 11 of book IV of the *Faerie Queene.*[41] His statement, however, seems to have inspired William Camden's Latin poem, the *De connubio Tamae et Isis,* 189 verses of which are dispersed through Camden's *Brittania,* a geographical and antiquarian compendium first published in 1586. Camden's poem, in turn, exerted influence upon the river marriage in Spenser's epic.

In the *De connubio,* the female river Tama and the male stream Isis meet and join their names, becoming the Tamisis, or Thames. In the 1600 edition of the *Brittania,* in the year following Spenser's death, a marginal note points out a precedent for this construction of the river's name out of its component branches: "So is it with *Ior* and *Dan* in the holy land, *Dor* and *Dona* in Gaul, whence Iordan and Dordan."[42] The Jor-Dan etymology can be traced back to Josephus and Jerome, and by the Renaissance it is a commonplace, probably inspiring the etymology of the similar-sounding Dordan (Dordogne).[43] It is suggestive that Spenser's chief contemporary competitor in the genre saw the model for the marriage of rivers in the Jordan.

There is less indication in Camden's poem of the idea of an oceanic source, although the source-cave of the Isis is decorated with a painting of Cynthia, the moon which rules the seas and a complimentary allusion to Elizabeth, and with the figures of five great rivers: the Ganges, Nile, Amazon, Ister, and Rhine, all of which appear as guests at the marriage of Thames and Medway.[44] But it seems to be Spenser's invention that his river marriage should also represent the source of all rivers. Spenser's rivers, among which are the four traditional rivers of paradise and Columbus's Edenic river, the Orinoco[45]—now part of Raleigh's Guiana—have come to wait attendance upon the wedding couple at the ceremony in the Hall of Proteus. On first reading, this scene simply suggests that all rivers finally flow into the ocean. But this confluence can also depict the rivers flowing back to their common

156

origin at the point where Thames and Medway meet. That river
junction actually lies in the Thames estuary, where the Thames has
become an oceanic freshwater stream. In the Proem to book VI,   **157**
Spenser glosses his earlier fiction in his encomium to Elizabeth, the
source of Courtesy.

> Then pardon me, most dreaded Soueraine,
>> That from your selfe, I doe this vertue bring,
>> And to your selfe doe it returne againe:
>> So from the Ocean all riuers spring,
>> And tribute backe repay as to their King.   [VI.Proem.7]

This Ocean is the river Oceanus, which is both the source and
destination of the rivers of the earth. Spenser's river marriage identifies this circular, global stream with the Thames, Elizabeth's royal
river.

The catalogue of English and Irish rivers which acknowledge the
Thames "as their Principall" (30)—even the longer and larger Humber
and Severn pay him homage—depicts the political unification and
consolidation of England under the central royal government of the
Tudors in London. The arrival of the foreign river guests, moreover,
asserts the claims of the emergent English nation-state to world-
empire. Like la Boderie's oceanic Seine, the Thames has become the
latest resting place of the *translatio imperii*. (Spenser's fiction prefigures
the depiction of the Thames as the center of a mercantile empire and of
a network of free trade in Pope's *Windsor Forest*, 329 ff., another
version of the messianic river of Isaiah 66). The description of the river
bridegroom brings into play a Virgilian imperial typology.

> And on his head like to a Coronet
> He wore, that seemed strange to common vew,
> In which were many towres and castels set,
> That it encompast round as with a golden fret.

> Like as the mother of the Gods, they say,
>> In her great iron charet wonts to ride,
>> When to *Ioues* pallace she doth take her way:
>> Old *Cybele*, arrayd with pompous pride,
>> Wearing a Diademe embattild wide
>> With hundred turrets, like a Turribant.
>> With such an one was Thamis beautifide;
>> That was to weet the famous Troynovant,
> In which her kingdomes throne is chiefly resiant.

> [IV.xi.27.6–9; 28]

The simile of the mural-crowned Cybele is taken from the underworld episode of the *Aeneid* (6.784 ff.), where Anchises prophesies the grandeur of Rome, the first new Troy, which will have empire over the entire earth. London, the residence of Elizabeth, is figured here as Troynovant, the newest Troy. But Troy fell, as the sea-god Nereus, a guest at Thames's wedding (19), had once prophesied, and Virgil's Rome had fallen too. The Cybele passage had already been placed in the ironic perspective of history by Joachim du Bellay in the sixth sonnet of the *Antiquitez de Rome,* a sequence which Spenser himself translated as the *Ruines of Rome.*

> Such as the *Berecynthian* Goddesse bright
> In her swift charret with high turrets crownde,
> Proud that so manie Gods she brought to light;
> Such was this Citie in her good daies fownd:
>   This Citie, more than that great *Phrygian* mother
> Renowm'd for fruite of famous progenie,
> Whose greatnes by the greatnes of none other,
> But by her selfe her equall match could see:
>   *Rome* onely might to *Rome* compared bee,
> And onely *Rome* could make great *Rome* to tremble:
> So did the Gods by heauenly doome decree,
> That other earthlie power should not resemble
>   Her that did match the whole earths puissaunce,
>   And did her courage to the heauens aduaunce.

While Anchises had looked forward to a future Roman empire, du Bellay looks back retrospectively on the greatest city on earth that is no more. Moreover, the sonnet, in which Rome may only be compared to herself, insists upon the uniqueness of the city as a historical event: a translation of empire, understood as a continuous, progressive historical movement, is not really possible. Spenser's twofold literary allusion in the *Faerie Queene* suggests, on the one hand, that England's power and civilization have made London the heir to Trojan Rome, and, on the other, that any analogy between the two is vitiated by their common historicity. Human history, the history of empire, does not, in fact, repeat itself except in its constant mutability and change, and the patterns of continuity which are found in it are fictions. The figure of the mother-goddess Cybele ascribes to the civilization which has risen beside the Thames the energy of natural generation, but that simile also implies decline and decay. An earlier passage in book III describes quite a different relationship between the Thames and Troynovant. The river has here assumed the character of pure flux.

It *Troynouant* is hight, that with the waues
  Of wealthy *Thamis* washed is along,
  Vpon whose stubborne neck, whereat he raues
  With roring rage, and sore him selfe does throng,
  That all men feare to tempt his billowes strong,
  She fastned hath her foot, which standes so hy,
  That it a wonder of the world is song
  In forreine landes, and all which passen by,
Beholding it from far, do thinke it threates the skye.

                      [III.ix.45]

The city is viewed here as a triumph over a contingency which it
nonetheless cannot fully control. The river responds in anger and
makes its waters dangerous to sailors. But, in turn, Troynovant seems
to have embodied the animal energy of the Thames and has become a
giant which "threates the sky." Spenser is again recalling his translation of du Bellay's sonnet sequence and a Rome "which did threate the
skies."[46] The myth of the titans and their unsuccessful assault upon the
heavens runs through the *Antiquitez*—in the sonnet cited above, Rome
"did her courage to the heauens aduaunce"—describing the city
which has grown too great and which must inevitably begin to
decline.[47] Spenser later appropriates the myth for his titaness Mutabilitie. In his complicated vision, civilization and empire cannot be
separated from the historical forces to which they provisionally give
order and ultimately accede.

In the figure of the Thames, Spenser celebrates his historical
moment while acknowledging its human contingency; with the Medway he weds to that moment the presence of consecrated nature.

Her goodly lockes adowne her backe did flow
  Vnto her waste, with flowres bescattered,
  The which ambrosiall odours forth did throw
  To all about, and all her shoulders spred
  As a new spring: and likewise on her hed
  A Chapelet of sundry floweres she wore,
  From vnder which the deawy humour shed,
  Did tricle downe her haire, like to the hore
Congealed little drops, which doe the morne adore.

                      [IV.xi.46]

While dew is an attribute of marine deities—Neptune (11) and the old
river Thame (25) have dewy locks and beards—the simile in the final
verses of this description of Medway, or Medua as she is called in
stanza 45, brings the dew in her hair into high relief. She shares in the

typology of divine grace which Spenser first depicts in the restorative dew of the Well of Life. Medway's portrait, moreover, echoes the earlier description of the Mount of Venus which rises in the midst of the Garden of Adonis; its myrtle trees

> like a girlond compassed the hight,
> And from their fruitfull sides sweet gum did drop,
> That all the ground with precious deaw bedight,
> Threw forth most dainty odours, and most sweet delights.
>
> [III.vi.43.6–9]

The bride is associated with the fragrant garden, throwing forth its odors—and with the fertile moisture of her own womb (mons Veneris.) Such an association is also the typological centerpiece of the Song of Songs.

> My sister my spouse *is as* a garden inclosed,
> as a spring shut up, *and* a fountaine sealed vp.
>   Thy plantes *are as* an orcharde of pomegranates
> with swete frutes, as camphire, spikenarde
>   Even spikenarde, and safron, calamus & synamon
> with all the trees of incense, myrrhe and aloes,
> with all the chief spices.
>   O fountaine of the gardens, o well of living
> waters, and the springs of Lebanon.   [4:12–15; Geneva Bible]

Solomon compares the sexual parts of his beloved to a garden containing the waters of life; biblical commentators noted the typological identity of this figurative garden with Eden and its fountainhead.[48] The "well of living waters" which describes Solomon's bride is the closest verbal parallel in the English Bible to the "Well of Life" in Spenser's Eden.

This typology depicts woman's body as a paradise, and could suggest how marriage recovers a prelapsarian state of being. In conjugal love every husband finds his own Eden and the sanctified wellsprings of life. Spenser's fiction expresses a similar idea, for his river marriage—set in an underground natural matrix—reconstitutes the "fons" of Genesis 2:6.[49] Exegetical tradition had described that source as an oceanic river rising in Eden and conflated it with the typology of the Jordan. The wedding of Thames and Medway reveals a new location in England of the confluent oceanic source of rivers. The relationship between Spenser's two versions of the source, each of which contains sacral dew, is emphasized by the symmetry of the two three-book installments of the *Faerie Queene*. The Well of Life appears in I.xi; Thames and Medway occupy IV.xi. The different sources reflect the subject matter of their respective books: what is portrayed as one and whole in the Legend of Holinesse is depicted as many and united in the Legend of Friendship.

In the *De partu Virginis*, Proteus journeyed to the source of the Jordan; in the episode of Thames and Medway, the source comes to Proteus, for the rivers are married inside the seer's hall. Like Sannazaro, Spenser rearranges the motifs of the *Fourth Georgic* in order to join the timelessness of the source to a Protean world of history and nature. The river marriage itself appears to repeat this same idea, wedding the poet's contemporary history, the rise of English empire figured in the Thames, to an order of grace embodied by the Medway. The marriage rite invests that history with a significance that both looks back to Eden and forward toward a new Eden at the end of time. For the moment, Spenser's allegory suggests that a paradise-in-history, like reconstituted elements of Eden's geography, can be found *now* in Elizabeth's England.

Its insistence upon the present moment lends Spenser's historical allegory a peculiar contingency that can be measured by a comparison with the poems of la Boderie cited at the opening of this chapter. There, the translation of empire and the arts to France and to the Seine is a cyclical return of history to its origin, an eschatological event which reveals France to be both the first and the last Eden. Spenser's praise of English empire has no such finality. It finds an anticipation *in history* of a future apocalyptic fulfillment, and locates its source of allegorical meaning in the specific event of Elizabeth's reign. This source can only be provisional. As the literary fortunes of the Cybele figure attached to the Thames suggest, history will go on, bringing change. Empires rise and fall, and the Faerie Queene may prove mortal.

Moreover, the celebration of the particular time in which he lives leaves the Spenserian poet open to the charge of time-serving. Allegory invites skepticism when it is used for political propaganda, conflating or confusing the categories of timeless truth and temporal power. In Ariosto's hands, this conflation became a reduction, and his refusal to see any distinction between that which is rendered to Caesar and that which is rendered to God enabled him to move beyond a satire on courtly panegyric to attack the metaphysical basis of allegorical practice. Spenser's encomiastic fiction raises the issue directly: does the historical Elizabeth, in fact, embody divine virtue and truth or has her patriotic poet instead paid her the most hyperbolic of compliments? In the latter case, his epic fiction would be, as Bruno remarks of poetry in praise of unworthy objects, a kind of idolatry, while his historical allegory, based on no meaning outside the poem's invention, would finally refer only to itself.

The skeptical criticism which insists upon the disparity between the poem's fictions and historical fact is given a monstrous and satanic embodiment within the *Faerie Queene* by the Blatant Beast, which is conquered only to escape again into the world in book VI, canto xii.[50] Calidore confronts this creature as it brings to light the real abuses of the cloister (24). The Beast, however, does not know where to stop.

> And spake licentious words, and hatefull things
> Of good and bad alike, of low and hie. [VI.xii.28]

The Blatant Beast speaks ill of everyone, and what may have begun as satirical exposure of hidden filth now becomes indiscriminate slander, muckraking turned to mudslinging. Calumny invents the corruption it cannot find. The targets include "the gentle Poets rime" (40), and the Beast's new release signals the end of the six books of the *Faerie Queene* which Spenser completed. Under attack, the poet bitterly pledges to write in a new mode.

> Therfore do you my rimes keep better measure,
> And seeke to please, that now is counted wisemens threasure.
> [VI.xii.41]

Spenser's narrator proposes henceforth to conform to what presumably is the Blatant Beast's idea of the poet: the flatterer who heaps praise on unworthy objects—from the Beast's point of view no object can be truly worthy. As long as he is to be calumniated as a self-interested pleaser of the great, the poet may as well be one in earnest and reap the benefits.

This declaration amounts to a farewell to poetry, or at least to the historical allegory of the *Faerie Queene*. If credit is given to the Beast's thoroughgoing backbiting—"Ne Kesars spared he a whit, nor Kings" (28)—neither Elizabeth nor any other mortal can live up to the poet's glorification, and the foundations of his allegory in history would be revealed to be built on sand. Moreover, even if the Beast's calumny is *not* believed, it may still insidiously undermine the poet's work. The slanderer's detraction presents itself as a rival or alternative version of the poetic compliment; if calumny is groundless and merely invented, it implicitly accuses the poetry of praise of the same fictional inauthenticity. Some Renaissance literary theorists saw detraction and praise as the two original subdivisions of poetry itself, the interchangeable rhetorical poses of the prosecutor and advocate.[51] Common sense asserts that the truth about Elizabeth must lie somewhere in the middle, but common sense is the literalist enemy of allegory.

Although the Blatant Beast's charges are represented as a slander against the poet and his fiction, they might also reflect a real change in Spenser's attitude toward the queen. The rebellion in Ireland from which the poet fled in the last year of his life may have shaken his confidence in Elizabeth's power and produced events which could not be accommodated into the providential historical scheme his poem had designed for her. Under the guise of Diana, Elizabeth will leave the Irish landscape of the *Mutabilitie Cantos*, marking an end to Spenser's historical allegory. To what extent her removal is due to the poet's changing his mind about her or to the larger change—including revolutionary change—which is the fragment's titular subject matter is difficult to determine. There is some continuity, however, between the act that causes this desertion or expulsion of Elizabeth and the earlier skeptical attacks of the Blatant Beast that caused the poet to renounce his former poetry. Elizabeth disappears from the *Mutabilitie Cantos* after she has been exposed and seen for what she is, a Diana glimpsed naked among her nymphs.

The subplot in which Faunus, a sylvan demigod, sees Diana in her nakedness and laughs—either from the sheer, uncontainable pleasure of the sight or from the satirical discovery that the empress has no clothes—also contains a second river marriage. Faunus has bribed the Irish river nymph Molanna to grant him a vision of the goddess at her bath by promising to obtain for Molanna the hand of Fanchin, another stream flowing in the vicinity of Arlo Hill. The indignant Diana abandons her favorite watering spot, which, "Sprinkled with wholsom waters, more then most on ground," (vi.38), may distantly recall the holy water of the Edenic Well of Life that excelled Silo, Jordan, Bath, and Spa (I.xi.30). There are overtones of the Fall in the "Queene-apples" Faunus uses to entice Molanna (43); that they are queene-apples may also suggest the political nature of the offense. The story depicts Ireland's double fall from grace, conflating the earlier loss of an Edenic state with a more recent withdrawal of the royal presence: the Irish rebels are repeating Original Sin.

These two stages have already been separated out in the progress of Spenser's allegory, where the overarching plan of salvation history outlined in book I is replaced by an Elizabeth-centered historical allegory. The queen's presence allows for a partial, compensatory recovery within contemporary history of an original significance that has once been and is yet to come in Eden. But Diana's flight from Arlo Hill removes this second, historical dispensation of meaning from Spenser's allegory as well. What remains, the last compensatory vision left to the poem in this process of reduction, is the eventual wedding of Molanna and Fanchin. This second river marriage looks back in direct contrast to the marriage of Thames and Medway, which had assumed the figure of an oceanic source in order to celebrate the historical presence of Elizabeth. The wedding of the Irish rivers comes about rather as a result of Elizabeth's absence: a sign that the source is no more. Yet if this marriage follows the removal of one kind of allegory from the poem's fiction, the personified Molanna and Fanchin have not altogether lost their figural quality. The two streams continue to meet up to the poet's present day, and their indissoluble marriage is a permanent fact in the Irish landscape.[52]

In the absence of meaningful historical patterns, the *Mutabilitie Cantos* fall back precisely on such evidence as the river marriage in order to find some image of stability within the constant process of nature. Natural, rather than human, history remains the last reserve of meaning, and physical allegory, previously one among several levels of Spenser's allegory, is now the one level left intact when others are stripped away by time and change. The arguments of the would-be usurper Mutabilitie are countered by the very evidence she marshals to advance her case: the procession of seasons and months that gives a shape to the year and defines natural change as a series of ever-renewing cycles.[53] In her final verdict at the assembly on Arlo Hill, Dame Nature asserts that change does not rule over her creation but is, rather, the essential means by which that creation maintains its being. As was earlier the case of Adonis (III.vi.47), the undying father of created forms who lives in a constant state of metamorphosis, Spenser's final fiction celebrates that which is "eterne in mutabilitie," a self-perpetuating natural order. The more things change, the more they stay the same, a sign of the Creator's abiding presence in His creation.

The celebration of nature's cyclical repetition brings Spenser's fiction close to the orbit of ideas from which Bruno draws the doctrine of the *Eroici furori*.[54] Mutabilitie, whose beauty is appreciated by Jove himself (vi.31), is finally perceived, like Bruno's "magnifica vicissitudine," as the instrument through which nature works its perfection. Spenser's Diana, figuring the historical Elizabeth, disappears from the first of the *Mutabilitie Cantos* to be replaced in the second by the goddess Nature. Bruno's allegory of Diana has already dehistoricized Elizabeth, casting her as the Monad which contains all created nature.

The *Mutabilitie Cantos* portray the loss of a historical source of allegorical meaning which leaves the poet to find meaning in the timeless workings of nature. And yet, human history is reinvoked, if only negatively, in the "vnperfite," two-stanza-long canto 8, which forms a coda to the fragment. The constancy discovered within natural change anticipates an eschatological permanence, and the cycles of hours, days, and years do not merely keep nature running in place, but argue for the existence of a greater cycle of Nature which will eventually close upon itself. Whereas Bruno insists that the Christian millennium should be understood as a stage in a recurrent never-ending cycle, the eternal process by which nature perfects itself, Spenser conceives of this perfection as a finite act, the apocalyptic restoration promised to the poet in "that Sabaoths sight." In its finitude, Spenser's natural history finds a point of tangency with human history, both of which will be made perfect at the end of time. Critics have pointed out that the disappearing Elizabeth reappears obliquely in the last lines of the fragment infolded in the Sabbaoth God—Eli Sabbaoth;[55] the same may be said for the goddess Nature, who vanishes and leaves the field open to Mutabilitie at the end of canto 7, but whose divinity, unveiled at last, will be manifested in her Creator, seen face to face.

The emergence of the narrative "I" (When I bethinke me . . .) in canto 8 suggests that the switch to an eschatological perspective may comprise an effort to salvage the human identity of the poet's voice once his fiction can no longer locate itself historically. Bruno's poet had sacrificed his individual identity in the act of praising an infinite God and His eternal creation. Spenser's "I" reasserts an individual personality which looks forward to its own recovery at the resurrection of the flesh. But the potential loss of personality in a poetic meditation on an apparently timeless nature may account in part for the elegiac quality of the *Mutabilitie Cantos*, the sense in which they constitute a farewell to a former poetic self and an ending, intended or not, to Spenser's epic. The ending seems inevitable once the Faerie Queene herself withdraws her presence, and the Nature who takes her place carries the fiction only one canto further before she, too, disappears (vii.59.9). The *Mutabilitie Cantos* acknowledge the precariousness of an allegory founded on a historical moment that is bound to pass away. Sensing that a glory has passed or is about to pass from the earth, their tone is nostalgic for the source of meaning which the earlier books of the *Faerie Queene* were able to discover in human history. The joining of two rivers in the fallen Irish landscape looks back to the emblematic representation of this source: in retrospect, the marriage of Thames and Medway is a high water mark, a fleeting moment of plenitude, in Spenser's poem.

6

Rabelais: From Babel to Apocalypse

Je diray plus. Icelle herbe moyenante, les substances invisibles visible-
ment sont arrestées, prinses detenues et comme en prison mises; à leur
prinse et arrest sont les grosses et pesantes moles tournées agilement à
insigne profict de la vie humaine. Et m'esbahys comment l'invention de
tel usaige a esté par tant de siecles celé aux antiques philosophes, veue
l'utilité impreciable qui en provient; veu le labeur intolerable que sans elle
ilz supportoient en leurs pistrines.

Icelle moyenant, par la retention des flotz aërez sont les grosses
orchades, les amples thalameges, les fors guallions, les naufz chiliandres
et myriandres de leur stations enlevées, et poussées à l'arbitre de leur
gouverneurs.

Icelle moyenant, sont les nations, que Nature sembloit tenir abs-
conces, impermeables et incongneues à nous venues, nous à elles: choses
que ne feroient les oyseaulx, quelque legiereté de pennaige qu'ilz ayent et
quelque liberté de nager en l'aër que leur soit baillée par Nature. Tapro-
bana a veu Lappia; Java a veu les mons Riphées: Phebol voyra Theleme;
les Islandoys et Engronelands boyront Euphrates; par elle Boreas a veu le
manoir de Auster; Eurus a visité Zephire.

De mode que les Intelligences celestes, les Dieux, tant marins que
terrestres, en ont esté tous effrayez, voyans par l'usaige de cestuy benedict
Pantagruelion les peuples arctiques en plein aspect des antarctiques
franchir la mer Athlantique, passer les deux Tropicques, volter sous la
Zone torride, mesurer tout le Zodiaque, s'esbattre sous l'Æquinoctial,
avoir l'un et l'autre Pole en veue à fleur de leur orizon.

Les dieux olympicques ont en pareil effroy dict: "Pantagruel nous a
mis en pensement nouveau et tedieux, plus que oncques ne feirent les
Aloïdes, par l'usaige et vertus de son herbe. Il sera de brief marié, de sa
femme aura enfans. A ceste destinée ne povons nous contrevenir, car elle
est passée par les mains et fuseaulx des soeurs fatales, filles de Necessité.
Par ses enfans (peut estre) sera inventée herbe de semblable energie,
moyennant laquelle pourront les humains visiter les sources des gresles,

les bondes des pluyes et l'officine des fouldres, pourront envahir les regions de la Lune, entrer le territoire des signes celestes et là prendre logis, les uns à l'Aigle d'or, les aultres au Mouton, les aultres à la Couronne, les aultres á la Herpe, les aultres au Lion d'argent, s'asseoir à table avecques nous, et nos déesses prendre à femmes, qui sont les seulz moyens d'estre déifiez.

En fin ont mis le remede de y obvier en deliberation et au conseil.[1]
[*Tiers Livre*, chap. 51]

[I will say more. By the use of this herb, invisible substances are visibly arrested, taken, detained as if placed in prison; by their capture and arrest great and heavy mills are easily turned to the signal profit of mankind. And it astonishes me how an invention of such usefulness had been for so many centuries hidden from the ancient philosophers, in view of the inestimable benefit which has come from it, in view of the intolerable labor which they had to endure in their mills without it.

By its use, by the retention of waves of air, great merchantmen, broad chambered barges, strong galleons, ships of a thousand or ten thousand men take leave of their moorings, and are driven forward under the guidance of their pilots.

By its use, nations which Nature seems to have kept hidden, unreachable, and unknown have come to us, and we to them: something birds could not do, whatever lightness of feathers they have and whatever liberty to swim through the air that Nature has granted them. Ceylon has seen Lapland, Java has seen the Riphaean mountains, Phebol will see Theleme, Icelanders and Greenlanders will drink from the Euphrates; by it Boreas has seen the mansion of Auster, Eurus has visited Zephyr.

As a result, the heavenly Intelligences, the Gods, marine as well as terrestrial, have all taken fear, seeing how, by the usage of this blessed Pantagruelion, arctic peoples, in full view of antarctic peoples, cross the Atlantic ocean, pass the two Tropics, turn about beneath the torrid Zone, measure the Zodiac, frolic below the Equinoctial line, have both Poles in view on either end of their horizon.

In similar fear the Olympic gods have said: "Pantagruel has given us something new and troublesome to think about, more than the Aloides did of old, by the usage and power of his herb. He will soon be married, and will have children by his wife. We cannot contravene this destiny for it has passed through the hands and over the spindles of the sister Fates, the daughters of Necessity. By his children (perhaps) will be discovered an herb of similar energy, by use of which, men will be able to visit the source of the hail, the flood-gates of the rain, and the smithy of the thunderbolts, to invade the regions of the Moon, enter the territory of the heavenly signs, take up lodgings there, some at the golden Eagle, others at the Ram, others at the Crown, others at the Harp, others at the silver Lion, sit down at table with us, and take our goddesses for wives, which are the only means of becoming deified."

169

In the end they sought a means to prevent this in deliberation and in counsel.]

The wonderful plant Pantagruelion is the token of a steady forward march of human knowledge toward a divine goal, a prospect which dismays the Olympian gods at the close of the penultimate chapter of Rabelais's *Tiers Livre* (1546). The passage revises several thematic motifs encountered in our earlier chapters. Like Tasso's Magus of Ascalon, Pantagruel's descendants may obtain some of that knowledge of the secrets of nature which Job 38 ascribes to the cosmocrator alone: "les sources des gresles" (Job 38:22: aut thesauros grandinis aspexisti?); "les bondes des pluyes" (Job 38:25: Quis dedit vehementissimo imbri cursum?); "l'officine des fouldres" (Job 38:35: Numquid mittes fulgura?). Rabelais is also aware of the tradition from the apocryphal Book of Enoch, according to which the giants of Genesis 6:4 invent technology and the occult sciences as a byproduct of their idolatry and wickedness.[2] Rabelais has rewritten both biblical myths. (1) The secrets of creation may ultimately be reached by scientific pursuit. And, unlike Tasso and his Magus, Rabelais sees no discontinuity between such scientific learning and divine wisdom. (2) The Rabelaisian giants do not seek knowledge and mastery over nature out of prideful impiety, but rather as God's partners in the saving plan of Christian history. The Pantagruelion chapters (49–52) are a hymn to an advancing technology which culminates in the apocalyptic vision of the giants successfully storming heaven: restoring man to paradise.

Rabelais has also reinterpreted the classical myth of the gigantomachy. For Spenser, as for most writers of the sixteenth century, the assault of the Aloides was an emblem of human limitation, of the pride of empire and civilization laid low by the mutability of history.[3] Rabelais describes the cyclical historical pattern of *translatio imperii* in the first chapter of the *Gargantua*, arriving, like la Boderie and Spenser, at the appropriate nationalistic conclusion.

> des Assyriens en Medes,
> des Medes es Perses,
> des Perses es Macedones,
> des Macedones es Romains,
> des Romains es Grecz,
> des Grecz es Françoys.

[From the Assyrians to the Medes, from the Medes to the Persians, from the Persians to the Macedonians, from the Macedonians to the Romans, from the Romans to the Byzantines, from the Byzantines to the French].

Translatio imperii, with its related idea of *translatio studii,* may be understood either as a series of discrete cycles of growth, achievement, and decline, or as a continuous historical progress in which each new center of civilization builds upon the contributions of its predecessors. Spenser, it has been argued above, inclines to the former idea. With a faith in the ongoing process of history that is especially characteristic of his fiction, a faith born of the perspective of the modern measuring the achievement of his age against those of antiquity ("Et m'esbahys comment l'invention de tel usaige a esté par tant de siecles celé aux antiques philosophes"), Rabelais adapts the latter, progressive view of historical development in his version of a *second* gigantomachy in which the giants and human history successfully reach their heavenly goal.

The doubling of the myth of the giants, moreover, alludes to two specific events in biblical history, and provides a typological setting in which Rabelais's own giant fiction may be understood.

An exegetical tradition beginning as early as Josephus makes Nimrod (Genesis 10:8–10) both a giant and the builder of the Tower of Babel.[4] Inevitably, the biblical episode of aspiring giants thwarted in their venture to raise themselves to heaven was assimilated with the classical gigantomachy; Dante places Nimrod in Hell side by side with the rebellious Titans.[5] The two stories are fully conflated in the early sixteenth century by the Dominican friar, Peter Lavinius, in his commentary on Ovid's *Metamorphoses* (1503). Lavinius reads Ovid's version of the gigantomachy (1.151–62) as a direct retelling of the incidents at Babel.

> And the people were separated out by their languages and dispersed throughout the earth: who at length were gathered together again in the unity of the faith by the apostles speaking different languages. Indeed Ovid prettily describes this gigantomachy of Nimrod and the building of the tower when he pretends that the giants placed mountains on top of mountains.[6]

Rabelais surely read Lavinius, as he makes fun of the friar's commentary in the prologue to the *Gargantua,* comparing him, as one Frère Lubin, to the ancient allegorists of Homer. Nonetheless, he incorporates Lavinius's allegorizations into his own fiction.[7]

If the earlier assault of the giants, the repulsed Aloides, corresponds to the confusion of languages and dispersal of humanity at Babel, then the second, successful scaling of Olympus by the Rabelaisian giants, Pantagruel's descendants, represents the typological inversion of Babel: the church's apostolic mission to reunite the world in Christian faith. The unity of language lost at Babel is compensated by the spiritual gift of tongues at Pentecost (Acts 2:1), which enables the Apostles to preach the gospel to all the nations of the earth. The mission to spread the Word continues throughout human history until the Apocalypse, when the saints gathered at the Supper of the Lamb will include members "from every race, tribe, people and language" (Revelation 7:9: ex omnibus gentibus et tribubus et populis et linguis.) This is the messianic banquet promised to all peoples on Mount Zion in the eschatological prophecy of Isaiah 25:6: "Et faciet Dominus exercituum omnibus populis in monte hoc convivium vindemiae, pinguium medullatorum, vindemiae defaecatae." Thinly disguised in classical garments, the historical course presaged by the Pantagruelion culminates in an apocalyptic scenario. The giants find their homes in the stars, turning the constellations into taverns where they drink— the central activity of the Rabelaisian hero—at a divine banquet.

The placement of eschatological prophecy at the end of the eulogy of the Pantagruelion links the advancement of human learning and technology to the unfolding of salvation history. This link is enunciated early on in the Rabelaisian books in the letter from Gargantua to Pantagruel in chapter 8 of the *Pantagruel*. Prescribing to the young Pantagruel a thorough immersion in the new humanist education, the letter begins with a meditation on the generations of man. Gargantua sees himself reborn in his son at the same time he bequeathes to him a cultural inheritance which the heir is expected to augment in a period that has not only restored classical learning from the gothic dark ages of his grandfather Grandgousier, but has surpassed the classical past as well. Gargantua cites the examples of printing and artillery, two of the three modern inventions traditionally used by Renaissance men to assert the advance their age had made over antiquity, and he declares that the possibilities for study in his day excel those available to Plato, Cicero, or Papinian. The praise of procreation in marriage, which partially restores what has been lost by Original Sin ("est aulcunement instauré ce que nous feut tollu par le peché de nos premiers parens"), gives the humanist program a context within a progressive movement of history that leads to a full apocalyptic restoration.

> Mais par ce moyen de propagation seminale, demoure es enfans ce que estoit de perdu es parens, et es nepveux ce que deperissoit es enfans, et ainsi successivement jusques à l'heure du jugement final, quand Jesu-Christ aura rendu à Dieu le pere son royaulme pacifique hors tout dangier et contamination de peché, car alors cesseront toutes generations et corruptions, et seront les elemens hors de leurs transmutations continues, veu que la paix tant desirée sera consumée et parfaicte, et que toutes choses seront reduites à leur fin et periode. [*Pantagruel* 8]

> [But by this means of seminal propagation there remains in the children what was lost in the parent, and in the grandchildren what perished in the children, and so on in succession until the hour of the Last Judgment, when Jesus Christ will have returned to God the Father His peaceful kingdom, free from all danger and contamination of sin, for then all generation and corruption will cease, and the elements will be free from their continual transmutations, since the peace so greatly desired will be consummated and perfected and all things returned to their end and period.]

This second paragraph of Gargantua's letter has been ignored by critics early in this century who tried, on the basis of the letter, to make Rabelais into a freethinker, and by more recent commentators who have read the letter as a satire on the exaggerated claims of humanist pedagogy.[8] The language of the letter suggests an analogy between the eventual restoration of God's kingdom on earth and the restoration of good learning ("la lumiere et dignité a esté de mon eage rendue es lettres. . . . Maintenant toutes disciplines sont restituées, les langues instaurées;" "light and dignity have been returned to letters in my age. . . . now all good disciplines have been reconstituted, the knowledge of languages restored"). Christ's restitution to God the Father of a realm whose peace will be "consumée et parfaicte" provides the larger model for the accounting which Pantagruel is to make when he returns to Gargantua after completing his education, an enterprise his father urges him to "parfaire et consommer." Placed within the larger plan of Christian history, human learning and the development of the practical arts are sacralized, described by the eucharistic formula, "manne celeste de la bonne doctrine" ("heavenly manna of good learning"). The progress of knowledge continues to the final revelation of the Last Judgment, and the manifold disciplines of study which Gargantua catalogues are to be explored not merely by his son but by all his posterity. The insistence upon procreation as the means of forward historical growth toward better and better things reappears in the episode of the Pantagruelion, where the future achievements of human science depend upon Pantagruel's own marriage and begetting of children. This marriage theme finds its apocalyptic fulfillment in the prophecy that Pantagruel's descendants will wed goddesses and become divine.

Pantagruelion is a kind of hemp. The Rabelaisian narrator relates various technological uses of hempen rope, but what specifically has the Olympian gods worried is its employment in contemporary navigation. Commentators have noted that Rabelais twists inside out a passage in the *Natural History* of Pliny where the Roman author describes the manufacture of linen sails from the lowly flax plant and then proceeds to execrate Daedalus, the inventor of mast and sail, for having made possible a "daring life, full of transgressions."[9] Pliny suggests that man was never meant to sail. Rabelais rejects this pessimism about human limitations while he celebrates the new accomplishments of Renaissance seamanship.[10] Navigation to the New World was the third advance, along with printing and gunpowder, which the Renaissance boasted over antiquity. Rabelais, however, is not merely repeating another modern claim for superiority to the ancients: this latest technological breakthrough has a direct evangelical application and provides a specific contemporary context for the apocalyptic expectations to which the Pantagruelion gives rise.

Christopher Columbus, who "discovered" the river of Eden in the Orinoco, regarded himself as a harbinger of the messianic age. He wrote: "God made me the messenger of the new heaven and the new earth of which He spoke in the Apocalypse by St. John (Revelation 21:1), after having spoken of it by the mouth of Isaiah."[11] The Isaian prophecies (65:17, 66:22) refer to the eschatological restoration of Mount Zion, a project which became a dream and fixation for Columbus throughout his life. Having found what he took to be King Solomon's mines at Veragua, he urged Ferdinand and Isabella to use the New World gold to rebuild Solomon's temple. For his part, Columbus promised to transport preachers to convert the emperor of China, whose kingdom, he remained convinced, lay just beyond Hispaniola.[12] This missionary commitment, in fact, lay at the basis of the apocalypticism both of Columbus and of other Renaissance men confronting the new achievements of navigation. The sea routes west to the Americas and east around Africa opened up the real possibility of a worldwide apostolic movement. The spreading of the gospel to the "four corners of the earth" (Isaiah 11:12, Ezekiel 7:2, Revelation

7:1) would signal the completion of the church's historical mission and the imminence of the Last Judgment. Influenced by Joachimite millenarian schemes, Columbus and such mystical thinkers as Egidio da Viterbo and Guillaume Postel identified the Age of Discovery with the beginning of the apocalyptic age.[13] John Liddy Phelan has described this train of thought.

> Christianity for the first time could implement its universal claims on a world-wide basis. The gospel could be brought to all peoples and all races. It could be preached in every tongue that man spoke. Christianity could be global as well as universal. To those of mystical temperament this possibility appeared as a vision which was so blinding and radiant that its fulfillment must inevitably foreshadow the rapidly approaching end of the world. It seemed to these mystics that after all the races of mankind had been converted nothing further could happen in this world; for anything else would be an anticlimax.[14]

The geographical explorations taking place as Rabelais wrote fostered apocalyptic expectations—expectations shared by his Olympians, who contemplate in alarm human ships sailing to the ends of the earth, North wind journeying to South, East to West. The meeting of nations, reversing the diaspora of Babel, looks forward to a final day when all mankind, united in one faith, will take up the assault upon the heavens.[15] This assault, in fact, has been under way for some time. Jesus Himself said that, "A diebus autem Ioannis Baptistae usque nunc regnum caelorum vim patitur, et violenti rapiunt illud" (Matthew 11:12). Heinrich Bullinger's commentary (1542) on the Matthew passage describes this spiritual assault as an ongoing evangelical process.

> Indeed the Lord seems to be saying something like this: the prophets foretold the future Christ as the object of longing and expectation of the people, of sinners, of the wretched, and of the most afflicted, and, accordingly, at the coming and revelation of the Messiah, such men will hasten with great ardor to the kingdom of heaven more as if they were taking it by storm than receiving it. For Micah says, imitating Isaiah, that this will come to pass on the last of days, that the mount of the temple will be placed on top of the mountain peaks, and be raised higher than the mountains, and that the people will flock together to it. Many nations will go forth and will say, Come and let us ascend to the mountain of the Lord, and to the temple of the God of Jacob, etc. (Micah 4:12) On the other hand, you have known that, since the days of John the Baptist, that is from that time in which he began to preach Christ, sinners, publicans,

soldiers, prostitutes, gentiles, whoever is most miserable, as if a battle-
line has been drawn up, and with something like its force, eagerly seize
upon and, as it were, plunder, that is, drink up avidly the grace of the
gospel. Of this the pharisees and scribes are themselves witnesses,
repeatedly indignant that Christ freely allowed publicans and sinners to
approach Him. We now infer from these words the following: Let the
whole world therefore acknowledge Jesus to be the Christ, nor hereafter
is another Messiah to be expected: this very time in which Christ said
these things was itself the Messianic Age, and in those days the kingdom
of heaven arose, which through succeeding ages and the preaching of
the apostles has been spread throughout the entire globe of the earth.[16]

Bullinger removes the Messianic Age from the last days and places it
back within the Christ event and the continuing history of the Church.
Jesus takes the place of the eschatological Zion of Isaiah and Micah,
and brings the Kingdom of Heaven down to earth, where it goes
forward through the spreading of the gospel first preached by John.
Conflating the historical revelation of Jesus with the Old Testament
prophecies more normally identified with His second coming, Bullinger asserts the continuity of spiritual experience. The convert to the
Word is already participating *now* in the spiritual events reserved for
then, the end of time. The assault of the Rabelaisian giants is an
emblem of those apocalyptic events—the ascent of a restored Zion into
the Kingdom of Heaven—which complete salvation history after
progressive advances in human learning and technology have
brought the evangelical mission of Christianity to its fulfillment. But
the scene may also describe the individual experience of the Christian
in history, who, by the gift of grace and the Holy Spirit, takes heaven
by storm. A later Renaissance exegete, Cornelius a Lapide (1629),
would compare the spiritual violence of Matthew 11:12 to how "the
poets fable that heaven was once invaded by giants."[17]

The gods' seriocomic prophecy is qualified by the parenthetical
"peut estre" and by their decision to forestall the striving giants "au
conseil." This apparent allusion to the opening of the Council of Trent
a year before the publication of the *Tiers Livre*, and the book's final
chapter, which describes the resistance of Pantagruelion to fire, checks
any sense of excessive optimism in the Rabelaisian vision. The fiery
furnace from which the Pantagruelion emerges "renouvelé et nettoyé"
is a familiar typological figure for the trials by which God tests His
people in the Bible. The stake which could await the incautious
reformer gives the figure an appallingly real application in Rabelais's

176

contemporary France. The threat of a reactionary counterreform reminds the reader that, despite the prospect of messianic peace and festivity, man remains subject to the vicissitudes of present history. This pattern of apocalyptic promise followed by qualification also appears in the final chapters of the *Gargantua* and the *Quart Livre*. In the *Gargantua*, the utopian monastery of Theleme (chap. 52–58), with its several reminiscences of the heavenly Jerusalem of Revelation 21–22, seems to be a haven outside of history for those of perfected will. But the "Enigme en prophetie" found at Theleme in chapter 58 appears to foretell a new wave of religious persecution.[18] In a similar sequence, chapters 63–65 of the *Quart Livre* portray Pantagruel's companions "solving" a series of problems they have proposed by sitting down together at a joyful feast, a eucharistic foretaste of the messianic banquet at the end of time. But chapters 66–67 bring one more confrontation with the theological adversaries at Gannabin and the scatological finale caused by Panurge's all-too-human fear.[19]

These switches of perspective at the endings of the Rabelaisian books preclude any easy fictional resolution. Just as Spenser summons Redcrosse away from his marriage to Una in order to resume his quest, Rabelais concludes his books by drawing back from a narrative closure identified with apocalyptic fulfillment and peace. Its open-endedness returns the fiction to the processes of history which are still incomplete and urges the reader to the task of further interpretation. For if history is redeemed in the Rabelaisian books as the staging ground for man's salvation and eventual ascent to the heavenly seats of the gods, it is simultaneously a realm of contingency, of problematic events and riddling signs whose meaning has not yet been revealed, of the confusion which is Babel.

Initially, the Rabelaisian text seems to be the product of this confusion. In its first sentence, the opening chapter of the *Pantagruel* self-consciously examines the genesis of its own fiction.

> Ce ne sera chose inutile ne oysifve, veu que sommes de sejour, vous ramentevoir la premiere source et origine d'ont nous est né le bon Pantagruel: car je voy que tous bons hystoriographes ainsi ont traicté leur Chronicques, non seullement les Arabes, Barbares, et Latins, mais aussi Gregoys, Gentilz, qui furent buveurs eternelz.

> [It will be no useless nor idle matter, seeing that we are at leisure, to remind you of the first source and origin from which the good Pantagruel

has been born to us, for I see that all good historians have thus treated their chronicles, not only the Arabs, Barbarians, and Latins, but also the Greeks and Pagans, who were eternal boozers.]

While the last phrase, "qui furent buveurs eternelz," is a loaded one in the larger Rabelaisian context—it replaces a reference to Matthew and Luke in earlier editions—the parodic intentions of the text are clear. In place of a solemn history, the chapter proceeds to describe the monstrous creation of the giants in an absurd once-upon-a-time, beneath impossible astrological conjunctions, when men ate medlars fertilized by the blood of the slain Abel. The nonsensical genealogy that follows jumbles the names of giants from the Bible, classical myth, ancient history, and chivalric romance together with names made up by Rabelais's punning imagination—purely verbal beings. The parody of Old and New Testament genealogies, like Pulci's beginning his *Morgante* with the Word of God, establishes the human author as an autonomous creator by the word. The claim, later advanced in the first chapter of the *Gargantua,* to have unearthed this giant genealogy from a lost book—just as Ariosto follows the chronicles of Turpin or Cervantes edits the translated history of Cide Hamete Benengeli—invents a transparently fictional source in order to assert authorial control and autonomy. Sir Philip Sidney praises the poetic imagination which produces "forms such as never were in nature, as the Heroes, Demigods, Cyclops, Chimaeras, Furies."[20] He might have added Ariosto's compound word and beast, the hippogriff, or the Rabelaisian giant whose mouth contains a whole other world. But the ultimate result of the freedom of language to form a world of its own is nonsense, the nonsense genealogy, the nonsense of the Library of St. Victor, of the nonexistent languages which Panurge speaks, of the coq-à-l'âne lawcourt scenes in chapters 11–13 of the *Pantagruel,* of the mock scholastic debate with signs in chapter 19. Lawyers and Sorbonne theologians are of course the butt of Rabelais's satire—they do in fact talk nonsense—but his own linguistic exuberance almost makes him a partner to their abuses. The Library of St. Victor is both a satire on scholastic learning and a not-so-distant ancestor of Borges's labyrinthine library where books and verbal meaning proliferate unendingly. In pointed contrast to the vast, diversified, but ultimately coherent educational program outlined one chapter later in Gargantua's letter, the ridiculous titles of the Library of St. Victor suggest how learning may be splintered up into a scholastic discourse ever capable of making new distinctions and inventing new relationships, no longer subject to any reality outside its own logical and linguistic structures. Yet at the same time the library seems to celebrate the inexhaustible resources of Rabelais's literary invention. Like other humanists, Rabelais attacks the scholastics for being engrossed in the purely verbal disputes occasioned by their jargon and impure, "monkish" Latin. But, as a literary artist in love with words, he appears to be of the scholastics' party.

This impulse toward autonomy in the Rabelaisian text bears the mark of Cain: what replaces a direct claim to the authorship of its giant fiction in the first chapter of the *Pantagruel* is the murder of Abel, from whose blood—through the intermediary medlars—the giant race derives its origin. Rabelais reverses the Ovidian myth (*Metamorphoses* 1.156–62) where it is mankind which springs up from the earth soaked with the blood of the overthrown Titans. This new race, according to Ovid, followed the giants' violence and impious ways, and Jove, like the Old Testament God, wiped them out with a flood. Lavinius moralizes: "Our first parent became a sinner: and rendered all his posterity liable to sin: and begot the fratricide Cain, whose descendants were given to all sorts of crimes, as if drawing birth from blood, that is to say, from sin, they did not degenerate from their ancestry."[21] If the blood of the Ovidian giants begets a race of Cain, Rabelais's giants owe their existence to Cain's bloodshed. Cain's punishment, which makes him a wanderer across the earth, is the same as his fratricidal crime: a violation of human community. Saint Augustine describes Cain as the typological founder of Babel-Babylon, the earthly city of confusion.[22] The violence which accompanies the genesis of the Rabelaisian books suggests the potential for any linguistic discourse to estrange itself from its audience, to become sufficient unto itself, nonsense to others.

But the blood that fertilizes the medlars, which in turn produce gigantism and giants, belongs to the innocent victim Abel: the "sang du juste." The phrase is biblical but derives from the New rather than the Old Testament. It translates Christ's curse against the Pharisees in Matthew 23:35, "ut veniat super vos omnis *sanguis iustus* qui effusus est super terram *a sanguine Abel iusti* usque ad sanguinem Zachariae filli Barachiae, quem occidistis inter templum et altare." By this invective, Jesus links Himself to the slain prophets and makes Abel's death prefigure the Passion.[23] Hebrews 12:24 describes Abel's blood as an inferior type for the mediating blood of Christ. Christ's blood continues to perform its sacrificial role in the wine of the Eucharist, and the eating of the medlars grown from Abel's blood is compared to Noah's discovery of wine. The sacrament of Communion gathers back a dispersed humanity as members of Christ's body, the Church. Rabelais appears deliberately to contradict the biblical text (Genesis 4:11–12), where the earth soaked with Abel's blood will not yield any fruits to Cain, in order that Abel's sacrifice may from the outset counteract the effects of Cain's sin. In *The City of God*, Saint Augustine fits the sequence of the births of Cain and Abel into the progress both of universal and individual human history.

> Of these two first parents of the human race, then, Cain was the first-born, and he belonged to the city of men; after him was born Abel, who belonged to the city of God. For as in the individual the truth of the apostle's statement is discerned, "that is not first which is spiritual, but that which is natural, and afterward that which is spiritual," whence it comes to pass that each man, being derived from a condemned stock, is first of all born of Adam evil and carnal, and becomes good and spiritual only afterwards, when he is grafted into Christ by regeneration: so was it in the human race as a whole.[24]

According to Augustine's scheme, Abel, the second-born son, represents the possibility of spiritual rebirth in Christ, the second divine dispensation after the Fall. In Rabelais's fiction, the eucharistic medlars that spring from Abel's blood reverse the effects of the forbidden fruit of Eden, which they verbally recall ("elles estoient belles à l'oeil et delicieuses au goust"; "they were lovely to the eye and delicious to taste"). The spiritual gifts of the Sacrament—a superabundant, divine supplement to the human—are comically figured in the gigantism which swells the bodies of the medlar eaters and eventually produces the Rabelaisian giants.

This complex pattern of biblical allusion points up the essential doubleness of the Rabelaisian act of literary creation.[25] The birth of an individual style, insofar as it appropriates to itself the source of signification and expresses meaning in a new form, is at first an act of violence against the understanding of its audience, a transgression, like Cain's fratricide, which leads to the confusion of Babel. But Rabelais's fiction symbolizes in the redemptive blood of Abel its claim to originate as a eucharistic gift of the Spirit, the same Spirit which descended at Pentecost with the gift of languages and whose historical mission is to gather together the human community. Insofar as the Rabelaisian text contributes to a transcendent significance, it may be shared with its reader; for all its apparent nonsense, the text claims to possess an *interpretable* meaning. Conversely, the extent to which the text gives edification to a community of interpreters is the measure of its spiritual inspiration. The Rabelaisian books claim to create just such a community, the groups of Pantagruelists ("toutes bonnes compaignies de Pantagruelistes") addressed by the prologue to the *Gargantua*.

This community of interpretation exists and evolves *in history*, carrying forward the work of the Spirit. The assimilation of the initially puzzling Rabelaisian text into a shared body of meaning is part of that much larger historical process by which Abel's City of God—Jerusalem, the Church—is built out of the confusion of Babel. For Rabelais, the growth of this city through history until it becomes identical with the New Jerusalem at the end of time coincides with a progressive unfolding of spiritual knowledge. It is toward the fulfillment of this knowledge that the Church works as an interpretative community, and its missionary commitment aims both to share its tradition with others and, by increasing the number of interpreters, to add to its own edification. This ecclesial model is the basis for Rabelais's confident inclusion of humanist learning and the discoveries of Renaissance science as parts of a continuing divine revelation. And this model guides the interpretation of his fiction. Like the Pantagruelion it celebrates, the Rabelaisian text is a pledge of greater things to come, a future fullness of meaning which it both participates in and contributes to. In this futurity lies the text's claim to truth and efficacy, and those examples of misappropriated and unproductive discourse which appear in Rabelais's fiction are linked with attempts to stop or reverse the progress of history. If Pantagruel traces his genealogy back to a hodgepodge of ancestors, where meaning is confused with nonsense, his descendants, according to Gargantua's letter and the alarmed prophecy of the Olympian gods, form a genealogical chain leading to the perfect world of the Last Judgment.

The assimilation of the text into a historical community of interpretation is a cooperative effort, and the interpreter must work as hard, if not harder, than the author. If the text *should* be offered in the proper spirit—Pantagruelism—it *must* be accepted in that spirit if it is to edify. Rabelais demonstrates how the Pantagruelism of the interpreter can overcome even the ultimate threat of Babelic nonsense in chapter 9 of the *Pantagruel*. Panurge enters the book speaking fourteen languages. Three are imaginary and only the last—French, his mother tongue—succeeds in communicating his need for food. Panurge argues repeatedly, in the Dutch, Danish, and Greek which cannot be

understood, that language should in fact be superfluous, given his
famished appearance. But instead language gets in the way; it becomes an obstacle between the speaker and the satisfaction of his
desire. Behind this comedy, as well as the larger Rabelaisian meditation on interpretation and community, lies the text of chapters 12–15 of
1 Corinthians. Paul is discussing the distribution of spiritual gifts
among the members of the church, and in chapter 14 he distinguishes
between "glossolalia," the gift of speaking in strange tongues, and
"prophetia," the ability to interpret spiritual truths for the community.

> Sectamini caritatem, aemulamini spiritalia, magis autem ut prophetetis.
> 2Qui enim loquitur lingua non hominibus loquitur, sed Deo; nemo enim
> audit, spiritu autem loquitur mysteria. 3Nam qui prophetat, hominibus
> loquitur ad aedificationem et exhortationem et consolationem. 4Qui
> loquitur lingua semetipsum aedificat; qui autem prophetat, ecclesiam
> Dei aedificat.

> 10Tam multa, ut puta, genera linguarum sunt in hoc mundo, et nihil sine
> voce est. 11Si ergo nesciero virtutem vocis, ero ei cui loquor barbarus, et
> qui loquitur mihi barbarus. 12Sic et vos, quoniam aemulatores estis
> spirituum, ad aedificationem ecclesiae quaerite ut abundetis. 13Et ideo
> qui loquitur lingua, oret ut interpretetur.

Paul urges the speaker in tongues to remain silent unless an interpreter is present (14:28). Panurge has no such inhibitions. He misuses
his linguistic gifts and reduces the various real languages he speaks to
the nonsense of the made-up ones. His virtuoso performance reverts
language back to the situation of Babel where every man speaks only
for himself and becomes a stranger ("barbarus") to others.[26] Rather
than mediate between the speaker and the goal of his desire,
Panurge's verbal dexterity in fact defers satisfaction of his hunger and,
to the extent that he plays with language for its own sake, it begins to
take the place of the food he needs. Panurge's audience is caught up in
his linguistic display. Epistemon recognizes Panurge's Hebrew; Car-
palim, the Greek; and Pantagruel thinks he understands the imaginary Utopian tongue. Epistemon praises Panurge's pronunciation,
and none of the company seems to go beyond this superficial appreciation of his linguistic performance to act on the meaning of his words.
They withhold the charity Panurge asks for in his unintelligible Dutch.
Yet for Paul, no language is without meaning ("nihil sine voce est"),
and in the same Dutch, Panurge claims to speak in none but Christian
languages.[27] Language may always—potentially—carry out the work
of the Spirit, and even if the speaker misappropriates the gift of

languages, no utterance can be truly autonomous. His audience, through a creative act of interpretation, may derive spiritual meaning from his words. Paul identifies interpretation itself as one of the gifts of the Spirit distributed among the members of the Christian community (1 Cor. 12:10), who must share them together in order to receive maximum benefit, just as the various parts of the human body cooperate (12:11–30)—a passage which Panurge will later echo in his eulogy of debts and praise of the codpiece in the *Tiers Livre*.[28] For all the comic misdirection of his multilingual performance, Panurge does finally receive charity. He is made an Achates to Pantagruel's Aeneas, and despite his selfish and unproductive behavior in the subsequent Rabelaisian books, he is always accommodated within the giant's community.

A similar accommodation is demanded of the reader of Rabelais's fiction, even at its most seemingly nonsensical. The prologue to the *Gargantua* enjoins the reader's active participation in uncovering its hidden doctrine ("doctrine plus absconce"), but then proceeds to mock the allegorizers of classical poetry—including Lavinius—for finding meanings that the authors never intended; and it questions the reader's belief ("Croiez vous en vostre foy . . . Si ne le croiez") in the existence of any allegorical meaning beneath the book's comic surface. These contradictory signals cannot be simply reconciled and the reader's attitude can only be formed by the amount of esoteric meaning he actually does find within the narrative of the *Gargantua*. The prologue itself becomes another of the riddles of the book which the reader must interpret.[29] Such riddles cannot be escaped: the prologue asserts that even an allegorical reading should not bypass the literal level of the fiction, which is often puzzling and grotesque. This insistence upon the letter can partly be understood as the author's defense of the integrity of his work. But it is also in keeping with Rabelais's vision of history as a sacralized process through which divine meaning can be unfolded, with the insistent focus of his fiction upon the instrument of history—the body—and its natural processes. To allegorize the text at the expense of its letter would not only deny its human individuality but would remove it from the historical continuum that gives it meaning. Human history and the Rabelaisian text each provide a model for how to interpret the other: the model is incarnational, the irreducible link of letter and spirit. By reading allegorical meaning into the text, the interpreter may overlook the meaning already available in its historical letter—the meaning present now in the midst of history. Meaning in the Rabelaisian text must be sought within a letter which may be confusing and frequently does violence to the understanding. But the text in this respect mirrors the reader's experience before the violence and confusion which exist in his own history and through which he must recover a significance that is still in the making and is ultimately eschatological.

This incarnational model of interpretation which the Rabelaisian books apply to history and by which they ask to be read is more specifically based upon the Eucharist, the sacramental joining of the letter to a superabundant spirit. In its grandest claims, the prologue to the *Gargantua* promises to reveal to the reader "de tres haultz sacremens et mysteres horrificques," or the *mysteria* of the Sacrament, but it will find these outside as well as inside a context that is traditionally defined as sacramental: "tant en ce que concerne nostre religion que aussi l'estat politicq et vie oeconomicque"; ("as much in those matters which concern our religion as in matters of state and domestic life"). The idea that sacramental experience—conceived above all as an interpretative experience—may be applied or replicated in other spheres of human activity can be found in Erasmus. At the end of *The Praise of Folly*, the Eucharist emerges as the central hermeneutic event in the life of the Christian believer. The efficacy of the Sacrament depends upon its reception by the communicant, who will receive no benefit and may even be harmed unless he reaches for a spiritual meaning, the sacrifice of Christ, which is represented in the visible signs of the ceremony ("nisi id quod est spiritale accesserit, nempe hoc quod signis illis visibilis repraesentatur. Repraesentatur autem mors Christi"; "unless that which is spiritual is added, namely that which is represented by those visible signs, for the death of Christ is so represented").[30] The pious Christian extends this way of interpreting the Eucharist, which Folly, in a stunning Erasmian pun, claims merely to have offered exempli gratia, to all aspects of his or her life. ("Nec in his tantum, quae dumtaxat exempli gratia proposuimus, sed simpliciter in omni vita refugit pius ab his quae corpori cognata sunt, ad aeterna, ad invisibilia, ad spiritalia rapitur"; "Nor just in these matters, which I have merely presented as an example, but in all aspects of life the pious man flees from those things which are related to the body and is rapt by eternal, invisible, and spiritual things").[31] Conversely, in his colloquy, the *Convivium Religiosum* (1522), Erasmus suggests how the activity of a community of spiritual interpreters—their concerns brought down to earth from Folly's Platonizing rapture to matters of scriptural exegesis, reading the book of nature, and moral philosophy—may approximate the eucharistic meal.[32] Rabelais presents the same idea at the end of the *Quart Livre* (63–65).

The Eucharist, instituted at the moment of Christ's physical disappearance from Earth, looks forward prophetically to His second coming: the liturgy addresses the Host: "Benedictus qui venit in nomine Domini."[33] The spiritual interpreter of *The Praise of Folly* enjoys a foretaste of the knowledge that will become full only at the resurrection of the body, droplets from the fountain of life ("minutissima quedam stillula est, ad fontem illum aeternae felicitatis . . . futurae felicitatis tenuis quaedam degustatiuncula"; "the most minute droplet compared to that fountain of eternal happiness . . . a sort of diluted little taste of that future happiness").[34] The incompleteness of prophetic understanding within an eschatological perspective is discussed by Paul in a famous section from the same passage of 1 Corinthians.

> Ex parte enim cognoscimus et ex parte prophetamus; [10]cum autem venerit quod perfectum est, evacuibitur quod ex parte est.[11] Cum essem parvulus, loquebar ut parvulus, sapiebam ut parvulus, cogitabam ut parvulus; quando autem factus sum vir, evacuavi quae erant parvuli.[12] Videmus nunc per speculum in aenigmate, tunc autem facie ad faciem; nunc cognosco ex parte, tunc autem cognoscam sicut et cognitus sum. [1 Corinthians 13:9–12]

The full meaning of the Christ event is still to be revealed, and the present findings of the interpreter can only be imperfect: "Ex parte enim cognoscimus." Their partial nature accounts for the need of community: the Church in which spiritual gifts may be exchanged. The Rabelaisian text describes its genesis as a gift produced from a eucharistic sacrifice (the blood of Abel) and then asks that it should itself be read according to the hermeneutic model of the Sacrament: the writer and the reader of the text are thus engaged in the same interpretative activity. The authority claimed for the text is partial, the product of an individual, historical author, who is merely one in a larger community of spiritual interpreters.[35] The collaboration of that community—which for Rabelais progresses through history toward more and more perfect understanding—is required to integrate the meaning of his text into a continuing unfolding of significance. The text's affirmation of meaning now in present history—because both that history and the text itself are contributing toward a future, fuller meaning—depends upon the text's reception by its Pantagruelist readers and their successive generations.

If this cooperative ecclesial model for the relationship of the text to **185** its reader allows Rabelais a prophetic claim to authority, it also has an urgent contemporary application. Toward the end of his treatise on human language, the *Lingua* (1525), Erasmus considers the religious disputes of his day.

> Today, in truth, when we see the schools of philosophers disagree with so many opinions, and all Christians at sword's point with so many different dogmas, do we not reproduce the building of the tower of Babel?[36]

Erasmus cites the texts of Philippians and 1 Corinthians and imitates both the language and the metaphor of Paul's description of the body of Christ in the latter epistle. He contrasts the dissension in the ranks of the sixteenth-century Church to the cooperation of the apostolic community.

> If member is torn from member, what will become of the body? If the body is separated from its head, what will happen to its life? This doubtless is what Paul says of us called together into the society of the Son of God, for we are ingrafted by faith into that body, which is the church: the church really means congregation, not division. Yet because we cannot adhere to the head, unless we consent among ourselves, let us be held together by mutual charity, as he says, "Thirst to be perfect," that is, an integral body, not a mutilated or rent one, but solid and joined together in Christ, by the chain of His Spirit. Paul disapproves of what these voices of discord were heard to say among the Corinthians: "I am for Paul, I for Apollo, I for Cephas, I for Christ." What would he say if he heard the confused languages of men in this age: I am a transalpine theologian, I a cisalpine one, I a Scotist, I a Thomist, I an Ockhamist, I a realist, I a nominalist, I of Paris, I of Cologne, I a Lutheran, I a Karlstadtian, I an Evangelical, I a Papist? It makes me ashamed to name them all. O house, how you are dispersed, o community, how you are torn asunder, O body, where is now that happy ενάς (unity), from which whoever is excluded is not in Christ?[37]

Erasmus asserts that even if Christians cannot fully agree on matters of doctrine, they can remain joined together in one church. His solution to the discord set in motion by the Reformation is to transcend individual differences in a communal spirit of charity. The typological figure by which he urges ecclesiastical unity and reconciliation is a familiar one for Rabelais.

Therefore let us cease to build up the tower of Babel, the tower of pride and dissension, and let us begin to restore Jerusalem and the fallen temple of God.[38]

The goal of the Rabelaisian text is to place itself within a continuing community of interpretation. Simultaneously, the text aims to create this community by teaching *how* to interpret. The Rabelaisian books repeatedly thematize the problems and processes of interpretation: in the *Pantragruel*, the hero's judgment at the Lawcourt in chapters 11–13 is followed by the debate with signs (18–20) and the cryptic message from the Parisian lady (24). Two riddles, the "Fanfreluches antidotées" (2) and the "Enigme en prophetie" (58), frame the narrative of the *Gargantua*. Interpretation becomes the central, explicit theme of the *Tiers Livre*, where the inconclusive consultations with a series of authorities on the question of whether Panurge should marry generate the narrative that will turn into the sea-quest of the *Quart Livre* and *Cinquième Livre* before reaching the oracular word of the Dive Bouteille. A justly celebrated and much written-upon episode that takes up the problem of interpretation is the apparition of the *paroles gelées*, the frozen words, in chapters 55–56 of the *Quart Livre*.[39] Pantagruel and his companions at sea suddenly hear mysterious sounds, voices and words in the air around them. Panurge, characteristically afraid of anything new and strange, wants to run away, but Pantagruel attempts to find the meaning of this verbal assault. He offers a series of explanations for the phenomenon.

> . . . J'ay leu qu'un Philosophe, nommé Petron, estoyt en ceste opinion que feussent plusieurs mondes soy touchans les uns les aultres en figure triangulaire aequilaterale, en la pate et centre des quelz disoit estre le manoir de Verité, e là habiter les Parolles, les Idées, les Exemplaires et protraictz de toutes choses passées et futures: autour d'icelles estre le Siecle. Et en certaines années, par longs intervalles, part d'icelles tomber sus les humains comme catarrhes, et comme tomba la rousée sus la toison de Gedéon; part là rester reservée pour l'advenir, jusques à la consommation du Siecle.
>
> Me souvient aussi que Aristoteles maintient les parolles de Homere estre voltigeantes, volantes, moventes, et par consequent animées.
>
> D'adventaige Antiphanes disoit la doctrine de Platon es parolles estre semblable, lesquelles en quelque contrée, on temps du fort hyver, lors que sont proferées, gelent et glassent à la froydeur de l'air, et ne sont ouyes. Semblablement ce que Platon enseignoyt es jeunes enfans, à peine estre d'iceulx entendu lors que estoient vieulx devenuz.

Ores seroit à philosopher et rechercher si forte fortune icy seroit l'endroict on quel telles parolles degelent. Nous serions bien esbahiz si c'estoient les teste et lyre de Orpheus. Car après que les femmes Threisses eurent Orpheus mis en pieces, elles jecterent sa teste et sa lyre dans le fleuve Hebrus. Icelles par ce fleuve descendirent en la mer Pontique, jusques en l'isle de Lesbos tousjours ensemble sus mer naigeantes. Et de la teste continuellement sortoyt un chant lugubre, comme lamentant la mort de Orpheus; la lyre à l'impulsion des vents mouvens les chordes accordoit harmonnieusement avecques le chant. Reguardons si les voirons cy autour. [*Quart Livre* 55]

[. . . I have read that a Philosopher named Petron was of the opinion that there existed many worlds touching one another in the figure of an equilateral triangle, in the marrow and center of which he said was the abode of Truth, and there dwelt the Words, Ideas, Exemplars, and portraits of all things past and future: and surrounding them was the Age, the world of time and history. And in certain years, at long intervals, part of these fall on mankind like distillations, as the dew fell on the fleece of Gideon, part remains up there reserved for the future, until the consummation of the Age.

I also remember that Aristotle maintains that the words of Homer are fluttering, flying, moving, and therefore animated.

Moreover, Antiphanes said that the doctrine of Plato was similar to words which in some country, in times of deep winter, at the moment they are uttered, congeal and freeze in the cold air and are not heard. In the same way, that which Plato taught to young children was hardly understood by them until they had become old.

Now it would be worth philosophizing and inquiring if by chance this is the place where such words thaw out. We would be taken aback indeed if these were the head and lyre of Orpheus. For after the Thracian women had torn Orpheus into pieces, they threw his head and lyre in the river Hebrus. They descended by this river into the Pontic sea, reaching the island of Lesbos, swimming ever together above the waves. And from the head there issued continuously a lugubrious song, as if lamenting the death of Orpheus; with the force of the wind moving its strings, the lyre accorded harmoniously with the song. Let's see whether we catch sight of them hereabouts.]

Pantagruel's first and last explanations for the presence of the frozen words set forth the two poles of meaning and nonmeaning between which the Rabelaisian fiction operates. At first, Pantagruel offers a Christianized version of a passage in Plutarch's essay, *On the Obsolescence of Oracles*. The Platonic *eide* residing in the eternal abode of Truth outside of history are assimilated with the Christian Logos, the Logos that once descended to earth like the dew which fell on the fleece of Gideon. The episode in Judges 6:37–40 was treated by late patristic commentators as a prefiguration of the birth of Christ.[40] Sannazaro mentions Gideon's fleece among several Old Testament prophecies of the Nativity in book 2 of the *De partu Virginis* (68–69). The full disclosure of truth, however, is reserved for the apocalyptic end of time—"la consommation du Siècle." If this interpretation would turn the disembodied words into forms of the Incarnate Word, Pantagruel's alternative suggestion that they may issue from the dismembered head of Orpheus reduces them to lifeless objects. Orpheus's fate reveals the ultimate meaninglessness of his poetry in the face of the historical forces that destroy him. The words of the poet continue to sound in an autonomous literary existence of their own, but they only signify human loss: it is as if, Pantagruel suggests, they were mourning for Orpheus's death.

Between these antithetical models of discourse, first full and then emptied of meaning, Pantagruel offers another interpretation: Plato's teachings are said to have fallen upon children like frozen words unheard. Since, as the following chapter reveals, the words that appear to the giant and his companions are indeed frozen, this interpretation merits close attention. In fact, it mediates between and harmonizes the two other explanations he has offered. Initially, to the child who cannot understand them, the words of Plato may as well belong to a foreign language. The adult, however, may eventually come to appreciate their significance. This metaphor for an interpretation which requires temporal process is the same one Paul uses ("cum essem parvulus") to describe the continuing operation of the Spirit in history between the first and second comings of Christ. Marked by its historical moment, human discourse cannot be complete in itself like the divine Logos. But its very historicity allows such discourse to insert itself within an ongoing process of human interpretation that overcomes the impasse portrayed in the Orpheus myth and leads toward a final revelation of the Word of God. The promise of an eschatological closure to history endows all human meaning with a prophetic dimension which can only emerge through the movement of time.[41]

The reconciliation of the apparently double impulses in the Rabelaisian text—to reify itself as an autonomous "frozen" linguistic object or to subject itself to the temporal "thawing out" process of interpretation—is once again accomplished by shifting the emphasis to the reader. The doubleness inheres less in the text than in the possible responses it may receive. Within the fiction, Panurge is the figure of the bad reader. In chapter 56, he asks to have a look at the frozen words.

> Mais en pourrions nous veoir quelqu'une. Me soubvient avoir leu que, l'orée de la montaigne en laquelle Moses receut la loy des Juifz, le peuple voyoit les voix sensiblement. [*Quart Livre* 56]

> [But could we see some of them? I remember having read that, at the edge of the mountain on which Moses received the law of the Jews, the people saw voices in sensible form.]

Panurge refers to Exodus 20:13: "Cunctus autem populus videbat voces et lampades et sonitum bucinae montemque fumantem; et perterriti ac pavore concussi, steterunt procul." Patristic exegetes coupled this passage with the description of the lightning and thunder in Sinai in 19:16–19. The same exegetes saw in the flames of the Sinai theophany an Old Testament prefiguration of the tongues of fire that accompany the descent of the Spirit and the gift of tongues at Pentecost, a festival which, in fact, commemorated the giving of the Law fifty days after Passover. In his homily on the eve of Pentecost, Bede discusses the typological correspondences between the two biblical events. Noting, as does Panurge, that the terrified Israelites beheld the divine voices at a distance ("l'orée de la montaigne"), Bede draws out the moral.

> For on the fiftieth day after the slaying of the lamb the Law was given, and God descended on the mountain in fire, and in like manner on the fiftieth day after the resurrection of our Lord, which is today, the grace of the Holy Spirit was given to the disciples gathered at table. Appearing as a fountain of visible fire, the Spirit invisibly irradiated their breasts with the light of knowledge, and kindled them with the ardor of unextinguishable charity. . . . For the people of Israel, content with the surface of the carnal letter, stood to hear the heavenly word as if from the outside and from below; but now that the grace of the Holy Spirit has been given more extensively, the hearts of the faithful are raised up to understand in a higher way, and at the same time, to be filled more perfectly with the sayings of the Holy Gospel. In the first instance, among the flames of fire and the flashing of lightning, there sounded the crashing of thunder and the noise of trumpets; in the second with the sight of the fiery tongues, the sound, as it were, of the vehement spirit similarly came from heaven.

But while in both dispensations, of the Law and of Grace, a sound was heard on the outside, in the second instance, the virtue of the heavenly gift more miraculously accompanied the hearing of sound, for it taught soundlessly inside the hearts of the disciples.[42]

Panurge's desire to see the frozen words in the manner of the Israelites—whose terror at Sinai he repeats when the words first approach Pantagruel's ship—indicates his literalist disposition to prefer the external sign over any further spiritual significance to which the sign may point. Panurge entered his marriage quest in the *Tiers Livre* with his right ear pierced "a la Judaique," a symbol not only of his bondage to lust but also of a willing subjection to the letter of the Law—to a world of immediate and palpable meaning—and a rejection of the evangelical freedom of the Spirit preached by Erasmus and Luther.[43] In the latter three Rabelaisian books, Panurge consistently shows his sympathy for those aspects of Catholicism which Erasmian reformers attacked for their superstitious or ceremonial "Judaicizing" tendencies. Christianity traditionally misrepresents Judaism's worship of an Old Testament Law, which it regards as definitive for all time, as a turning away from history—and the historical supercession of the Law by the Spirit—into idolatry.

The connection between adherence to the letter and an unwillingness to trust in historical process is thematized in Panurge's marriage quest itself. The consultations with the various authorities of the *Tiers Livre* are repeated attempts to obtain a sign that will resolve once and for all Panurge's decision to marry. Panurge hesitates because he fears that he may be cuckolded as he grows older and becomes unable to satisfy the sexual desires of his wife—a comic emblem for the larger recognition of individual mortality attendant upon marriage and the begetting of children. Panurge's self-love refuses to acknowledge his own temporality and is the cause of his spendthrift prodigality, living for the present moment only, in the second chapter of the *Tiers Livre*. He cannot decide to enter the succession of generations which the Rabelaisian books describe as the progressive movement of salvation history. He wants, in effect, both to marry and not to be replaced by his children, in contrast to Gargantua who writes of the consolation for mortality which he finds in his son. Panurge thus seeks to impose an inauthentic closure upon his life—a promise that he will live happily ever after—which he associates and confuses with the illusory temporal stability of the linguistic sign. He wishes to read into the unchanging sign a confirmation of his own immunity to time and change; but in spite of the sophistry with which he twists the words and signs offered by the authorities he consults until they fit his predetermined interpretation, Panurge can never quite convince himself, and his quest goes on. His rhetorical ingenuity is a major source of the book's comedy and a carry-over from the linguistic virtuosity of his entrance into the *Pantagruel*. If in that earlier episode his self-indulgence in language deferred the satisfaction of his hunger, in the later Rabelaisian books Panurge's quest for a sign virtually replaces his initial sexual desire and postpones his marriage indefinitely. To the extent that words and signs become an end in themselves, they are an unproductive dead end, repeatedly frustrating Panurge as he moves from one noncommunicating language to the next or from one authority on marriage to another. Panurge's desire to possess the letter here and now and be done with the process of interpretation arises from a fear of historical contingency which is at odds with a stoic, spiritual Pantagruelism—a "certaine gayeté d'esprit conficte en mespris des choses fortuites;" ("certain gaiety of spirit preserved in disregard for fortuitous events"). His attitude toward the frozen words, which reflects a larger wish to freeze meaning in the same way that a language uttered in time can be "frozen" or reified, is sharply contrasted with the sage Pantagruel's refusal to make a fetish of words. Pantagruel rejects the narrator's wish to preserve the frozen words in oil.

Yet Panurge can hardly be blamed for wanting some surety of meaning in the midst of the confusion of history. His initial fear seems partly justified when the frozen words are revealed to be the horrifying sounds of battle. These are "motz barbares" in "languaige barbare"—if Paul cannot make himself understood, he becomes a "barbarus" to other men—and here the absence of communication is explicitly linked to violence. The only intelligible words at the end of a series of disjointed syllables are *goth, magoth,* which, as Florence Weinberg has demonstrated, connect the uncharitable use of language to the apocalyptic enemy Gog and Magog (Revelation 20:7–8).[44] The chapter ends, too, with a comic miniature of linguistic misunderstanding as Panurge takes Frère Jean at his word ("au mot") when he least expects it. This literalism angers Frère Jean and for a moment threatens the peace of Pantagruel's little community. Panurge ends the chapter with a plaintive cry, "Pleust à Dieu que icy, sans plus avant proceder, j'eusse le mot de la dive Bouteille!" ("Would to God that here, without proceeding any further, I had the word of the holy

Bottle!"). Panurge wants the full meaning of the divine Word now, without having to experience any further the confusion and violence of human history. But he does not yet understand the nature of his quest. The word of the Dive Bouteille will not allow him to escape from history by offering definitive meaning, but will rather exhort him to accept history and the continuing process of spiritual interpretation.

At the end of their underground descent in the closing chapters of the *Cinquième Livre*, Pantagruel and his companions reach the great fountain of the Temple of Bacchus, to which is adjoined the shrine of the Holy Bottle.[45] The mechanics of the fountain, which will turn out to be the real goal of their quest, take the shape of the human heart. Bacbuc, the sybilline priestess, comments:

> Vos Philosophes nient estre par vertu de figures mouvement fait; oyez icy, et voyez le contraire. Par la seule figure limaciale que voyez bipa[r-]tiente, ensemble une quintuple infoliature mobile à chascune rencontre interieure (telle qu'est la ve[n]e cave au lieu qu'elle entre le dextre ventricule du coeur), est ceste sacrée fontaine excolée, et par icelle une armonie telle que elle monte jusques à la mer de vostre monde. [*Cinquième Livre* 42]

> Your philosophers deny that movement can be caused by the power of figures; listen here and learn the contrary. Merely by the two-part corkscrew figure that you see, together with the five-fold leafwork moving at each interior joint (such is the hollow vein at the point where it enters the right ventricle of the heart), the sacred fountain is emptied, whence arises a harmony that rises to the seas of your world.]

This description of the fountain, whose waters sound as if they come from far off and underground ("comme de loin venant et soubterrain"), appears to link it to the figure of the subterranean oceanic source, communicating to the seas of the earth. The analogy between the rivers and the channels that flow beneath the earth and the blood which courses through the arteries and veins of the human body is made by Seneca (*Naturales quaestiones* 3.15 ff.) in a passage which F. M. Cornford suggests may have been influenced by the *Phaedo*'s myth of Oceanus.[46] Leonardo da Vinci explains the upward movement of water from the depths of the earth to mountainside springs in terms of the blood which courses from the sea of the heart to the head.[47] The analogy could work both ways, and the discovery of the circulation of the blood inspired one of the latest Renaissance poetic versions of the oceanic river-source, this passage from Henry More's panegyric poem on William Harvey.

> Scilicet Oceanis ut subterraneus undis
> Fit cursus, caecae resecans penetralia Terrae,
> Dum liquor è magno prorumpens fortiter alveo
> Per cava pérque poros sinuoso tramite ductus
> Intùs ad Imaum pergit gelidúmque Niphatem,
> Alpes ac Rhodopen, niveum & candoribus Aemum:
> Mox tamen è madidis algenti rore Cavernis
> Per juga transudant latices, quos excipit Indus
> Et Tigris Rhodanúsque atque auro turbidus Hebrus,
> Axius atque Erigon, guttarum qui agmina ripis
> Rursus ad Oceanum referunt; pérque extima Terrae
> Innumero repetit humor Mare refluus Amni:
> Sic sanguis qui à corde fluit propulsus & intrò
> Labitur occultos quócunque Arteria rivos
> Ducit, conspicuis mox ad cor tendere venis
> Cernitur, assidui signans vestigia cursûs
> Caeruleis, queis tota nitet cutis extima, ramis.[48]

[Just as a subterranean course is made by the waves of the Ocean, cutting through the dark insides of the earth, while the water, breaking powerfully out of the great cavity, and led in a winding path through hollow channels and passages, proceeds into the insides of the Imaus mountains and the icy Niphates, of the Alps and the Rhodopean range, of the snowy, white peaks of Haemus: thereupon out of caverns dripping with cold moisture fountainheads soak through the mountain ranges, which are followed by the Indus, the Tigris, the Rhone, and the Hebrus [Maritza] muddy with gold, the Vardar, and the Tzerna, which carry their droplets in an onslaught back to the Ocean; through the farthest reaches of the Earth the refluent water returns to the Ocean in numberless streams—so does blood march out, flowing propelled from the heart and gliding through hidden Arterial rivers, then is seen to bend its course back to the heart in visible veins, marking traces of its perpetual course with purple tributary branches, with which the skin glistens through all its outermost reaches.]

Just as the rivers of the earth (Indus, Tigris, Rhone, Maritza, Vardar, and Tzerna) rise out of the underground stream of Ocean only to flow back into its waters, so, More writes, the blood leaves in arterial rivers from the heart to which it returns in its circular course through the veins. The fountain of the Dive Bouteille may evoke a similar analogy. It may also look back to Panurge's eulogy of debts in the *Tiers Livre* (4).

Panurge depicted the human microcosm replicating the charitable order of the cosmos and the harmony of the spheres ('O quelle harmonie sera parmy les reguliers mouvements des cieulz!"); the heart distributes blood ("La vie consiste en sang") and nourishment among the cooperating members of the body. The waters which flow from the heart-shaped fountain produce a universal harmony and provide Pantagruel and his men with a sustenance that is spiritual rather than physical. Panurge described the everyday miracle by which bread and wine are changed ("transmue") into life-giving blood. The underground fountain of life ("la vivificque fontaine") points to the greater mystery of the Eucharist.

At first Pantagruel and his company drink from the fountain and taste only water. They have come to the shrine with insufficient thirst, and Bacbuc brings on a banquet of salty Rabelaisian delicacies before ordering them to drink again. The reception of the fountain's waters depends upon the disposition of the drinker. Bacbuc explains that this disposition varies from one individual to another.

> Jadis un Capitaine Juif, docte et chevaleureux, conduisant son peuple par les desers en extreme famine, impetra des cieux la manne, laquelle leur estoit de goust tel, par imagination, que par avant realement leur estoient les viandes; icy de mesmes, beuvans de ceste liqueur mirifique, sentirez goust de tel vin comme l'aurez imaginé. Or imaginez et beuvez. [*Cinquiène Livre* 42]

> [A Jewish captain of old, learned and chivalrous, leading his people across the desert in extreme hunger, besought manna from the heavens, which tasted to them, through their imaginations, as their foodstuffs had actually tasted in times past; here, in the same way, drinking this miraculous liquor, you will find the taste of whatever wine you have imagined. Now imagine and drink.]

The water now tastes to each of the drinkers like his favorite wine. The scene reenacts the miracle at Cana where Jesus transformed the water of the Law into the New Wine of the Spirit. The Spirit, however, takes many forms among the members of the Christian community: "Divisiones vero gratiarum sunt, idem autem Spiritus" (1 Corinthians 12:4). The taste of the water/wine depends upon the individual imagination, and each interpreter shares in the Spirit with different results. Erasmus had used the example of the many-flavored manna to describe how scripture generates multiple interpretations—each of value in its own way.[49] The manna and the wine of Cana prefigure the bread and wine of the Eucharist, and the Sacrament is the paradigm for all spiritual experience throughout the final episode of the Dive Bouteille. Panurge's initiation into the mysteries of the oracle, which teaches the correct way to drink, can be understood as an education in how to think and interpret sacramentally.

Moreover, the different responses of Pantagruel's men to the fountain's water may reflect contemporary controversies over the nature of the Eucharist, which by mid-century had become one of the causes of schism. If so, Rabelais's position remains both evangelical *and* catholic. Although it is crucial that the liquor of the Sacrament be accepted with the proper thirst so that it be spiritual wine and not water, the drink of "Judaicizing" literalists, the exact nature of the Eucharist must be left to individual tastes. If the Sacrament may mean different things to different Christians, all belong, however, to the same community. The behavior of the Rabelaisian characters toward the varying interpretations which arise from drinking at the spiritual fountain provides a model for one church whose members may disagree but who agree to stay together.

As Bacbuc proceeds (chap. 45) to prepare Panurge for his initiation, Rabelais's tone moves in and out of satire. While scholars have attempted to explicate the esoteric symbolism of Panurge's outlandish costume and the numerology of his nine trips around the fountain, three pretty leaps in the air, and seven bum-bumps on the ground, the episode clearly pokes fun at Renaissance occultism.[50] Panurge performs more rituals than were ever invented by the lawgivers Numa Pompilius and Moses, or by the Etruscan Cerites, from whose name the word *ceremony* derives. Panurge's solemn shenanigans are thus part of a legalistic, ceremonial religion, the kind attacked by evangelical reformers for its lack of spirituality. The scene is reminiscent of Panurge's debate with signs in the *Pantagruel* (18), another instance in which Rabelais satirizes the Neoplatonic occultists as seekers after a new letter.[51] For Rabelais, the pagan cults of initiation and purification, like the Judaism of the Old Testament, have been superseded by Christianity; Epistemon remarks in the *Tiers Livre* (24) that the ancient oracles became mute as fishes at the coming of Christ, a statement which Panurge will echo when he asserts in prophetic verse that the true oracle resides not in Delphi but in the Dive Bouteille (*Cinquième Livre* 45). The syncretic fusion of Hermetic philosophical lore and Christian religion which had fascinated Ficino and Giovanni Pico is practiced in the *Cinquième Livre* with the uneasy unawareness that it can cause a backsliding into idolatry.

196

Nevertheless, the recollection, often comic and parodic, of the ancient mysteries and oracles can serve religion by pointing to the authentic Christian *mysterion*—the Sacrament—and the true oracle of the Spirit. The Bacchic paraphernalia throughout the episode recalls the Dionysian mysteries, and the happy retelling of the story of Ceres and Proserpina in the last chapter evokes the cult of Eleusis. As the Pantagrueline company descends into the temple of the oracle (35), the text alludes twice to a third ancient ritual which combined the functions of oracle and mystery, the cave of Trophonius in Boetia. It is likely that Panurge's elaborate preparations for the Dive Bouteille recall Pausanias's account of the purification of the initiate for Trophonius's oracle; perhaps more significant for Rabelais's fiction is the statement of Philostratus that the oracle of Trophonius was "the only oracle which gives responses through the person himself who consults it."[52] Erasmus had described the cave of Trophonius in the *Adagia*, grouping it, as does Rabelais, with the cave of Saint Patrick in Ireland. Erasmus explains the proverbial tradition that the visitor to the oracle—which seems to have revealed the secrets of Hades—left without the ability to laugh. Pausanias recounts that the initiate emerged from his experience paralyzed with terror; eventually, however, he regained the power of laughter.[53] Either version indicates the frightful confrontation with death that seems to have been the central therapeutic event in all the ancient mysteries. Cicero writes that from the Eleusinian rites he "gained the power not only to live happily, but also to die with a better hope," and perhaps the chief benefit which the initiate received was an end to his fear of death.[54] This fear is at the basis of Panurge's marriage dilemma, and his inspired decision to marry after consulting the Dive Bouteille signals a new ability to trust in the future. The issue of laughter, deprived or restored, in the mysteries of Trophonius may have been of special interest to the comic artist Rabelais. In his Bacchic enthusiasm after having interpreted the most joyous oracle Bacbuc has ever heard the Bottle deliver, Panurge breaks into verse and then into laughter: "Trinquons, dist Panurge, de par le bon Bacchus / Ha, ho, ho etc." (45).

From the Dive Bouteille there first emerges a bubbling sound "tel que font les abeilles naissantes de la chair d'un jeune taureau occis et accoustré selon l'art et invention d'Aristeus" (44; "a sound such as bees make that are born from the flesh of a young bull killed and prepared according to the art and invention of Aristaeus"). The allusion to the *bugonia*—another pagan mystery of death and rebirth— of the *Fourth Georgic* may point specifically to the effects of the Eucharist. In Guillaume Michel's moralization of the *Georgics* (1519), the sacrificed calf represents Jesus Christ and the bees are the "new men regenerated in his blood."[55] The tragic ending of Virgil's poem, where the story of Orpheus depicts the human individual alienated from the collective regeneration of nature represented by the *bugonia*, is rewritten by the Dive Bouteille's invitation to spiritual life and by Panurge's eventual application of its oracle, his decision to enter a sanctified process of marriage and generation.

197

The word of the Bottle, in contrast to Panurge's detailed ritual preparations, is simple and straightforward: it clinks out onomatopo- etically the single word: "Trinch." The last injunction of Erasmus's Folly to her initiates ("mystae") is the same: "Bibite." The exhortation to drink in the spirit, whether it is figured in the living water promised to the Samaritan woman or by the new wine at Cana, has a long history in Christian thought and symbolism that can be traced back through the Johannine writings to Judaeo-Christian origins.[56] Am- brose's call to the faithful to drink in Christ has already been cited in my third chapter (see above, p. 74). Augustine develops the theme in the seventh tractate of his *Commentary on the First Letter of John*, a text which may underlie the fiction of the *Cinquième Livre*. Erasmus edited the *Commentary*, which went under the alternate title of *De Caritate*, in 1529, and he must have found particularly timely and congenial to his eirenism Augustine's argument that charity is most perfectly exempli- fied in the unity of the church, the body of Christ. Rabelais derived the rule—"FAY CE QUE VOULDRAS"—of the Abbey of Theleme, the model community of charity, from the famous tag "Dilige, et quod vis fac" (or, in its vulgarized form, "Ama, et fac quod vis") in Augustine's seventh tractate.[57] This tractate begins with a rewriting of Paul's homily (1 Corinthians 10:1–5) upon the source which flowed to the Israelites from the rock in the desert (Exodus 17:6).

> This world is for all the faithful who seek their homeland what the desert was for the people of Israel. Certainly they were still wandering [errabant] and looking for their homeland: but with God for their guide they could not mistake their way [errare non poterant]. Their way was the commandment of God. For in their forty years of wandering, their route was made up of a very few campsites, and it is known to all. If they delayed, it was because they were being tested, not abandoned. What

God promises us now is an ineffable sweetness and a good, which Scripture calls and you have heard us remind you is 'that which the eye has not seen, the ear has not heard, and which has not dwelt in the heart of man.' We are tested by temporal travails, and we are taught by the temptations of this present life. But if you do not wish to die of thirst in this desert, drink in charity. This is that source which God has wished to place here, lest we fail on the way: and we shall drink from it in abundance, when we shall have arrived in our homeland.[58]

If for Paul the rock in the desert was Christ, for Augustine the water which now springs to the faithful is the charity through which His Spirit manifests Itself in man. Charity and the Spirit, Augustine affirms, are one and the same.

When, therefore, the Apostle says, 'The charity of God is diffused in our hearts through the Holy Spirit which has been given to us' [Romans 5:5], let us understand in love the essence of the Holy Spirit. For the Holy Spirit Itself is that which the wicked cannot receive: It is that source of which Scripture speaks: 'Make your source of water your own property, and let no stranger share it with you.' [Prov. 5:15–16] All those who do not love God are strangers and antichrists. And while they may enter churches, they cannot be counted among the sons of God; that source of life does not belong to them. The wicked man too may be baptized: the wicked too may possess prophecy. We find that King Saul possessed prophecy: he persecuted the holy David, and he began to prophesy. The wicked man too can receive the sacrament of the flesh and blood of our Lord: for of such it is said: 'Who eats and drinks unworthily, eats and drinks his own condemnation' [1 Cor. 11:29]. The wicked man can bear the name of Christ: that is, he can be called a Christian; of those it is said: 'They prophaned the name of their God.' [Ez. 36:20] Therefore the wicked man, too, can possess all these sacraments, but it is not possible to possess charity and be wicked. Charity, therefore, is one's own special gift, this is the unique source. The Spirit of God exhorts you to drink from this source; the Spirit of God exhorts you to drink from the Spirit Itself.[59]

These two Augustinian passages contain a series of doctrinal topoi that reappear in Rabelais's episode and which define the act of spiritual drinking. The homily about the Christian replenishing himself as he wanders the desert of the world in search of the Promised Land where he will drink in abundance establishes the prophetic structure of spiritual experience. The gift of the Spirit is a foretaste now in history of a future eschatological fullness of meaning. Rabelais has expressed this idea in one of the "propos des bien yvres," back in the *Gargantua*.

Non moy, pecheur, sans soif, et si non presente, pour le moins future, la prevenant comme entendez. Je boy pour la soif advenir. Je boy enternellement. Ce m'est eternité de beuverye, et beuverye de eternité. [*Gargantua* 5]

[Not without thirst am I, a sinner, and if not a present thirst at least a future one: I am forestalling it, you understand. I drink for the thirst to come. I drink eternally. For me eternity is drinking and drinking eternity.]

The drunkard anticipates the future joys of eternity in a comic confusion of topery and the sacramental drinking of the new wine of the Spirit. Augustine asserts that the Eucharist, while it may provide a central occasion for the operation of the Spirit, is not the spiritual source from which man is to drink—that source lies within, in the charitable heart of each believer. Augustine identifies the water in the privately owned "cisterna" and "fontes" of Proverbs 5:15–16 as the spiritual wellspring that lies inside every individual, and Erasmus would adapt this patristic gloss to discuss how the reader of scripture should interpret by himself.[60] If the Spirit expresses Itself in a selfless charity that works for the good of the community—the church—Its operation is nonetheless private and internal. This spiritual individualism is borne out in Rabelais's fiction when Bacbuc leads Panurge from the oracle of the Bottle to the temple fountain.

Levez vous, allons au chapitre, en la glose duquel est le beau mot interpreté. [Cinquième Livre 44]

[Get up, let us go to the chapter, by whose gloss the fair word is interpreted.]

Panurge now drinks again from a flask shaped like a breviary, by which he can find the "chapter" which will gloss the oracle's injunction to drink. He himself must provide this gloss, just as his imagination had earlier determined the flavor of the water-changed-to-wine. Bacbuc explains: "La Dive bouteille vous y envoye, soyez vous mesmes interpretes de votre entreprinse" (45; "The Holy Bottle sends you there, be yourselves the interpreters of your enterprise"). Each seeker is sent back from the oracle to his own inner spiritual resources. The oracle's word is definitive only in that it insists upon the necessity of further, individual interpretation. Such spiritual interpretation is prophetic: Bacbuc compares drinking from the fountain to Ezekiel swallowing the book of God (Ezekiel 3:13), an action that is repeated by the author of Revelation (10:8–10).[61]

The temple fountain, moreover, is the source of literary creation. Panurge, Pantagruel, and Frère Jean drink from its liquor and burst into Bacchic, poetic furor. Giovanni Pico had paired the nine Bacchuses of the Orphic hymns with the nine Muses and conflated Bacchic frenzy with poetic inspiration.[62] Both represent the gift of the Spirit in Rabelais's fiction. Just as the Rabelaisian books begin by deriving the genealogy of Pantagruel from the eating of medlars sprung from the sacrificial blood of Abel, they now close with a reenactment of their own generation from a smiliar eucharistic origin. This scene of literary genesis, moreover, places the author of the books in the same position as the reader to whom he addresses the prologue of the *Tiers Livre*. Rabelais initially presents his fiction as a Diogenic tub ("tonneau")—a grotesque object like the Silenus of Alcibiades—but the tub punningly turns out to be a tun of wine, and, again like the Silenus, its contents are precious.

> Tout Beuveur de bien, tout Goutteux de bien, alterez, venens à ce mien tonneau, s'ilz ne voulent, ne beuvent; s'ilz voulent et le vin plaist au guoust de la seigneurie de leurs seigneuries, beuvent franchement, librement, hardiment sans rien payer, et ne l'espargnent. Tel est mon decret. Et paour ne ayez que le vin faille, comme feist es nopces de Cana en Galilée. Autant que vous en tireray par la dille, autant en entonnerary par le bondon. Ainsi demeurera le tonneau inexpuisible. Il a source vive et vene perpetuelle. [*Tiers Livre* Prologue]

> [Let all good thirsty drinkers and tasters (or: gouty men) who come to my cask choose not to drink if they do not wish to; if they wish and the wine pleases the taste of their lordly lordships, let them drink frankly, freely, boldly without paying, and let them not be sparing. This is my decree. And have no fear lest the wine run out, as it did at the marriage of Cana in Galilee. As much as I draw for you at the tap I shall replenish at the bung. Thus the cask will remain inexhaustible. It has a living source and a perpetual stream.]

Rabelais refers to himself in the *Tiers Livre* prologue, as he did earlier on the title page of the *Pantagrueline Prognostication* (1532–33), as an "architriclin," the title of the steward at the marriage feast at Cana (John 2 : 8–10), who first tasted the water that had been turned to wine. He offers his fiction as the living water ("source vive") and new wine of the Spirit, that is, as an occasion for the reader to exercise *his own* gift of interpretation. The fiction has itself been created through an individual act of drinking (interpretation) from the water-wine of the

Spirit—the fountain of the Dive Bouteille. To write and read the Rabelaisian text are one and the same spiritual action performed within a community of interpreters. In Pauline terms, the text is a prophecy which authenticates its own inspiration in the Spirit to the extent that it can edify the community and itself become the source of further prophetic interpretation. Rabelais offers his fiction to his readership in the same spirit in which he created it: to drink in the Spirit, as Augustine insists, is to drink in charity.

Charity does not, however, lead to any immediate agreement within the community of interpreters. While Panurge elects to wed, Frère Jean, drinking from the same spiritual source, refuses to marry and forego his liberty. His decision receives a vituperative denunciation from Panurge—and it is likely enough that Rabelais approved of clerical marriage—but Panurge has the last word only because Frère Jean does not care to argue any further. Every man must interpret as he is moved from within by the Spirit, and his finding will be subsequently colored by his personal affects and historical circumstances. The result is a series of individual interpretations that may seem superficially indistinguishable from the fragmentary dispersion of meaning produced by the situation of Babel where self-love made every man speak for himself alone. How is one to separate the utterance of the spiritually inspired Panurge from the sophistry of the Panurge seduced by the evil spirit? Drinking in the Spirit produces a gloss which must, in turn, be glossed, a proliferation of meaning which may appear to be endless and to move no closer to a definitive truth.[63]

Rabelais's final chapter, however, places the process of interpretation within a narrative framework that turns what might otherwise seem an infinite regress of meaning into a plan of historical progress. The closure of interpretation is provided by the finite structure of history itself: the motto over the temple gates had earlier proclaimed: "TOUTES CHOSES CE MEUVENT A LEUR FIN" (36; "All things move toward their end"). The final chapter reimports the thought and eschatological perspective of the Pantagruelion episode. Bacbuc exhorts Pantagruel and his company to undertake "le chemin de la congnoissance divine et chasse de sapience" ("the path of divine knowledge and the pursuit of wisdom"), coupling together *sapientia* and *scientia*, spiritual knowledge with the pursuits of human learning and science. In Rabelais's version of the Fortunate Fall, Bacbuc describes how Pluto ravished Proserpina and made knowledge of the underworld available to man, a source of new and greater technological discoveries.

Vos philosophes qui se complaignent toutes choses estre par les anciens escriptes, rien ne leur estre laissé de nouveau à inventer, ont tort trop evident. Ce que du ciel vous apparoist, et appellez Phenomenes, ce que la terre vous exhibe, ce que la mer et aultres fleuves contiennent, n'est comparable à ce qui est en terre caché.

Pourtant est equitablement le Soubterrain Dominateur presques en toutes langues nommé par epithete de richesses. Ils quant leur estude addoneront et labeur à bien rechercher par imploration de Dieu souverain, lequel jadis les Egyptiens nommoient en leur langue l'Abscond, le Mussé, le Caché, et par ce nom l'invoquant supplioient à eux se manifester et descouvrir, leur eslargissant cognoissance et de soy et de ses créatures, par aussi conduits de bonne Lanterne. (*Cinquième Livre* 47)

[Your philosophers are too evidently wrong who complain that all things have been written about by the ancients, leaving them nothing new to discover. Those things which appear to you from the heavens, and which you call Phenomena, what the earth displays to you, what the sea and other rivers contain is not comparable to that which is hidden inside the earth.

Therefore the Lord of the Underworld is justly named almost in all languages by the epithet of Riches. The philosophers devote their study and labor to diligent investigation by imploring the Lord God, whom the Egyptians of old named in their language, the Hidden, the Veiled, the Concealed, and by invoking this name prayed that He would manifest and discover Himself to them, enlarging their knowledge of Him and of His creatures, through the guidance of a good Lantern.]

Once again Rabelais takes heart in the scientific advancements which the moderns of the Renaissance have made over the ancients, and opens up vistas of future, continuing discovery. The investigation of the concealed secrets of creation is represented as part of the search for a hidden godhead. Such an evangelical view of science, it was pointed out earlier, is denied by the experience of Tasso's Magus of Ascalon, and the *Liberata*, with its melancholy insistence upon the theme of concealment, presents a Platonized version of the *Deus absconditus*, a God who withdraws, inaccessible and unknowable, from the confines of the sensible universe. Rabelais revises the idea of a hidden God and seems to anticipate Francis Bacon's description of the relationship of God and scientist in *The New Organon* (1620): "Even as though the divine nature took pleasure in the innocent and kindly sport of children playing at hide-and-seek and vouchsafed of his kindness and goodness to admit the human spirit for his playfellow at that game."[64] Rabelais's God similarly allows man to come and find Him where He is concealed in His works. He thus behaves like the author Rabelais, who urges his reader to uncover the "doctrine plus absconce" of his fiction. Reading the hidden meaning of his book—with all its riddles and hermeneutic puzzles—and reading the Book of Nature are analogous spiritual activities, and both, in turn, have a model in the drinking from the fountain of the Dive Bouteille. Having been taught to interpret in the proper, sacramental way, Pantagruel's company and Rabelais's Pantagruelist reader are sent out to put their spiritual gifts to use.

Rabelais's attempt to instruct his reader in the problems of interpretation is reminiscent of Bruno's use of the allegory of the *Eroici furori* as a kind of mental training in the structure of spiritual understanding. Bruno, it may be recalled, invokes the gospel injunctions that the thirsty should come and drink and that he who seeks will find. In a formula later dear to Bruno, Bacbuc describes God as an infinite sphere whose center is everywhere (47). She thereby relocates the source of spiritual meaning that is manifested in the Dive Bouteille throughout all of creation and in every aspect of human experience to which the enlightened interpreter turns his attention—ultimately the source lies within the interpreter himself. But though Rabelais and Bruno both draw on the same traditional metaphors in order to urge their readers forward on a continuing spiritual quest, their definitions of that quest radically diverge. The search for Bruno's infinite godhead is itself endless, an ahistorical, unchanging gnosis which is its own reward and objective. By contrast, the Rabelaisian quest progressively changes while it moves through a finite history toward an eschatological goal. Bruno's seeker is an isolated contemplative; Rabelais turns the quest for knowledge into a collective effort of charity, carried out by a community or tradition of individual interpreters.

Bacbuc earlier explained the significance of the word *sac* as the emblem of human interdependence (chap. 45),[65] and now she asserts the necessity of human companionship ("compagnie d'homme") on the road to knowledge. She also emphasizes the historical structure of the quest by citing the story of the Egyptian king Thales, who was asked where wisdom was to be found. He answered:

> 'On temps'; car par temps ont esté et par temps seront toutes choses latentes inventées; et c'est la cause pourquoy les antiens onto appelé Saturne le Temps, pere de Verité, et Verité fille eut Temps. Infaliblement aussi trouveront tout le savoir, et d'eulx et de leurs predecesseurs, à peine estre la minime partie de ce qui est et ne le scavent. [*Cinquième Livre* 47]

[In time, for by time have been and by time will all hidden things be found; and this is the reason why the ancients called Saturn, Time, the father of Truth and Truth the daughter of Time. They will find without fail that all of their knowledge and that of their predecessors is scarcely the smallest part of that which exists which they do not know.]

The movement of time is required for a progressive unfolding of human knowledge, which will be incomplete until the end of time when eternal Truth will be revealed. In the *Adagia*, Erasmus includes the saying that Truth is the daughter of Time in his treatment of the proverb, "Tempus omnia revelat," and then harmonizes the wisdom of the ancient poets with the eschatological promise of the gospel: "Nihil est opertum, quod non revelabitur, et occultum quod non scietur" (Matthew 10:26).[66] The prospect of a final revelation guarantees the outcome of the pursuit of knowledge through history and gives the continuing operation of the Spirit, each human interpretation succeeding and engendering others, the shape of an intelligible narrative. From a future retrospect, the limitations of present understanding will be clear, but so will the extent to which present findings contribute prophetically to an ultimate significance. Once again, Rabelais ends his book, and now his entire five books, by depicting his characters in the possession of an apocalyptic foretaste, participating now as interpreters in a future closure of meaning—and then by drawing both those characters and his reader back into the incomplete, still open-ended processes of history. The quest for the Grail-like Dive Bouteille ends by urging the seeker to continue on the quest of human history.[67]

By placing his book within this ongoing spiritual quest, Rabelais resolves in a unique way the opposition arising in Renaissance literature from a double reading that wants to understand the literary text both as an individual and historical human creation *and* as a vehicle of truth grounded in a source of authority outside itself. If Renaissance literary texts characteristically demonstrate the incompatibility of these two readings by sacrificing one, partly or entirely, in favor of the other, the Rabelaisian books allow both fully to coexist. The prophetic authority of Rabelais's text derives from its claim to participate in the historical operation of the Holy Spirit. This operation has its source within the inner experience of each human interpreter, and, by presenting his literary creation as a form of prophetic interpretation, Rabelais sanctions the individuality of his style and thought. His text provides a particularly good example of how an evangelical insistence upon spiritual freedom could complement and furnish a metaphysical basis for those humanist rhetorical doctrines which encouraged self-expression and innovation: both are manifestations of a larger individ- **205** ualism of the age. At the same time, Rabelais acknowledges the limitations which the individuality and historicity of his text impose upon the prophetic authority to which it lays claim, and he presents the text as one interpretation among many. For him no spiritual meaning exists that is not mediated through human interpretation subject to the contingency of history and to the imperfect, confusing processes of language and communication that have been mankind's lot since Babel. He therefore accepts a historical relativism of meaning that an acute critic like Giovanni Pico had seen to be the subversive consequence of humanism's recognition of literary individuality. But if interpretation is relative through human history, history for Rabelais is itself a sacred process, and he is, no less than Pico, a "princeps concordiae." The history of individual interpretations can and must be brought into a community of meaning—this is the true work of the Spirit which gathers a dispersed humanity into the charitable body of the church. Each spiritual interpretation is relative to a prophetic tradition that is ongoing through history, and Rabelais goes beyond Pico's syncretism by arguing that this tradition is progressive, moving closer and closer to a final revelation. The authority of his own text is measured by its contribution to this tradition, a measurement that must be made by the reader, who, by exercising his own spiritual gifts, places himself as well as the Rabelaisian text within the unfolding tradition.

But Rabelais's books rarely, if ever, obtained from his contemporaries the kind of reading they enjoin—they were roundly condemned on one side by Calvin and by the mystical but authoritarian Catholic Postel on the other.[68] The failure of the books to find a community of response except, ironically enough, in the shared hostility which united these religious opponents against the conciliatory middle, suggests that their meaning—and the literary solution that they find between the competing claims of authorial individuality and divine authorization—were even more historically determined than Rabelais would have been able or willing to admit. His hermeneutics depend upon a distinctive ecclesiology: that Erasmian church, at once Evangelical and Catholic, which would allow for maximum differences of viewpoint within its unified community and which would foster continuous debate and reform while advancing an apostolic tradition.

By Rabelais's death at mid-century, the dream of a reconciliation among Catholics and Protestants was fast receding, and its diminishing prospect accounts for the darkening tone of the religious satire of the *Quart Livre*. The first Huguenot war broke out in 1562, two years before the publication of the posthumous *Cinquième Livre*. (When the Huguenot poet Agrippa d'Aubigné, probably writing in the 1580s, included a version of the oceanic source myth in *Les Tragiques,* he gave a grisly turn to the analogy between the rivers of the earth and the circulatory system of the heart: his personified Ocean turns back the rivers of France and makes them flow backward upon their sources, like the sanctified Jordan, when he finds them trying to purge themselves of the blood of Protestant martyrs.)[69] In the later years of the century, Rabelais's relativistic conception of spiritual truth would be treated with little patience by men ready to fight and die for one or another absolute Truth. Likewise, the evangelical sanctions which he found for his individual literary creation would lose their force when the time came to choose sides. The poet, whether Tasso anxious to satisfy the Inquisition or Spenser celebrating the Anglican settlement, would claim authorization from the established doctrine of church and state, not as an individual interpreter adding to the tradition of spiritual knowledge. Individual claims to prophecy would be regarded—correctly—as threats to the political order, and when authors of the defeated opposition like d'Aubigné or the puritan Milton made such claims, they adopted the alienated voice of the Old Testament prophets speaking for a small saving remnant against the larger community. Rabelais's pluralistic vision aimed to preserve the largest possible community: his peculiarly modern assertion of the value of human difference, the fullest, most inclusive expression of an Erasmian humanism that drew together a new historical awareness of the individual with the doctrine of spiritual liberty, marked a moment in the history of Renaissance thought that was not to be repeated.

7

Epilogue: From Origin to Originality

> There was a place,
> Now not, though sin, not time, first wrought the change,
> Where Tigris at the foot of Paradise
> Into a gulf shot under ground, till part
> Rose up a fountain by the tree of life;
> In with the river sunk, and with it rose
> Satan involved in rising mist, then sought
> Where to lie hid.   *[Paradise Lost, 9.69–76]*

In order to enter Eden unseen and to effect the Fall of Adam and Eve, Milton's Satan adopts one of his manifold disguises. The fountain beside the Tree of Life is, as Tasso's and Spenser's fictions have shown us, the Fountain of Life and the source of the earth's waters—from which a mist originally rose (Genesis 2:6) to water the earth after its creation. This fountain is the traditional figure for the originary dispensation of the Word of God. By placing himself in and at the Edenic source, Satan emblematically reenacts the sin which caused his own fall and which is the paradigm for all sin in the Judaeo-Christian theology: his denial of his secondary status as God's creature, his desire to be *like* God, autochthonous and original, "self-begot, self-raised," (5.860). Satan had willfully misread the first historical event of *Paradise Lost*, the begetting and proclamation of the Word—the intelligibility of history itself—out of eternity. He refused to accept the trinitarian paradox that the Word, begotten in time—and after the creation of Satan himself—could be simultaneously timeless and originary; he rejected Abdiel's orthodox contention (5.835) that the Son was copresent as God's creative Word from the beginning. Or rather, Satan's historicist, literal reading turned the equality between God and His Word on its head. He reasoned backwards from the apparently secondary, temporal status of the Word that the Father which It reveals must be equally secondary. For Satan, the proclamation of the Son is merely God's self-authorizing fiction, a piece of political propaganda which, like the encomiastic Renaissance court spectacle, attempts to give a mask of legitimacy to the present regime. Satan concludes that signification is an autonomous system controlled arbitrarily by the powers that be, and he aspires to that power himself: it is his word against the Word of God.

The further implication of Satan's dissenting position is to deny, at the very moment it is revealed, the Judaeo-Christian linear concept of history that begins and ends in the Word of God, the Alpha and Omega, and to substitute in its place the idea of the Platonic Year and its cycle of creation and destruction, a creative process through which he, God, and the angels all came into being at the same moment (5.861–63). In such a universe no claims to authority can be made on the basis of priority or of an originary dispensation. Satan would be free to take matters into his own hands and create his own political order, based on raw power.

> Our puissance is our own, our own right hand
> Shall teach us highest deeds, by proof to try
> Who is our equal.   [5.863–65]

This rugged individualism fails, and Satan learns to his cost that he is not God's equal, that he cannot overcome his secondariness and make himself original, that neither history nor significance is arbitrarily made by creatures but rather given by the divine Creator.

If Satan's immersion in the mist of the Edenic fountain is an emblem of his desire to usurp God's position as the source of intelligibility in the universe—a usurpation which seems possible once Satan denies God's originary nature and reduces Him to his own secondary, creaturely status—the poem has already shown Satan searching for an alternative source of his own. The topos of the oceanic source finds a last great version in Renaissance fiction—although in parodic form—during Satan's journey to Chaos in book 2. Setting out from the gates of Hell, Satan, Sin, and Death behold the shapeless realm of Chaos.

> Before their eyes in sudden view appear
> The secrets of the hoary deep, a dark
> Illimitable ocean without bound,
> Without dimension, where length, breadth, and highth,

And time and place are lost; where eldest Night
And Chaos, ancestors of Nature, hold
Eternal anarchy, amidst the noise
Of endless wars, and by confusion stand.
For Hot, Cold, Moist, and Dry, four champions fierce
Strive here for mastery, and to battle bring
Their embryon atoms.   [2, 890–900]

By describing Chaos as an ocean, Milton alludes, as he does several
times in the voyage episode of book 2, to the *Os lusíadas* (1572), the
Portuguese epic of Luís de Camões.[1] In book 6 of Camões's poem, the
god Bacchus descends to the cavernous depths of the ocean where the
palace of Neptune lies. On its sculpted gates he beholds reliefs of
Chaos and the four elements.

> E vê primeiro, em côres variadas,
> Do velho Caos a tão confusa face;
> Vem-se os quatro elementos trasladados
> Em diversos oficios occupados.[2]   [6.10]

[And he first sees, depicted in various colors, the confused features of
ancient Chaos, and the four elements are seen represented there taking
part in their different functions.]

There follows a description of the sculptures of Fire, Air, Earth, and
Water. The ecphrasis of the gates connects Neptune's abysmal realm
with cosmogonic origins, and illustrates the doctrine of Thales that
water is the animating principle of material life. We may also recall
how at the oceanic source of the *Fourth Georgic* Clymene sang of the
loves of the gods from the time of Chaos, an account of the emergence
of creation from the confused state of prime matter. While Camões
locates the chaotic source of material creation in the Ocean's depths,
Milton's Chaos is a kind of Ocean, "the hoary deep." Here, however,
matter has not yet been disposed into elemental forms: "neither sea,
nor shore, nor air, nor fire" (912). Milton's emphasis lies as much upon
the entropic as the creative potential of this Chaos. For Tasso, the
primordial abyss of the oceanic source was the "grembo immenso /
de la terra che tutto in sé produce." Milton describes the "wild abyss /
The womb of nature and perhaps her grave" (910–11). The "source" to
which Satan makes his way is deprived of any creative, originary
power of its own.[3] It is merely the uncreated Deep of Genesis 1:2,
lacking the presence of the Holy Spirit whom Milton addresses at the
opening of his poem.

> thou from the first
> Wast present, and with mighty wings outspread
> Dove-like sat'st brooding on the vast abyss
> And madest it pregnant. [1.19–22]

In the absence of an informing Spirit, Chaos remains merely the raw material of creation, available should God decide to make new worlds (915–16).

The Spirit whom Milton asks for internal illumination is the authorizing source of the poetry of *Paradise Lost*. Satan's journey to Chaos and its antisource also contains a parodic scene of inspiration.

> At length a universal hubbub wild
> Of stunning sounds and voices all confused
> Borne through the hollow dark assaults his ear
> With loudest vehemence: thither he plies,
> Undaunted to meet there what ever power
> Or spirit in that nethermost abyss
> Might in that noise reside, . . . [951–57]

Satan looks for a "spirit" in the noise of Chaos but finds only Babel, "voices all confused." This Babel, in fact, parodies its typological inversion, the advent of the Spirit and the gift of tongues at Pentecost (Acts 2:2). In the Vulgate version, which Milton knew and studied, the gathering apostles are startled by the "sonus tamquam advenientis spiritus vehementis."[4] The vehement Spirit is replaced in Chaos by the "loudest vehemence" of its distorted utterances.

Satan's "inspiration" is appropriately Babelic. By rejecting God and His Word and making signification into an autonomous system open to his own manipulation, Satan reduces meaning to the purely arbitrary state of Chaos, where "high arbiter/Chance governs all" (909–10), and ultimately to nonsense. Milton again suggests the consequences of Satan's denial of historical sequence. Chaos, where the dimension of time is lost, is the true version of that universe imagined by Satan where there would be no before and after, and where the reign of God could not be upheld on the basis of His priority. Without temporal sequence, however, an ordered syntax is impossible, and the unformed state of Chaos corresponds at the grammatical level to a language which, lacking syntactical coordinates, struggles in vain to create significance and turns into Babel.

Babel and its implications are already suggested in the description of Satan's heavenly dwelling.

> his royal seat
> High on a hill, far blazing, as a mount
> Raised on a mount, with pyramids and towers
> From diamond quarries hewn, and rocks of gold
> The palace of great Lucifer, (so call
> That structure in the dialect of men
> Interpreted) which not long after, he
> Affecting all equality with God,
> In imitation of that mount whereon
> Messiah was declared in sight of heaven,
> The Mountain of Congregation called.　　　　[5.756–66]

In this elaboration of Isaiah 14:13–14, Milton appeals to the same typological opposition between the Tower of Babel and Mount Zion that we saw operative in the fiction of Rabelais. The biblical source for the exaltation of the Son on the Mountain of God is Psalm 2:6: "Yet have I set my king upon my holy hill of Zion." The heavenly mountain of Milton's God is a combination of Zion and Sinai.[5] The "pyramids and towers" of Satan's palace recall an earlier passage which, describing the building of Pandemonium, similarly couples "Babel, and the works of Memphian kings" (1.694). The comparison to "a mount / Raised on a mount," suggests the traditional conflation, which was exploited by Rabelais, of the story of Babel and the classical myth of the giants piling Pelion on Ossa to storm Olympus. In this light, Raphael's peculiar parenthetical aside about the name of Satan's palace "in the dialect of men / Interpreted" seems to be a reminder that Satan's first sin and rebellion carries within it the principle of Babel, whose consequences in human history are linguistic multiplicity and the confusion of tongues.

This Babelic confusion, moreover, has a literary corollary, and Satan becomes the figure of the autonomous, original author. By trying to find an alternative source to the Holy Spirit which sanctions Milton's verse, by constituting *himself* as that source, Satan embodies a rival form of poetry. Such poetry no longer claims an authorized origin—indeed, it does away with the idea of such an origin and sees all discourse as equally secondary. The author attempts to assert his own primacy through the power and originality of his rhetoric, but places himself in a proliferating series of original authors and a world of proliferating meanings. The end result is Babel.

To portray this originality as Satanic is, of course, to condemn it. *Paradise Lost* proceeds, moreover, to demonstrate that meaning—

including poetic meaning—can never be purely autonomous or self-created, that meaning always depends upon the originary dispensation of the divine Word. Even as Satan steps into the mist of the source, he merely assumes a preexistent typology. Like all secondary creatures, he is condemned to imitation, and his attempt to be original only produces counterfeit replicas of the divine order he wishes to usurp. Like Tasso in the *Gerusalemme liberata*, Milton reduces the demonic mode of existence to parody. Yet both poets recognize the considerable power of the diabolic counterfeit that may pass current alongside the divine original. Satan can at least muddy the waters of the source, a process reflected in the subsequent career of the mist-figure in *Paradise Lost*. As Satan progresses through Eden, the mist becomes more sinister: he seeks out the serpent "like a black mist low creeping" (9.180); he already anticipates the serpent or, more properly, the serpent after the Fall, which will have to crawl on its belly. Then, having entered the serpent's body, he leads Eve to the forbidden fruit.

> Hope elevates, and joy
> Brightens his crest, as when a wandering fire,
> Compact of unctuous vapour, which the night
> Condenses, and the cold environs round,
> Kindled through agitation to a flame,
> Which oft, they say, some evil spirit attends
> Hovering and blazing with delusive light,
> Misleads the amazed night-wanderer from his way
> To bogs and mires, and oft through pond or pool,
> There swallowed up and lost, from succour far.   [9.633–42]

This simile shows Satan in his true colors. The mist has now become an "unctuous vapour," swamp-gas which casts a false and delusive light. This progressive transformation of Satan in the language of the poem is what one might expect, a separating out of the demonic copy from divine type—the Fountain of Life—whose form it had initially assumed. But when that divine type is reinvoked at the very end of *Paradise Lost* in the poem's last extended simile, it cannot seem to disassociate itself from Satan's parody. At the expulsion of Adam and Eve, the cherubim descend to guard the gates of Eden.

> on the ground
> Gliding meteorous, as evening mist
> Risen from a river o'er the marish glides

> And gathers ground fast at the labourer's heel,
> Homeward returning.   [12.628–32]

The simile links the divine guardians to the river mist of the Fountain of Life. But the "meteorous" brightness of the cherubim and the "marish" recalls the swamp-fire that earlier described the glistening serpent.[6] The gathering of the mist at the laborer's heel further evokes the serpent, cursed by God in Genesis 3:15: "it shall bruise thy head and thou shalt bruise his heel." The original type of the fountain—itself the figure of the originary Word—seems to have been infiltrated by Satan and sin.

The interference which Satan's secondary, counterfeit imitation succeeds in placing around an originary divine significance describes the general problem of meaning in the world after the Fall. It can also characterize the role of all earlier literature—classical and Catholic—in *Paradise Lost*. The literary tradition Milton inherits is similarly conceived as a series of shadowy imitations and distortions of the scriptural events which are his subject and which he can only reconstruct by reading backwards through the tradition's filter of human error and demonic falsehood. The attempt to recover those original events authorizes the revisionary strategies of *Paradise Lost* that have been the focus of recent Milton criticism. Milton's poem "corrects" the texts of his literary predecessors in order to reveal a true narrative of sacred history that lies embedded beneath layers of profane poetic fiction. Moreover, the return to origins, to the ab-original events that even precede the biblical account of Creation, reverses the relationship of priority between *Paradise Lost* and the tradition of earlier texts which it imitates. Those texts are now paradoxically recognized to be Milton's successors, to be secondary imitations of the archetypal story contained in his poem.[7] Thus, while *Paradise Lost* comes at the end of the epic tradition, it claims to be the original sacred epic—of which the tradition is a series of later desacralized copies. This desacralization of all literature outside of the Bible and his own poem constitutes Milton's Puritan rejection both of Renaissance syncretism and of the kind of community with ecclesial tradition that we have seen espoused in the Rabelaisian books.

Viewed from another perspective, however, this desacralization of tradition makes possible the appreciation of a purely literary originality. So long as literary tradition is vested with sacred authority, the writer may find it difficult to valorize his own individuality and innovation. By relegating his poetic predecessors to a secondary human status vis-à-vis the originary Holy Spirit which dictates his own unpremeditated verse, Milton is able, with one and the same gesture, to affirm both his unique authority and his authorial uniqueness. An inevitable analogy thus arises between Satan's attempts to be original, dramatized and criticized by *Paradise Lost*, and the poem's own brilliantly successful assertion of originality. Criticism returns to Blake's aphorism that Milton, the true poet, was "of the Devil's Party." The individuality of spiritual experience which is part both of Milton's faith and of his claim to singular poetic authority may be difficult to distinguish from the larger Renaissance individualism against which his poem polemicizes in the figure of Satan.

It is useful, then, to observe how another seventeenth-century text desacralizes literary tradition in order to valorize authorial originality—a strategy which, in this case, is not confused with the kind of religious claims that Milton makes for his poem. In 1622 the young French poet Jean Chapelain, later to be the author of the much awaited, much admired, and little read epic, *La Pucelle* (1655), wrote a prefatory letter to the *Adone* of Giovanbattista Marino. He sets out to extol a poem which, like *Paradise Lost*, proposes to be a summation— and, in Marino's case, borders closely upon a reductio ad absurdum— of its literary culture and tradition. Chapelain chooses to praise the *Adone* for its innovation: Marino has produced an almost unprecedented literary entity, an epic of peace. (And, for all its frivolity, the *Adone* does, in fact, set a literary precedent for the seventeenth-century epic, for Milton's epics of heroic patience and for Chapelain's account of the passion of Joan of Arc.) In order to assert the worth of Marino's departure from tradition, Chapelain defines two types of praiseworthy originality ("nouveauté").

la première *Parfaicte en sa Perfection* quand une chose non monstrueuse qui n'a jamais esté vient à esclorre; comme lors qu'en un lieu où jamais il n'avoit paru d'eau, l'on voit sourdre tout à coup quelque surgeon d'eau vive; l'autre *moins Parfaicte*, lors qu'en une chose des-ja trouvée on descouvre quelque perfection jus-qu' alors incongnuë, comme si en ceste mesme source trouvée, après quelque temps l'on venoit à remarquer quelque vertu particuliere, dont on ne se fust pas apperçeu devant.[8]

[the first kind, *Perfect in its perfection*, when something not monstrous which has never been before comes to be born; as when, in a place where water has never appeared, one sees a source of flowing water suddenly spring up; the other *less Perfect*, when in a thing which has already been discovered one finds a kind of perfection unknown until then, as if in this same discovered source, after some time has gone by, one came to note some particular properties which one had not perceived before.]

Chapelain uses the figure of the source to distinguish a primary, absolute ("parfaicte") originality from a secondary one ("moins parfaicte") that is dependent upon the first; the difference between the source itself, and the special qualities which may be derived from it. He then goes on to explain that primary originality corresponds to

l'invention premiere des arts et des sciences, comme en particulier la Poësie, mise en avant par Apollon en son temps ou par autre; et cette Nouveauté est la plus excellente, pource qu'elle ouvre le chemin à ceux qui viennent après d'en trouver les vertus speciales.

[the first invention of the arts and sciences, as the particular case of Poetry introduced by Apollo in his age or by some one else; and this Originality is the most excellent, because it opens the path to those who come later to discover special properties in it.]

The latecomers who follow the invention of poetry itself are able to enjoy a secondary, imperfect kind of originality that consists in

l'invention des especes, comme de l'Heroïque par Homere ou Orfée, de la Lyrique par Sappho: en laquelle invention, bien qu'il y ait moins d'excellence, si y en a-t-il neantmoins beaucoup, au regard de ceux qui en font la premiere recontre: et autant en est-il de celle des *Subalternes.*

[the invention of species, such as the Heroic by Homer or Orpheus, or the Lyric by Sappho, which invention, while it has less excellence, nonetheless has a considerable amount in the eyes of those who come across it for the first time: and so much excellence belongs to the invention of *subalterns.*]

These secondary, original poets discover the different genres and forms which poetry can assume. In their ranks belong tne first epic poet, Homer, the first lyric poet, Sappho, and, as Chapelain goes on to assert, the first writer of the epic of peace, Marino. What is most striking in Chapelain's argument is that it assigns *all* historical poets to this secondary status. The first kind of absolute originality may or may not be a divine attribute. Chapelain neatly skirts the issue by ascribing the invention of poetry to the mythical Apollo—or to somebody else. By contrast, the poets of Western literary tradition are all human, and their originality is neither transcendent nor absolute. These include Homer, the earliest bard whose works survive and the one most commonly accorded the status of divinity—an indication that his achievements are unattainable by the modern poet. Chapelain's strategy, similar to Vasari's assertion in the *Proemio* to the *Vite* that the arts existed before the first recorded artists, is to insist upon the human historicity that sets literary tradition at a secondary remove from a divine origin. When all works in this tradition are discovered to be secondary, and none, not even Homer's, can be set up as an absolute model, the competition between poets of the past and present can be conducted on a more equal footing. Originality is now only a relative quality of the poetic text and its value may fluctuate throughout literary history. For the moment, however, the originality of the modern poet Marino gives his poem a hearing. And, later in the century, during the period of the Quarrel between the Ancients and Moderns, Chapelain himself will be held up as the new French Homer.[9]

Chapelain and Milton share the same tactic: to assert the human secondariness of the literary tradition which precedes them and to separate it from a divine origin. Their motives are different; though, in Milton's case, they prove complementary. For in clearing away a tradition of error from his sacred source, Milton can simultaneously clear the field of potential rivals in order to make room for his own voice. Like Chapelain, Milton can assert the value of originality vis-à-vis tradition, and such an assertion is virtually a generic convention of epic, where each bard is required to overgo his predecessors: Milton's pledge to pursue "Things unattempted yet in prose or rhyme" (1.16) is itself a quotation from the *Orlando furioso*. In fact, the claim of *Paradise Lost* to divine authority is identical to and inseparable from its claim to originality. Which claim is the source of the poem's value, however, depends on the standards by which it is read. Milton would have us regard the poem's originality as a by-product of its prophetic inspiration, and he satirizes the quest for an autonomous literary originality in the character of Satan. Yet Milton may be behind the prevailing taste of his own time which, if Chapelain's letter is more representative, valorized the literary text's innovation and individuality to the relative disregard of its claims to truth. In 1704, thirty years after Milton's death, John Dennis would make originality the key criterion of his judgment of *Paradise Lost*; he would make it as well the primary motive of Milton's poetry.

> Milton was the first, who in the space of almost 4000 Years, resolved, for his Country's Honour and his own, to present the World with an Original Poem; that is to say, a Poem that should have his own Thoughts, his own Images, and his own Spirit. In order to this he was resolved to write a Poem, that, by virtue of its extraordinary Subject, cannot so properly be said to be against the Rules, as it may be affirmed to be above them all.[10]

Dennis acutely recognizes that the scriptural subject matter of *Paradise Lost*, Milton's recovery of the original events of sacred history, authorizes its originality. Yet he argues that Milton's desire for poetic originality, for personal glory and individual creativity, led to the choice of the subject matter in the first place.[11] Already Milton is being grouped in the Devil's Party.

In his *Conjectures on Original Composition* (1759), Edward Young qualifies this view of Milton as the successful original and presents a more radical concept of originality. Objecting to Milton's vast learning—which places the poet within the very tradition from which he struggles to escape—Young holds up the example of Shakespeare.

> Perhaps he was as learned as his dramatic province required, for whatever other learning he wanted, he was master of two books, unknown to many of the profoundly read, though books, which the last conflagration alone can destroy: the book of nature, and that of man. These he had by heart, and has transcribed many admirable pages of them, into his immortal works. These are the fountain-head, whence the *Castalian* streams of *original* composition flow; and these are often mudded by other waters, tho' waters in their distinct channel, most wholesome and pure: As two chymical liquors separately clear as crystal, grow foul by mixture, and offend the sight. So that he had not only as much learning as his dramatic province required, but, perhaps, as it could safely bear. If *Milton* had spared some of his learning, his muse would have gained more glory, than he would have lost, by it.[12]

Young's metaphor is peculiarly analogous to Milton's depiction of the Edenic fountain infiltrated by Satan and his corrupt secondary tradition. Here the texts of the past which force the poet into imitation, even of Milton's revisionary kind, muddy the source waters not of divine truth but of the original poetic imagination. Such an imagination, in the case of Shakespeare, ranges at its most free when it contemplates man and nature and garners from them contingent truths. These truths have their own validity, although Young admits that they will eventually be replaced by a revealed truth at the Last

Judgment. He is, in fact, careful to uphold an order of revelation which the original poetic genius cannot attain, and he cautions against the error of those "who set up genius, and often, mere *fancied* genius, not only above human learning, but divine truth."[13] He assigns to poetry an independent realm of its own.

> In the fairyland of fancy, genius may wander wild; there it has a creative power, and may reign arbitrarily over its own empire of chimeras. The wide field of nature also lies open before it, where it may range unconfined, make what discoveries it can, and sport with its infinite objects uncontrolled, as far as visible nature extends, painting them as wantonly as it will: But what painter of the most unbounded and exalted genius can give us the true portrait of a seraph? He can give us only what by his own or others eyes, has been seen; tho' that indeed infinitely compounded, raised, burlesqued, dishonored, or adorned: In like manner, who can give us divine truth unrevealed?[14]

Young grants the imagination its separate domain precisely because it should not and cannot meddle with sacred truth. The attempt to assume a prophetic mantle encounters just those problems which Milton, the painter of Seraphs, claims both to have met and overcome. The representation of divine being is controlled and "compounded" both by the human senses, the painter's own eye, and by the figures of the past—what has been seen through the eyes of others, a tradition of literalist error overlaying spiritual truth. In effect, Young suggests that this tradition blocks any return to a divine source and that a poetry which aspires to that source will only perpetuate the falsehoods of the past. Poetry is thus necessarily banished, in the name of religion, to its own imaginative spaces, where it seeks a new Hippocrene—unsullied by earlier drinkers—in nature, in human nature, and in the creative originality of the poet.

Young's *Conjectures* were written well after the close of the Renaissance and their wholesale rejection of tradition announces new Romantic attitudes that are foreign to Renaissance literary thought. But Young's separation of literature from revealed truth and his valorization of the writer's individuality represent the ultimate conclusions reached by a debate which began and was still very much in progress in Renaissance fiction. The texts which this study brings together because of their common treatment of the source topos belong to a body of literature that self-consciously measures the literary text's claims to allegorical truth in light of a new Renaissance awareness of history and human creativity. Such measurement generated a debate over the source of literary meaning and value; it opposed the desire to ground the text's fiction in an authorized origin against the impulse to originality, to grant its author a creative autonomy. The debate allowed an essentially secular view of literature to be entertained and disputed, and this view was eventually to prevail. Literature gave up its former allegorical sanctions amid a new appreciation (and incipient professionalization) of the individual author and amid growing skepticism and apprehension about human claims to grasp and represent sacred truth.[15] Milton depicts the end result of this process of secularization when Satan and the principle of Babel which he embodies take the place of the divine source. But the same result is celebrated in the writings of Chapelain and Young, where the figure of the source itself ceases to stand for a divine poetic origin and instead describes the poet's own originality. Milton himself had transformed all literature preceding *Paradise Lost* into a desacralized literary history; his own epic would soon be placed within that history by readers who admired its poetry but ignored its prophetic spirit. But what *Paradise Lost* might lose in divine authority would be offset by the deification of its author in the pantheon of original poets.

The new perception of the literary text that emerged at the end of the Renaissance both shared in and, more important, helped to shape a new mentality. Seeking authorizing origins in the past, Renaissance culture encountered its own human historicity. The consequences of this discovery were felt with a special force in its literature, for it was in literature that the contest between individual innovation and the authority of tradition was recast as a struggle for independence from sacred authority, and it was in literature that Renaissance thought first achieved an autonomous, secular identity. But the very nature of this achievement may have obscured the extent to which it contributed to an intellectual revolution. By obtaining a cultural autonomy from systems of authorized truth, literature gave up its right to be authoritative. It thereby found itself in a marginal position with respect to what would pass as the more central, more authentic disciplines of human thought: instead of being banished by philosophy, literature had exiled itself. Under the influence of idealist philosophy, intellectual historians have assigned the literary text a more or less passive role: literature reflects but does not embody, still less create, ideas. But the evidence suggests that the effort of the Renaissance literary text to reexamine the source of its authority, to define itself *as text*, is an event in intellectual history that intellectual history has not adequately understood or explained.

The Renaissance author emerged as original at the moment when a traditional and authoritative canon was historicized and relativized. And, in order to accommodate him—once innovation became the criterion for admission—the canon had to expand into the future. The impulse to originality came to inform all realms of human thought and discourse, formerly closed, now irreversibly open-ended. What Renaissance poets had begun to learn was learnt over and over again. There could be no return to the source. Originality had become the source of authority.

Notes

AHR   *American Historical Review*
AJPh *American Journal of Philology*
BHR   *Bibliothèque d'Humanisme et Renaissance*
CQ   *Classical Quarterly*
ER   *Etudes Rabelaisiennes*
JHI   *Journal of the History of Ideas*
JMRS *Journal of Medieval and Renaissance Studies*
JWCI *Journal of the Warburg and Courtauld Institutes*
MLN   *Modern Language Notes*
PG   *Patrologia graeca*, ed. J. P. Migne
PL   *Patrologia latina*, ed. J. P. Migne
PMLA *Publications of the Modern Language Association*
RenQ *Renaissance Quarterly*

CHAPTER 1

1   Giorgio Vasari, *Le vite de' più eccellenti pittori, scultori ed architettori*, ed. Gaetano Milanesi (Florence, 1881), 7: 148–49. A superlative edition of the *Vita di Michelangelo* alone is provided by Paola Barocchi in *La vita di Michelangelo nelle redazioni del 1550 e del 1558* (Milan and Naples, 1962), 5 vols. See, by the same scholar, *Michelangelo tra le due redazioni delle vite vasariane (1550–1568)* (Lecce, 1968). For a stimulating discussion of Miche-

langelo's conscious originality, see David Summers, "Michelangelo on Architecture" *The Art Bulletin* 54 (1972): 146–57.

2 Hans Baron discusses the case of Vasari, among others, in "The *Querelle* of the Ancients and Moderns as a Problem for Renaissance Scholarship," *JHI* 20 (1959): 3–22, reprinted in Paul Oskar Kristeller and Philip P. Wiener, eds., *Renaissance Essays* (New York, 1968), pp. 95–114. See also August Buck, *Die "Querelle des Anciens et des Modernes" im Italienischen Selbstverständnis der Renaissance und des Barocks* (Wiesbaden, 1973).

3 I am quoting from the edition of Martin de Riquer, *Don Quijote de la Mancha*, 2 vols. (Barcelona, 1971), p. 1055.

4 *Don Quijote* 2.3, p. 563.

5 Vasari, *Le vite*, 1: 222–23.

6 Ibid., 7: 135–36. For the celebration of Michelangelo's divinity and the ideology of his funeral, see Jacopo Giunta, *The Divine Michelangelo*, ed. and trans. Rudolf and Margot Wittkower (London, 1964).

7 See Ulrich Leo, *Angelica ed i "Migliori plettri": Appunti allo stile della Controriforma* (Krefeld, 1953).

8 To the failed mannerists, Vasari contrasts the example of Raphael, who wisely did not try to copy what was inimitable in Michelangelo but rather forged an original style of his own. *Le vite*, 4: 376.

9 The contribution of humanist philology to a new historical consciousness has been the subject of many seminal studies by Eugenio Garin. See the introduction to *Italian Humanism: Philosophy and Civic Life in the Renaissance*, trans. Peter Munz (New York, 1965), pp. 1–17; the essays, "Interpretazioni del Rinascimento" and "La storia del pensiero del Rinascimento," in *Medioevo e Rinascimento* (1954; Bari, 1973), pp. 85–100, 179–95; and the essays "L'ambiente del Poliziano" and "La nuova scienza e il simbolo del 'libro,' " in *La cultura filosofica del Rinascimento italiano: Ricerche e documenti* (1969; Florence, 1979), pp. 335–58, 451–65. See also Donald Kelley's study of French legal humanism, *Foundations of Modern Historical Scholarship: Language, Law, and History in the French Renaissance* (New York and London, 1970); A. Grafton, "On the Scholarship of Politian and its Context," *JWCI* 40 (1977): 150–88; George Huppert, "The Renaissance Background of Historicism," *History of Theory* 5 (1966): 48–60; and the review article of Joseph Preston, "Was There an Historical Revolution?" *JHI* 38 (1977): 353–64. Other factors in addition to humanist textual criticism were clearly at work in shaping a new awareness of the past. In *The Crisis of the Early Italian Renaissance* (Princeton, 1955), Hans Baron has argued that the republican political thought which was galvanized in early quattrocento Florence during her struggle with Milan fostered reappraisals of Roman and contemporary history. William J. Bouwsma has argued that life in the Renaissance city-republic, whose institutions could alter across time, produced a consciousness of change and an emphasis upon the writing of history; see *Venice and the Defense of Republican Liberty* (Berkeley and Los Angeles, 1968), pp. 17–24. A similar thesis, which also discusses how republican mercantilism created a mentality particularly alert to the problems of chance and contingency, is

developed at length in J. G. A. Pocock, *The Machiavellian Moment: Florentine Political Thought and the Atlantic Republican Tradition* (Princeton, 1975).

10   "Nam, sive quem haec Aeliana studia delectant; plurima est, et in omne
iure civili, et in pontificium libris, et in Duodecim Tabulis, antiquitatis
effigies, quod et verborum prisca vetustas cognoscitur, et actionum
genera quaedam maiorum consuetudinem vitamque declarant": *De oratore* 1. xliii. 193. *De oratore*, trans. E. W. Sutton and H. Rackham (Cambridge, Mass. and London: Loeb Classical Library, 1942), 1: 134.

11   ". . . sic ut non versus modo (ita enim Quintillianus ait) censoria quadam
virgula notare, sed libros etiam qui falso viderentur inscripti, tanquam
subdititios, submovere familia permiserint sibi"; *Praelectio in Priora Aristo-
telis Analytica cui titulus Lamia*, ed. and trans. (into Italian) Isidoro del
Lungo, in *Le selve e la strega: prolusioni nello studio fiorentino* (Florence,
1925), p. 222. The Quintillian passage is found in the *Institutio oratoria* 1. 4.
3.

12   See *The Treatise of Lorenzo Valla on the Donation of Constantine*, ed. and trans.
Christopher B. Coleman (New Haven, 1922). Casaubon's criticism of the
Hermetic texts is contained in his *De rebus sacris et ecclesiasticis exercita-
tiones XVI. Ad Cardinalis Baronii prolegomena in Annales* (London, 1614), pp.
70 ff. For a description of his method, see Frances A. Yates, *Giordano Bruno
and the Hermetic Tradition* (1964; New York, 1969) pp. 398–402. Both the
Donation and the Hermetic texts had long been suspected of being later
forgeries. Valla and Casaubon submitted them to rigorous historical and
philological examination; Casaubon's achievement suggests that the
study of Greek had begun to arrive at the level of the study of Latin.

13   See Remigio Sabbadini, *Storia del ciceronianismo e di altre questioni letterarie
nell'età della rinascenza* (Turin, 1885); G. W. Pigman III has written two fine
articles on Ciceronianism and related issues of imitation, "Imitation and
the Renaissance Sense of the Past, the Reception of Erasmus' *Ciceronianus*," *JMRS* 9 (1979): 155–77, and "Versions of Imitation in the Renaissance," *RenQ* 33 (1980): 1–32; see also Terence Cave, *The Cornucopian Text:
Problems of Writing in the French Renaissance* (Oxford, 1979), pp. 135–41;
J. H. M. Salmon, "Cicero and Tacitus in Sixteenth-Century France," *AHR*
85 (1980): 307–31. English translations of the *Ciceronianus* and of the
exchanges between Poliziano and Cortesi and between Pico and Bembo
are contained in Izora Scott, *Controversies over the Imitation of Cicero* (New
York, 1910). The Latin text of the Poliziano–Cortesi letters is printed in
Prosatori latini del quattrocento, ed. Eugenio Garin (Milan and Naples,
1952), pp. 902–10. The Bembo–Pico exchange has been edited by Giorgio
Santangelo in *Le epistole "De Imitatione" di Giovanfrancesco Pico della Mirandola e di Pietro Bembo* (Florence, 1954).

14   Juan Luìs Vives, *De tradendis disciplinis* (1540), 3. 6: "post quos Latinus
sermo ad luxum est et delicias cum moribus civitatis conversus, ut fucata
sint magis et adumbrata, quàm priora illa." *Joannis Ludovici Vivis Valentini
opera omnia* (1745; London, 1964), 6: 325.

15   Poliziano, *Oratio super Fabio Quintiliano et Statii Sylvis*: "nam si rectius
inspexerimus, non tam corruptam atque depravatam illam, quam dicendi

223

mutatum genus intelligemus. Neque autem statim deterius dixerimus quod diversum sit." Garin, *Prosatori latini*, p. 878. Tacitus *Dialogus de oratoribus* 18.

16 "Nam cum nihil in natura hominum sit ab omni parte beatum, plurium bona ante oculos ponenda, ut aliud ex alio haereat et quod cuique conveniat aptandum sit." Garin, *Prosatori latini*, p. 880.

17 See Poliziano's letter to Paolo Cortesi, in ibid., pp. 902–04; Scott, *Controversies*, pp. 17–19. For a brief discussion of Poliziano's method of imitation, see *The Stanze of Angelo Poliziano*, trans. David Quint (Amherst, Mass., 1979), pp. xii–xv.

18 Pico's letter is published in Garin, *Prosatori latini*, pp. 804–22. Along with Barbaro's reply and first letter, it has been translated, with an introduction, by Quirinus Breen, "Giovanni Pico della Mirandola on the Conflict of Philosophy and Rhetoric," *JHI* 13 (1952): 384–412. It is discussed by Hanna H. Gray, "Renaissance Humanism: The Pursuit of Eloquence," *JHI* 24 (1963): 497–514, reprinted in Kristeller and Wiener, *Renaissance Essays*, pp. 199–216. Gray's essay is slanted to Barbaro's point of view—the humanist rhetorician's insistence upon the inseparability of style and content—and, I think, makes too little of Pico's objections. Barbaro's reply to Pico is a learned joke, but Pico's letter, while urbane and witty, raises serious and troubling issues.

19 "Quaerebant quid abhorrens, quid receptum in natura, quid a Romanis interea non curabant." Garin, *Prosatori latini*, p. 820.

20 "Non quaerimus in pecunia qua moneta percussa sit, sed qua materia constet. Nec est qui purum aurum non malit habere sub nota Teutonum, quam sub romano symbolo factitium." Ibid.

21 On Pico, see Garin, *Giovanni Pico della Mirandola: Vita e dottrina* (Florence, 1937); Ernst Cassirer, "Giovanni Pico della Mirandola," *JHI* 3 (1942), reprinted in Kristeller and Wiener, *Renaissance Essays*, pp. 11–60, and *The Individual and the Cosmos in Renaissance Philosophy*, trans. Mario Domandi (1963; Philadelphia, 1972), pp. 115–21; Henri de Lubac, *Pic de la Mirandole* (Paris, 1974).

22 Good critical discussions of *The Praise of Folly* are offered by Clarence H. Miller in "Some Medieval Elements and Structural Unity in Erasmus' *The Praise of Folly*," *RenQ* 27 (1974): 499–511, and in the introduction to his translation of *The Praise of Folly* (New Haven and London, 1979), pp. ix–xxv. See also Walter Kaiser, *Praisers of Folly* (Cambridge, Mass., 1963); Marjorie O'Rourke Boyle, *Christening Pagan Mysteries* (Toronto, Buffalo, and London, 1981), pp. 27–61, Sister Geraldine Thompson, *Under Pretext of Praise: Satiric Mode in Erasmus' Fiction* (Toronto, 1973); Richard S. Sylvester, "The Problem of Unity in *The Praise of Folly*," *English Literary Renaissance* 6 (1976): 125–39; Wayne A. Rebhorn, "The Metamorphoses of Moria: Structure and Meaning in *The Praise of Folly*," *PMLA* 89 (1974): 463–76; and Lynda G. Christian, "The Metamorphoses of Erasmus' 'Folly' " *JHI* 32 (1971): 289–94.

23 In its distrust of rhetoric, *The Praise of Folly* bears a somewhat antithetical relationship to Erasmus's concept of a rhetorically structured theology.

For a persuasive demonstration of how this concept informs Erasmus's other writings and thought, see Marjorie O'Rourke Boyle, *Erasmus on Language and Method in Theology* (Toronto and Buffalo, 1977).

24 I am quoting from the text of *The Praise of Folly* contained in Erasmus von Rotterdam, *Ausgewählte Schriften*, ed. Werner Welzig (Darmstadt, 1975), 2:106–08.

25 Ibid., p. 48.

26 Ibid., p. 62.

27 Ibid., p. 48.

28 Ibid., p. 56.

29 *The City of God* 14. 28, *PL* 41. 436.

30 *Ausgewählte Schriften*, 2:136.

31 Ibid., pp. 150–52.

32 Ibid., p. 130.

33 Ibid., p. 156.

34 Ibid., pp. 66–68.

35 Ibid., p. 112.

36 Ibid., p. 116.

37 Ibid., p. 160.

38 Ibid., p. 158.

39 Ibid., p. 202.

40 For a discussion of the relationship between Erasmus's biblical scholarship and his exegetical method, see Henri de Lubac, *Exégèse médiévale: Les quatre sens de l'Ecriture* (Paris, 1964), vol. 4 (II, 2), pp. 427–87. See also J. B. Payne's comments, pp. 26–34, on the role of the scriptural letter in Erasmus's exegesis in "Towards the Hermeneutics of Erasmus," in J. Coppens, ed., *Scrinium Erasmianum* (Leiden, 1969), 2:13–49. On the method of Erasmus's biblical scholarship, see the still valuable chapter on his New Testament translation in Preserved Smith, *Erasmus: A Study of His Life, Ideals, and Place in History* (New York and London, 1923), pp. 159–88, and Albert Rabil, *Erasmus and the New Testament: The Mind of a Christian Humanist* (San Antonio, Tex., 1972), pp. 99–155.

41 *Ausgewählte Schriften*, 2:186.

42 Ibid., p. 188. Erasmus's choice of the Luke passage is polemical, for its interpretation had long been the subject of controversy. The two swords of Luke 22:38 had been used to justify the temporal as well as the spiritual power of the church, a reading which Erasmus is at pains to refute. For the history of the dispute over the passage, see Joseph Lecler, "L'Argument des deux glaives (Luc XXII, 38) dans les controverses politiques du Moyen Age: Ses origines et son developpement," *Recherches de science religeuse* 21 (1921): 299–339; 22 (1932), 151–77, 280–303.

43 Ibid., pp. 206–10. For an attempt to locate this passage within a tradition of Christian Neoplatonism, see M. A. Screech, *Ecstasy and "The Praise of Folly"* (London, 1980).

44 Such an allegorical structure corresponds to what Angus Fletcher calls "the oldest idea about allegory, that it is a human reconstitution of divinely inspired messages, a revealed transcendental language which

tries to preserve the remoteness of a properly veiled godhead." (*Allegory: The Theory of a Symbolic Mode* [Ithaca and London, 1964], p. 21.) Michael Murrin suggests that a divine source of allegorical meaning may be conflated with or replaced by the truths held self-evident by a community and enshrined in its memory of a nobler, virtuous past. See his *The Veil of Allegory* (Chicago and London, 1969), pp. 75–97.

45 *Ausgewählte Schriften*, 2:208.

46 See de Lubac, *Exégèse médiévale*, 4: 432, n. 1.

47 See Boyle, *Erasmus on Language and Method*, pp. 33–57, 114–17; Cave, *The Cornucopian Text*, pp. 85–86.

48 The ancient allegorizers of Homer, responding to the attacks of the philosophers, are discussed by Félix Buffière, *Les Mythes d'Homère et la pensée grecque* (Paris, 1956), and Jean Pepin, *Mythe et allégorie* (Paris, 1958). The Renaissance rediscovery of the Homeric allegorists is recounted in Don Cameron Allen, *Mysteriously Meant: The Rediscovery of Pagan Symbolism and Allegorical Interpretation in the Renaissance* (Baltimore and London, 1970), pp. 83–105.

49 Historicist and allegorical readings of the literary text are explicitly opposed in the *Ad Petrum Paulum Histrum dialogus* (1401) of Leonardo Bruni. In the first of two dialogues, the character Niccolò Niccoli uses a historical critique to attack the *Divine Comedy;* in the second, he turns around and defends Dante's poem on allegorical grounds (see Garin, *Prosatori latini*, pp. 68–70, 86–89). Roberto Cardini has studied and published a 1465 exchange of letters between the humanist Buonaccorso Massari, who defends a philological-historical method of reading, and Lorenzo Guidetti, a disciple of Cristoforo Landino, who advocates a more literary-rhetorical approach to the text (see Cardini, *La critica del Landino* [Florence, 1973], pp. 39–65, 265–286). Landino's method included allegoresis, for which he was subjected to a withering attack by Francesco Florido Sabino in book 2, chapter 24 of the latter's *Lectionum subcisivarum libri tres* (1540). Sabino does not deny the allegorical content of poetry, but he criticizes Landino's excesses and argues that passages which can be read literally in their context should not be allegorized. See Ianus Gruterus, ed., *Lampas, sive fax artium liberalium* (Frankfurt, 1602), 1:1156–61.

50 Thomas P. Roche has quoted Rosemond Tuve: "Allegory is a method of reading in which we are made to think about things we already know" (*The Kindly Flame* [Princeton, 1964], p. 30). That allegorical meaning requires an earlier text, or pretext, is the argument of Maureen Quilligan, *The Language of Allegory* (Ithaca and London, 1979). Because this intertextual structure lends allegory a self-consciousness about its own rhetoricity, allegory is privileged over the symbol by Paul de Man in his discussion of romantic tropes, "The Rhetoric of Temporality," in Charles Singleton, ed., *Interpretation: Theory and Practice* (Baltimore, 1969), pp. 173–91.

51 For the term *topos* which I am applying to the various depictions of the source, see Ernst Robert Curtius, *European Literature and the Latin Middle Ages*, trans. Willard R. Trask (1953; New York and Evanston, 1963), pp. 79–105.

52 Some other Renaissance versions of the source topos which lie outside this study appear in Pietro Bembo's Latin panegyric poem, *Benacus*, in Canto 1, lines 88–117 of the *Adone* of Giambattista Marino, in the Mummelsee fantasy of Book 6 of Johann von Grimmelhausen's *Simplicius simplicissimus*, in the final episode of the *Schaefferey von der Nimpfen Hercinie* of Martin Optiz: the topos is mercilessly burlesqued by Teofilo Folengo in book 23, vv. 40 ff. of the *Baldus*. Its most significant modern version is the Anna Livia Plurabelle section of *Finnegan's Wake*.

53 For critical discussions of the *Ode à Michel de l'Hospital*, see Grahame Castor, *Pleïade Poetics: A Study in Sixteenth-Century Thought and Terminology* (Cambridge, 1964), pp. 28–35, 38–40, and Cave, *The Cornucopian Text*, pp. 230–33.

54 All quotations from Ronsard are from the Pleïade edition of the *Oeuvres complètes*, ed. Gustave Cohen (Paris, 1950), 2 vols. The text of the *Ode à Michel de l'Hospital* is printed in vol. 1, pp. 386–406; the text of the *Response aux injures et calomnies* is found in vol. 2, pp. 595–621.

55 For a discussion of the relationship of allegory and anamnesis, see Murrin, *The Veil of Allegory*, pp. 90–94. The Muses are, of course, associated with sources: Castalia on Parnassus, Hippocrene on Helicon. Ronsard's fiction, where the Muses return to the source of sources, plays on a traditional myth of poetic inspiration frequently invoked in Renaissance Neo-Latin poetry. See Françoise Joukovsky-Micha, *Poesie et mythologie au XVIe siècle: Quelque mythes de l'inspiration chez les poètes de la Renaissance* (Paris, 1969), pp. 23–42, 119. These Muses could be interchanged with nymphs of the source (see pp. 73–120). See also Phyllis Pray Bober, "The Coryciana and the Nymph Coricia," *JWCI* 49 (1977): 223–39; Elisabeth B. MacDougall, "The Sleeping Nymph: Origins of a Humanist Fountain Type," *Art Bulletin* 57 (1975): 357–65.

56 For Ficino's description of the four furors, see the *In convivium Platonis de amore, commentarium* 7. 13, in his *Opera omnia* (1576; Turin, 1959), vol. 3 (II, 1), p. 1361; *In Phaedrum commentarium & argumenta* 4, *Opera omnia*, 3:1365; *De divino furore, Opera omnia*, vol. 2 (I, 2), pp. 612–15. For Ficino on the inspired nature of poetry and for the Renaissance view of the inspired, religious origins of poetry, see Charles Trinkaus, *"In Our Image and Likeness"; Humanity and Divinity in Italian Humanist Thought* (Chicago and London, 1970), 2: 479–82, 683–721.

57 I am quoting from the translation of R. Hackforth in *The Collected Dialogues of Plato*, ed. Edith Hamilton and Huntington Cairns (Princeton, 1963), p. 492.

58 Ronsard expresses his desire to achieve an originality that is also inspired in the *Hynne de la Mort*, vv. 24–42. He complains that the ancients have exhausted the waters of Helicon and asserts that the novelty of his present subject matter—a poem in praise of Death—entitles him to an untapped, exclusive poetic source.

> Je veux aller chercher quelque source sacrée,
> D'un ruisseau non touché, qui murmurant s'enfuit
> Dedans un beau vergier, loin de gens et de bruit,

Source, que le Soleil n'aura jamais cognue,
Que les oiseaux du Ciel, de leur bouche cornue,
N'auront jamais souillée, et où les pastoureaux
N'auront jamais conduit les pieds de leurs taureaux.
Je boiray tout mon saoul de ceste onde pucelle,
Et puis je canteray quelque chanson nouvelle,
Dont les accords seront, peut-estre, si tres-dous,
Que les siecles voudront les redire apres nous,
Et, suivant mon esprit, à nul des vieux antiques,
Larron, je ne devray mes chansons poëtiques,
Car il me plaist pour toy de faire ici ramer
Mes propres avirons dessus ma propre mer,
Et de voler au Ciel par une voye estrange,
Te chantant de la Mort la non-dite louange.

But perhaps the most striking aspect of this claim to originality is that it is itself an imitation of the opening of book 2, vv. 48–58, of the *Astronomica* of Manilius.

CHAPTER 2

1 Eduard Norden, "Orpheus and Eurydice," *Sitzungsberichte der Preussischen Akademie der Wissenschaften, Berlin, philosophisch-historische klasse* (1934): 628–83. A survey of the Servius-Gallus issue is to be found in L. P. Wilkinson, *The Georgics of Virgil* (Cambridge, 1969), pp. 108–11. A good analysis of the structure of the epyllion, locating the Orpheus story at its center, is presented in Brooks Otis, *Virgil: A Study in Civilized Poetry* (Oxford, 1963), pp. 187–214. Useful critical readings of the epyllion appear in Adam Parry, "The Idea of Art in Virgil's *Georgics*," *Arethusa* 5 (1972): 35–52; Charles P. Segal, "Orpheus and the *Fourth Georgic*: Virgil on Nature and Civilization," *AJPh* 86 (1966): 307–25; A. Wankenne, "Aristée et Orphée dans les Géorgiques," *Les Etudes Classiques* 38 (1970): 18–29; Friedrich Klingner, *Virgil* (Zurich and Stuttgart, 1967), pp. 326–63; Michael C. J. Putnam, *Virgil's Poem of the Earth: Studies in the Georgics* (Princeton, 1979), pp. 277–321.

2 All citations from Virgil's works are taken from *P. Vergili Maronis Opera*, ed. R. A. B. Mynors (Oxford, 1969).

3 The identification of Virgil's fiction with the *Phaedo* passage is discussed by E. A. Havelock, "Virgil's Road to Xanadu," *The Phoenix* 1, no. 1 (1946): 3–9; 1, no. 2 (1946): 2–7; suppl. to vol. 1 (1947), pp. 9–18. Aristotle criticizes the *Phaedo* myth and locates the sources of rivers in condensation and rainfall in the *Meteorologia* 1. xiii. 349b–350a. For the late survival of the oceanic source as a scientific idea, see Athanasius Kircher, *Mundus Subterraneus* (Amsterdam, 1665), pp. 226–43, and Alexander Caldecott, *Treatise on the Deluge* (London, 1768). Plato's myth is ridiculed in vol. 2, pp. 104–09 of Charles Perrault's *Paralelle des anciens et modernes* (1690), reprinted by H. R. Jauss (Munich, 1964), pp. 206–07.

4 *Metaphysics* 983b. In the *Homeric Questions,* the allegorist Heraclitus glosses the *Iliad* passage on Ocean with this doctrine of "Thales." See the *Allégories d'Homère,* ed. with a French translation by Félix Buffière (Paris, 1972), pp. 26–27. See also G. S. Kirk and J. E. Raven, *The Presocratic Philosophers* (Cambridge, 1957), pp. 11–19, 87–93.

5 *The Presocratic Philosophers,* pp. 60–65.

6 *Allégories d'Homère,* pp. 73–74. See also Buffière, *Les mythes d'Homère,* for a discussion of Heraclitus and his place in ancient mythography.

7 Wilkinson, *Georgics of Virgil,* p. 113; Norden, "Orpheus and Eurydice, pp. 652–54; Segal, "Orpheus and the *Fourth Georgic,*" p. 314.

8 As Circe will instruct Odysseus to consult Tiresias, so Eidothea instructs Menelaus to consult Proteus. Tiresias counsels Odysseus to sacrifice to Poseidon; Proteus tells Menelaus to offer hecatombs to the gods. Unlike Circe and Virgil's Cyrene, Eidothea plays no further role in the action. See John H. Finley, Jr., *Homer's Odyssey* (Cambridge, Mass. and London, 1978), pp. 149–52.

9 *Allégories d'Homère,* pp. 69–72. This cosmological interpretation of Proteus is also present in the Homeric scholia. See the commentary on *Odyssey* 4.384 [E.M.] in the *Scholia Graeca in Homeri Odysseam,* ed. Wilhelm Dindorf (1885; rpt. Amsterdam, 1962), 1:209.

10 Dionysius of Halicarnassus, *The Critical Essays,* ed. and trans. Stephen Usher (Cambridge, Mass. and London: Loeb Classical Library, 1974), 1:267.

11 *Republic* 382e. I am quoting from the Paul Shorey translation in Hamilton and Cairns, *The Collected Dialogues of Plato,* p. 630.

12 Plato's treatment of the Proteus myth is discussed by A. Bartlett Giamatti in "Proteus Unbound: Some Versions of the Sea God in the Renaissance," in Peter Demetz, Thomas Greene, and Lowry Nelson, Jr., eds., *The Disciplines of Criticism* (New Haven and London, 1968), pp. 437–75, 452–53.

13 *Ion* 541e. I am quoting from the translation of Lane Cooper in *The Collected Dialogues of Plato.*

14 See Giamatti, "Proteus Unbound." For the origins of the Proteus myth, see Marcel Detienne, *Les Maîtres de vérité dans la Grèce archaïque* (Paris, 1967), pp. 29–50.

15 The paradox of the source which cannot represent itself is explored by Jacques Derrida in an essay on Valéry's treatment of the metaphor of the source, "qual quelle: les sources de Valéry," in *Marges de la philosophie* (Paris, 1972), pp. 325–63. "Mais comment l'impossible est-il possible? Comment la source peut-elle se diviser—les sources dès le titre germinales—et donc d'elle même s'écarter pour se rapporter à elle même—qui est en tant qu'origine pure, l'irréference à soi? . . . Donc le malheur est d'avoir un sens, un seul invincible sens. C'est parce qu'elle a un sens que la source n'a pas de propre, de sens propre qui lui permette de revenir et s'égaler à elle même, de s'appartenir. C'est une sorte de nature ou plutôt de Dieu menacé, amoindri, impuissant en raison même de son originarité et de son indépendance de source" (pp. 337–38). Derrida's method here,

as elsewhere in his writings, is to start with a Platonic opposition between a timeless, self-identical fullness of meaning and the differentiating linguistic sign that is temporally displaced from that fullness—he speaks in terms of a negative theology—before substituting for that opposition Saussure's understanding of language as an autonomous process of differentiation where meaning is produced by oppositions within a whole system of signs; it is only through the sign's quality of being displaced from, and hence nonidentical to, an original significance that signs may be different from one another and that a play of signification *between* signs can take place. Virgil's fiction may contain a version of that Platonic opposition—between Cyrene's source and the differentiating forms of Proteus—which Derrida is out to deconstruct.

16 *Allégories d'Homère,* p. 72.
17 *Symposium* 179d. I am quoting from the translation of Michael Joyce in Hamilton and Cairns, *The Collected Dialogues of Plato,* pp. 533–34.
18 For a survey of the Orpheus-Eurydice myth in the literature of antiquity, see C. M. Bowra, "Orpheus and Eurydice," *CQ* 46 (1952): 113–26. For a reading that examines Virgil's linking of the Orpheus and Aristaeus myths in terms of ethnographic parallels, see Marcel Detienne, "Orphée au miel," in Jacques Le Goff and Pierre Nora, eds., *Faire l'histoire: Nouveaux objets* (Paris, 1974), pp. 56–75.
19 Cf. Segal, 318–19: "Aristaeus and the bees on the one side, Orpheus on the other stand in a complementary relation: Orpheus' *amor* does not further nature's aims of reproduction. He has *amor* without procreation, a peculiarly human, inward and soulful form of *amor;* the bees have procreation without *amor* (in the human sense)."
20 Max Wickert, in "Orpheus Dismembered: Operatic Myth Goes Underground," *Salmagundi* 38–39 (1977): 118–36, writes of an "uncertain wavering" in the Orpheus story "between the ideal of a Eurydice regained and that of a Eurydice renounced and apotheosized. . . . The very intensity with which he wants to give his desire for a special woman a privileged status has a tendency to make him enamored, not so much of that woman, but of his song" (p. 118). For the narcissistic implications of Orpheus's song, see Putnam, *Virgil's Poem of the Earth,* p. 308.

CHAPTER 3

1 Elegy I, 1 in Sannazaro, *Poemata* (Padua, 1719), pp. 100–01.
2 The inspiration for Sannazaro's elegy appears to have been another poem at the opening of a larger collection, Horace's dedication to Maecenas in book 1 of the *Odes* (see 1. 1, 22 ff.). A playful version of the struggle between genres is found at the beginning of Ovid's *Amores* (1. 1–4), where Cupid steals the last foot of the poet's epic hexameter and turns the verse into erotic Ovidian couplets.
3 See Ernst Robert Curtius, *European Literature and the Latin Middle Ages,* pp. 231–32; 201, n. 35.

4   William Empson has described this appropriation of pastoral conventions
    "to imply a beautiful relation between rich and poor" in *Some Versions of
    Pastoral* (1935; rpt. New York, 1960), p. 11. In a recent essay, Louis Adrian
    Montrose examines the use of pastoral symbolism in the literature and
    social rituals of Elizabethan England, " 'Eliza, Queene of shepheardes,'
    and the Pastoral of Power," *English Literary Renaissance* 10 (1980): 153–82.
    In literature the dressing up of aristocrats as shepherds seems to go as far
    back as the *Seventh Idyll* of Theocritus. Renaissance writers knew from
    Servius that Virgil's *Eclogues* contained topical allusions, and their own
    pastorals often transformed the bower into a vantage point on the urban,
    political world. But such pastorals appear to run counter to a more deep-
    seated impulse of a genre which seeks to evade—though it may still
    acknowledge—the public realm of history. For another view, however,
    see Michael J. K. O'Loughlin, " 'Woods Worthy of a Consul;' Pastoral and
    the Sense of History," in John H. Dorenkamp, ed., *Literary Studies: Essays
    in memory of Francis A. Drumm* (Worcester, Mass., 1973), pp. 143–71.

5   My view of what constitute the fundamental impulses and norms of
    pastoral follows closely Renato Poggioli's discussion of the genre in *The
    Oaten Flute* (Cambridge, Mass. and London, 1975). Poggioli writes: "From
    the very beginning pastoral poets seem to anticipate modern attitudes; to
    speak in Schillerian terms, they replace the 'naive' with the 'sentimental,'
    looking with more irony at life, and recoiling from the tragic and heroic
    sides of human experience. . . . Pastoral poets leave the theatre and the
    agora, to cultivate, like Candide, their own garden, where they grow
    other flowers than those of communal myth and public belief" (p. 4). See
    also Poggioli's examination of "The Pastoral of the Self," pp. 161–81.

6   Thomas Rosenmeyer, *The Green Cabinet: Theocritus and the European Pasto-
    ral Lyric* (Berkeley, Los Angeles, and London, 1973), p. 85.

7   See Paul Alpers on the self-reflexiveness of Virgil's pastoral poetry, in *The
    Singer of the Eclogues: A Study of Virgilian Pastoral* (Berkeley, Los Angeles,
    and London, 1979), pp. 244–49. "The essence of Virgil's pastoral suspen-
    sions is the poet's capacity to render and acknowledge truths and
    relations, but not to claim the power to resolve them" (p. 245).

8   A biographical study of the poet is included in Antonio Altamura, *Jacopo
    Sannazaro* (Naples, 1951).

9   "*L'Arcadia*: Storia e delineamento d'una struttura," in Saccone, *Il "sog-
    getto" del furioso e altri saggi tra quattro e cinquecento* (Naples, 1974), pp. 9–69
    (orig. publ. *MLN* 84 [1971]: 46–97). Saccone offers a thorough survey of
    the dating controversy and provides the outlines of a critical interpreta-
    tion of the *Arcadia* which at several points touches upon my own conclu-
    sions. Saccone notes the "carattere quasi violento con cui la realtà fa
    irruzione nell'immaginario" in Eclogue 10 (p. 53), and he sees the pastoral
    experience of the book as an evasion of the recognition of mortality
    (p. 60). He also notes the difference in tone between Eclogues 11 and 12
    (p. 62).
    The theory of a post-exile period of composition for the last two eclogues
    is advanced by Michele Scherillo in the introduction to his edition of the
    Arcadia (Turin, 1888), pp. xl ff. Scherillo's edition contains exhaustive

notes on Sannazaro's allusions and borrowings from classical and Italian authors, and is indispensable to serious readers of the book. Another study of Sannazaro's sources is Francesco Torraca, *La materia dell'Arcadia del Sannazaro* (Città di Castello, 1888). See also the critical discussion of the *Arcadia* in Vittorio Borghini's study of Sannazaro, *La più nobile umanista del Rinascimento* (Turin, Milan, Genoa, Parma, Rome, and Catania, 1943, pp. 99–217). The *Arcadia* is translated into English with an introduction by Ralph Nash, *Arcadia and Piscatorial Eclogues* (Detroit, 1966).

10 Saccone, *Il "soggetto" del furioso*, pp. 54–56.

11 All citations of the *Arcadia* are taken from Iacobo Sannazaro, *Opere volgari*, ed. Alfredo Mauro (Bari, 1961).

12 Panofsky, "*Et in Arcadia Ego*: Poussin and the Elegiac Tradition," in *Meaning in the Visual Arts* (Garden City, N.Y., 1955), pp. 295–320. Panofsky cites Sannazaro on p. 314.

13 The rhetorical effect of the anaphora "altri . . . altri" is discussed by Ellen Zetzel Lambert in *Placing Sorrow: A Study of the Pastoral Elegy Convention from Theocritus to Milton* (Chapel Hill, N.C., 1976), p. 96, and by Poggioli, *Oaten Flute*, p. 100. On pastoral apotheosis, see Rosenmeyer, *The Green Cabinet*, p. 117: "Virgil's 'Daphnis' locates the dead herdsman in a new and lasting bower, one that mirrors the bower and adds further glamor to it"; and Poggioli, p. 21: "No pastoral poet ever believes in man's return or ascent from the realm of the dead; the apotheosis closing a funeral elegy is always merely conventional and literary. The pastoral looks earthward, not heavenward." See also Alpers on Virgil's *Fifth Eclogue*, p. 200: "The creative power of Eclogue 5 is the power of human song."

14 For the laurel and for Petrarch's "attempt to exclude referentiality" and to create a purely intratextual fiction, see John Freccero, "The Fig Tree and the Laurel: Petrarch's Poetics," *Diacritics* 5 (1975): 34–40.

15 *Lament for Bion*, 115–26. *The Greek Bucolic Poets*, trans. J. M. Edmonds (1912; Cambridge, Mass. and London: Loeb Classical Library, 1970), p. 455.

16 The allusion to Creusa's disappearance may, in fact, be doubly allusive; it may return to the story of Orpheus and Eurydice which frames Sannazaro's fiction. The passage at the end of *Aeneid* 2 frequently echoes the *Fourth Georgic* epyllion, drawing an analogy between the loss of Creusa and the loss of Eurydice. Sannazaro would not have needed to know the passage in Pausanias (10.26.1) which recounts that Aeneas's wife was, in fact, named Eurydice in order to recognize a parallel between the two Virgilian episodes. See the commentary of R. G. Austin, *Aeneidos liber secundus* (Oxford, 1964), pp. 287–89.

17 The passage can be compared to Sannazaro's Latin poem (*Elegy* II, 9) on the ruins of Cumae (*Poemata*, pp. 146–47).

18 The *Meliseus* takes the form of a dialogue between two shepherds, Faburnus and Ciceriscus, who discuss the sorrow and eventual consolation of Meliseus, who represents Pontano himself. The eclogue is structured by the repeated juxtaposition of the human artifact and the forces of time and death. As Ariadne prepares to weave a cloth for her family, the

thread of her own life is cut short by Lachesis (49–62). Ariadne embroiders into her son's tunic an idyllic, sunlit portrait of woodland nature; a storm from the underworld, uprooting the very trees she depicts in the tunic, carries her off into a realm of darkness and night (102–20). Yet Meliseus finally consoles himself by making an artifact of his own: he weaves a basket in which he depicts the story of Orpheus raising up Eurydice. Three times, Meliseus repeats the refrain: "Orpheaque Eurydicenque sequentem intexite iunci/dum fiscella levi circumfrondescit acantho" (234–35). See Pontano, *Carmina*, ed. Benedetto Soldati (Florence, 1902), 2:30–36.

19 Petrarch's envois, however, may themselves contain more than merely conventional meaning. See Nancy J. Vickers, "Re-membering Dante: Petrarch's 'Chiare, fresche et dolci acque,' " *MLN* 96 (1981): 1-11, p. 11.

20 Altamura, *Jacopo Sannazaro*, p. 121. See also Borghini, *La più nobile umanista*, p. 443.

21 All citations of the *De partu Virginis* are taken from Altamura's critical edition (Naples, 1948). For a critical discussion of the poem, see Thomas M. Greene, *The Descent from Heaven: A Study in Epic Continuity* (New Haven and London, 1963), pp. 144–70. See also Borghini, *La più nobile umanista*, pp. 405–74; Giulia Calisti, *Il De partu Virginis di Jacopo Sannazaro* (Città di Castello, 1926). Francesco Tateo pertinently insists upon the poet's attempt to interject his own personality and historicity into the beginning and ending of the poem, in pp. 422–23 of "Per una lettura critica dell'opera latina del Sannazaro," *Convivium* 25 (1957): 413–27.

22 Gregory of Nyssa *On the Baptism of Christ, PG* 46.593. The passage is cited by Jean Daniélou in *From Shadows to Reality*, trans. Dom Wulstan Hibberd (London, 1960), p. 275. Daniélou's work is, in turn, cited and discussed by John Freccero in his essay that focuses on the identification of the Jordan and the Oceanus, "The River of Death: *Inferno* II, 108," in S. Bernard Chandler and J. A. Molinaro, eds., *The World of Dante* (Toronto, 1966), pp. 25–42. My discussion draws heavily on both studies.

23 Ambrose *Expositions on Luke, PL* 15.1665.

24 Sermon 38, attributed to Ambrose *On the Grace of Baptism, PL* 17.689. The passage is cited by Ferdinand Ohrt in *Die Altesten Segen über Christi Taufe und Christi Tod in Religiogeschichtlichen Licht* (Copenhagen, 1938), p. 167.

25 Gregory of Nyssa, *On Baptism, PG* 46.420–21. Daniélou, *From Shadows to Reality*, p. 272. Freccero, "The River of Death," p. 34.

26 Hippolytus, *Elenchos* 5. 7 (*PG* 16. 313–14). Daniélou, *From Shadows to Reality*, p. 273. Freccero, "The River of Death," p. 33.

27 The reflux of the Jordan is described by Psalm 114 (Vulgate 113), line 3, "Jordanis conversus est retrorsum." In the traditional iconography of the Baptism of Christ, the Jordan was personified as a river-god and was shown fleeing from the scene of the baptism. See Louis Réeau, *Iconographie de l'art crétien* (Paris, 1957), pt. 2, vol. 2, p. 299.

28 Origen, *Commentary on St. John* 6.42, *PG* 14.273. Daniélou, *From Shadows to Reality*, p. 268.

29 See Hugo Rahner, " 'Flumina de Ventre Christi': Die patristische Ausle-

gung von Joh 7, 37, 38," *Biblica* 22 (1941): 262–302, 367–403, and F.-M. Braun, "L'Eau et l'Esprit," *Revue Thomiste* 49 (1949): 1–30.

30 C. H. Dodd, *The Interpretation of the Fourth Gospel* (Cambridge, 1970), p. 56.

31 Ibid., pp. 297–300, 311–16.

32 Origen *Homilies on Ezekiel* 13.4, *PG* 13.764.

33 Ambrose *Explication of Psalm 1.* see 33, *PL* 14.940. This passage is cited by Rahner, p. 399.

34 Jerome *Commentary on Ezekiel* 14.47, *PL* 25.472.

35 See the chapters in Ohrt, "Der Weltjordan," pp. 177–80, and "Der Paradiesjordan," *Die Altesten Segen*, pp. 180–86. For the doubling of the Jordan in Christian iconography, see also Ferdinand Piper, *Mythologie der Christlichen Kunst* (Weimar, 1847–51), 2:511–14.

36 Athanasius, in *On the Incarnation of the Word*, p. 43, writes: "In all creation, only man conceived errors about God. Neither the sun nor the moon, nor the heavens, nor the stars, nor the water, nor the ether strayed from the path, but recognized the Word as their creator and sovereign, and remained as they had been created" (*PG* 25.172). The humanist rediscovery of the restoration theology espoused by such Greek patristic writers as Athanasius contributed to the almost Pelagian view of man's dignity and perfectability which characterized the theological climate in Rome before the sack of 1527, the atmosphere in which Sannazaro's poem was written. On the Pelagian tendencies of the *De partu Virginis*, see Greene, *Descent from Heaven*, pp. 157–58.

37 *P. Vergili Maronis opera omnia* (Venice, 1562), p. 119 verso.

38 See Emile Mâle, *Religious Art in France: XIII Century*, trans. Dora Nussey (London and New York, 1913), p. 169.

39 In Sannazaro's letter to Antonio Seripando of April 13, 1521, he compares his Proteus to Caiaphas, the high priest who unwittingly prophesies the sacrifice of Christ for mankind in John 11 : 49–52. Caiaphas, as commentators pointed out, is a Balaam figure, a prophet in spite of himself (Origen, *Homelies on Numbers* 14.4, *PG* 12.683). Sannazaro's comparison immediately follows his discussion of Virgil as a pagan prophet of Christ: "Io credo non errare se tengo che Dio volse essere bandito da tutto il mondo, e se non che la medesima paura di generare fastidio mi detenne, più di sei altri vaticinii delle genti nostre ci averia accomodati, e per uno, quello di Ovidio parlando di Augusto: *Prospiciet prolem sancta de Virgine natam*. E'l vaticinio di Caifas si accetta, *quia pontifex anni illius*. Proteo non possetti dire che fusse pontifice, ma, essendo chiamata vato da' poeti, mi parse non inconveniente che come dio marino predicesse quelle cose ad un fiume" (*Opere volgari*, p. 373). When Sannazaro produces another example of pagan prophetic poetry from *Metamorphoses* 15.836, he is perfectly aware that Ovid is writing about Augustus, not about Christ. But, through the inspiration of the Holy Spirit, Ovid's words have an allegorical meaning of which he is not aware.

40 Sannazaro's letter continues: "E dire che Proteo sempre avesse detto il vero, non mi parea consono con la religione. Cosi, per temperare la

fizzione poetica et ornare le cose sacre con le profane, mi parse provederci con dire: *mendax ad caetera Proteus, Hoc uno veras effudit tempore (carmine) voces.* Tanto più che Iordane dice esserli stato predetto molto tempo avanti, e sempre che reservo che in questo disse il vero, non importa che nel resto sia stato mendace. Virgilio fa il contrario: *Namque mihi fallax haud ante repertus, Hoc uno responso animum delusit Apollo"* (ibid.).

41 "Quid quod Uirginem fingit intentam praecipue sibyllinis uersibus, quod non apte Proteum inducit de Christo vaticinantem, quod nympharum, Hamadryadum, ac Nereidum plena facit omnia?" *Il Ciceroniano,* ed. and trans. (into Italian) Angiolo Gambaro (Brescia, 1965), p. 278.

42 "Quale porro sit, materiam piam ob hoc ipsum putere nobis, quod pie tractata sit? At pie tractari qui potest, si nunquam dimoueas oculos a Uirgiliis, Oratiis, ac Nasonibus." Ibid., p. 280.

43 Sannazaro does claim for himself a kind of originality in the address to his reedpipe at the end of the *Arcadia;* he is the first in his age to write pastoral poetry according to ancient norms: "Benché a te non picciola scusa fia, lo essere in questo secolo stata prima a risvegliare le adormentate selve, et a mostrare a' pastori di cantare le già dimenticate canzoni." But this originality is offered as an excuse for the *Arcadia*'s imperfections, for its failures to live up to the classical models it imitates. The passage itself recalls Horace *Odes* 3.30, 10–14.

44 See Gianfranco Folena, *La crisi linguistica del quattrocento e l'"Arcadia" di I. Sannazaro* (Florence, 1952).

45 Sannazaro's books thus belong to a body of Italian literature of the early sixteenth century the other works of which have been discussed by Mario Santoro in *Fortuna, ragione, e prudenza nella civiltà letteraria del cinquecento* (Naples, 1967). The impact of the French and Spanish invasions upon humanist literary culture is the subject of Santoro's first chapter, pp. 11–22, and is also the underlying theme of his study.

46 For the fortunes of the *Arcadia* and *De partu virginis,* see Borghini, *La più nobile umanista,* pp. 203–17, 450–53, 471–74.

CHAPTER 4

1 Pulci, *Il Morgante,* ed. Giuseppe Fatini (Turin, 1948), 1: 25.

2 Pulci's art elicits the following meditation by Leo Spitzer in the essay, "Crai, poscrai, posquaquera," in his *Romanische Literaturstudien* (Tübingen, 1959), pp. 609–10: "Language has become, with Pulci, as will later be more consistently the case with Rabelais, an independent autonomous reality, real as far as words can suggest reality, unreal as concerns their exact correspondence with outward reality. This emancipation of the word from that reality which it should submissively translate, this creation of an 'intermediate world,' half-real, half-unreal, with an autonomy of its own, is a reflection of the new humanistic emancipation from medieval ideals which had entailed a subjection to reality (though this could very well be of an unworldly, of a visionary or metaphysical kind, it

was none the less real for medieval man); *now* language dares be daring—capricious, bizarre, fantastic, 'nonworldly.' The human word posits a reality; why not exploit this power of language and, by a new coinage, posit a non-entity as an entity."

3 See Thomas M. Greene, *The Descent from Heaven*, pp. 130–31; but see also Patricia Parker, *Inescapable Romance: Studies in the Poetics of a Mode* (Princeton, 1979), p. 48: "Astolfo's journey to the Moon becomes in retrospect only one episode among many, as Renaissance illustrations of this canto so masterfully suggest."

4 See A. Bartlett Giamatti, *The Earthly Paradise and the Renaissance Epic* (Princeton, 1969), pp. 138–39, on Ariosto: "There is too much going on, impinging, underlying, ever to allow one man's set of standards or absolutes the final say. . . . Perhaps the only answer or standard or guide to life is that there is no answer, guide, or standard." On Ariosto's multiple perspective, see also D. S. Carne-Ross, "The One and the Many: A Reading of *Orlando furioso,* Cantos 1 and 8," *Arion* 5 (1966): pp. 195–234.

5 All citations of Ariosto are taken from the *Orlando furioso,* ed. Lanfranco Caretti (Milan and Naples, 1963).

6 The indebtedness of Ariosto's allegory to the *Somnium,* which was not printed until 1964, is discussed by Cesare Segre in *Esperienze ariostesche* (Pisa, 1966), pp. 85–95. I can take the occasion here to correct an earlier version of this chapter, published in *Yale Italian Studies* 1 (1977): 398–408, which asserted that the lunar junkyard was "new-minted by Ariosto's fantasy."

7 Yet even when Ariosto writes "traditional" allegory, his fiction qualifies and complicates traditional meanings. See William Kennedy, "Ariosto's Ironic Allegory," *MLN* 88 (1973): 44–67. For a discussion of how, in another passage, Ariosto's poem resists conventional allegorization, see Daniel Javitch, "Rescuing Ovid from the Allegorizers: The Liberation of Angelica, *Furioso* X," in Aldo Scaglione, ed., *Ariosto 1974 in America: Atti del Congresso Ariostesco—Dicembre 1974, Casa Italiana della Columbia University* (Ravenna, 1975), pp. 84–98.

8 *Inferno* 3.18. For Dante's condemnation of literary "immortality," see the episode of Brunetto Latini in *Inferno* 15. Brunetto's final words to the pilgrim concern the fate of his book: "Sieti raccomandato il mio Tesoro, / Nel qual io vivo ancora; e più non chieggio." (15.119–20).

9 The dissenting view of Homer's epics can be traced to Dio Crysostom, and Dido's chastity was a commonplace. See Don Cameron Allen, "Marlowe's *Dido* and the Tradition," in *Essays on Shakespeare and Elizabethan Drama in Honor of Hardin Craig* (Columbia, S.C. 1962), pp. 55–68. Parker (*Inescapable Romance,* pp. 41–44) demonstrates how Ariosto juxtaposes two conflicting authorities (Virgil vs. Ovid) in order to suggest the absence of an "authorized version."

10 Voltaire's opinion is recorded in *The Memoirs of Jacques Casanova de Seingault,* trans. Arthur Machen (New York, 1959–60), 3: 560–65. See also the preface to Voltaire's *La Pucelle d'Orléans.*

11 Robert Durling, *The Figure of the Poet in Renaissance Epic* (Cambridge, Mass., 1965), p. 149.

12 See Marcia Colish, "Seneca's *Apocolocyntosis* as a Possible Source for Erasmus' *Julius Exclusus*," *RenQ* 29 (1976): 361–68.

13 *Apocolocyntosis* 4.1. *L'Apocolocyntose du divin Claudius*, ed. and trans. into French René Waltz (Paris, 1934), p. 3.

14 Ibid., p. 4.

15 Durling has attacked the views of Croce (*Figure of the Poet*, pp. 250–51, n. 5) and Hegel (pp. 252–53, n. 22) on the *Orlando furioso*. "Hegel further fails to realize that 'distorting the subject matter' may be a way of commenting on the degree of reality of the 'real' world; in fact, behind his philosophical category lurks the inability of the nineteenth century to deal with the fictional modes of earlier periods," (p. 253). The same footnote contains Durling's remarks on the implications of Ariosto's "rejection of transcendental sanctions of narrative art" for the new form of the novel.

16 For the narrative dynamics of desire, see Eugenio Donato, " 'Per Selve e Boscherecci Labirinti': Desire and Narrative Structure in Ariosto's *Orlando furioso*," *Barocco* 4 (1972): 17–34, and, for a more general treatment, Giorgio de Blasi, "L'Ariosto e le passioni (studio sul motivo fondamentale dell' 'Orlando furioso')," *Giornale Storico della Letteratura Italiana* 129 (1952): 318–62; 130 (1953), 178–203. For the connection between Ariosto's narrative closure and the disclosure of human mortality, see David Quint, "The Figure of Atlante: Ariosto and Boiardo's Poem," *MLN* 94 (1979): 77–91.

17 See Tasso's letters (43–45) to Scipione Gonzaga (September 1575), and Luca Scalabrino (September 7 and 15, 1575) in *Le lettere di Torquato Tasso*, ed. Cesare Guasti (Florence, 1854), 1: 106–11.

18 See the appendix to Luigi Bonfigli's edition of the *Gerusalemme liberata* (Bari, 1930), p. 525.

19 See Tasso's letter (51) to Scipione Gonzaga, January 24, 1576, in *Le lettere*, 1: 125.

20 All citations from the *Gerusalemme liberata* are taken from vol. 3 of Tasso's *Opere*, ed. Bruno Maier (Milan, 1963).

21 See Kittley F. Mather and Shirley Mason, *A Source Book in Geology* (New York and London, 1933), pp. 7–11.

22 Garin, "Magia ed astrologia nella cultura del Rinascimento," and "Considerazioni sulla magia," in *Medievo e Rinascimento* (Bari, 1973), pp. 141–58, 159–78. For a masterly survey of the traditions of Renaissance magic, see D. P. Walker, *Spiritual and Demonic Magic from Ficino to Campanella* (1958; Neildeln / Liechtenstein, 1969). See also Wayne Shumaker, *The Occult Sciences in the Renaissance* (Berkeley, Los Angeles, and London, 1972).

23 See Tasso's letter (51) to Scipione Gonzaga, January 24, 1576, in *Le lettere*, 1: 125.

24 *Opere di Torquato Tasso*, ed. Giovanni Rosini (Pisa, 1821–32), 24: x. Michael Murrin has demonstrated the extent to which the scheme described in Tasso's *Prose Allegory* was integrated into the writing of his poem. See his *The Allegorical Epic: Essays in Its Rise and Decline* (Chicago and London, 1980), pp. 88–107.

25 Tasso, *Prose*, ed. Ettore Mazzali (Milan and Naples, 1959), pp. 840–41; *Le*

lettere, 2: 21–22. B. T. Sozzi discusses the 1579 letter in "Il Magismo di Tasso," in his *Studi sul Tasso* (Pisa, 1954), p. 317. It is very difficult to determine, given the disturbed nature of Tasso's psyche, whether the episode of the Magus reflects the conversion experience he describes here, or whether his account of this experience borrows from the fiction of the *Liberata*, completed by 1579. This may be a case of life imitating art.

26 *Prose*, p. 838; *Le lettere*, 2: 18.

27 Lactantius *Divine Institutes* 4.10, *PL* 6. 470–71; John Freccero, "The River of Death," p. 37.

28 Virgil, *Opera omnia* (1562), p. 118 recto.

29 See the Bonfigli edition, p. 526. While the Magus bathes Rinaldo, who has fainted, in the ocean, Rinaldo sees the Magus in a vision and is shown the rivers of Hell by him. "—Quel che l'onda ha di fiamma è Flegetonte; / sono Acheronte e Stige gli altri; e 'l nostro / oceano ha principio ov'io ti mostro.—"

30 For the opposition of "scientia" and "sapientia," see Eugene Rice, *The Renaissance Idea of Wisdom* (Cambridge, 1958), and, for a powerful critique of Rice, Antonio U. Romualdez, "Towards a History of the Renaissance Idea of Wisdom," *Studies in the Renaissance* 11 (1964): 133–50.

31 The majority of the *Liberata's* editors have mistakenly wished to refer the "egli" of verse 5 of octave 46 back to the "primo Vero" of verse 2; all third-person singular pronouns, as well as the "signor sommo e sovrano" of octave 47, verse 2, would refer to God. But these, in fact, refer to Peter the Hermit. The editors' confusion stems from the vagueness of a passage which seems to elide Tasso's God and the instrument of His revelation. It is Peter who has made the Magus see the light and who, only fifteen octaves earlier, tells Carlo and Ubaldo that he has prophesied their arrival to the Magus. Later in the poem (17, 88–89), the Magus disclaims any prophetic knowledge of his own and declares his dependency upon Peter the Hermit. See the annotations in the editions of Maier, p. 480; Anna Maria Carini (Milan, 1961), p. 328; and Lanfranco Caretti (Bari, 1961), p. 461.

32 Cicero *De re publica* 6.16–26.

33 The key texts for the Neoplatonic theory of love in the Renaissance are the *De amore* of Marsilio Ficino, the *Dialoghi d'amore* of Leone Ebreo, *Gli asolani* of Pietro Bembo, and the speech of the character Bembo in the fourth book of Castiglione's *Il cortegiano*. Some minor treatises are collected by Giuseppe Zonta in *Trattati d'amore del cinquecento* (Bari, 1912). Tasso's own *Conclusioni amorose* are permeated by Neoplatonic conceits, as Mazzali's excellent notes demonstrate (see the *Prose*, pp. 296–302). See also John Charles Nelson, *Renaissance Theory of Love: The Context of the Eroici Furori* (New York, 1958).

34 See Greene, *Descent from Heaven*, pp. 192-202, for a discussion of Tasso's attempt to elevate his God in the description of Michael's descent in canto 9. Murrin, *The Allegorical Epic*, pp. 121–27, describes how Tasso's Platonic epistemology produces an "opaque allegory."

35 *Prose*, p. 357.

36 Letter (79) to Scipione Gonzaga, June 15, 1576. *Le lettere,* 1: 195.

37 *Prose,* p. 367.

38 Ibid., p. 368.

39 Letter (80) to Scipione Gonzaga, June 23, 1576. *Le lettere,* 1: 197.

40 Letter (57) to Luca Scalabrino, March 12, 1576. *Le lettere,* 1: 136 (see Greene, *Descent from Heaven,* pp. 207–08): "But actually his poem's historicity counts for little; in this respect the romance tradition proved too strong. The great weakness of second-rate literary epic ever since Apollonius Rhodius was that it cut itself off from history and became a closed system, relevant to nothing but itself. . . . Tasso tried much harder to be historic and failed. When his poem succeeds, it succeeds through the intensity of his imagination, unaware of the vacuum in which it is working."

41 See Durling, *Figure of the Poet,* p. 195; "What is at stake for Tasso, in his struggle with the problem of the truth of poetry, is ultimately the claims of the individual poet's subjectivity against the massive institutionalization and formulation of doctrine that was then taking place in Italy." My argument is particularly indebted to Durling's chapter on Tasso, pp. 182–210, which discusses Tasso's ambivalence toward the idea of divine poetic inspiration.

42 See Eugenio Garin, *Italian Humanism,* pp 1–4 and, for Tasso's own period, pp. 170–82. See also the essay of Paul Oskar Kristeller, "The Moral Thought of Renaissance Humanism," in his *Renaissance Thought II: Papers on Humanism and the Arts* (New York, Evanston, and London, 1965), pp. 20–68.

43 *Opere di Torquato Tasso* (1821–32), 24:vii.

44 See Murrin, *The Allegorical Epic,* p. 120. For a view of the duel between Tancredi and Argante as a kind of *psychomachia,* see Fredi Chiappelli, "Una possibile scomposizione di fonti in due personaggi della *Gerusalemme liberata,"* *Etudes de Lettres* IV, 1, no. 2-3 (1978): 49–58.

45 For a discussion of Goffredo's dilemma, see Dante della Terza, *Forma e memoria: Saggi e ricerche sulla tradizione letteraria da Dante a Vico* (Rome, 1979), pp. 7–9.

46 *Opere di Torquato Tasso* (1821–32), 24:ix.

47 Hrabanus Maurus *On the Universe* 11.19, *PL* 111.328.

48 This point is also made by Andrew Fichter in "Tasso's Epic of Deliverance," *PMLA* 93 (1978): 265–74, p. 273.

49 For the theme of narcissism, see Giamatti, *The Earthly Paradise,* pp. 203–05.

50 Armida's quotation of Luke is foreshadowed earlier in canto 16 when she pleads with Rinaldo to take her with him back to the Christian camp, even as his bondservant: "mostrando me sprezzata ancella a dito" (16.48.8). Greene, (*Descent from Heaven,* pp. 209–11), discusses the hierarchy of the Christian army in terms of a Platonic ladder. The trio of Goffredo, Rinaldo, and Armida suggests the tripartite structure of the Platonic soul, which is only balanced when reason governs the spirited part, and both, in turn, govern the concupiscent appetite.

51 The best surveys of the complex history of the critical debate over the *Liberata* are contained in Bernard Weinberg, *A History of Literary Criticism in the Italian Renaissance* (Chicago and London, 1961), 2:954–1073, and Eugenio Donadoni, *Torquato Tasso* (Florence, 1921), 2:7–53. My discussion of the *Conquistata* is indebted to Donadoni's three fine chapters in the same volume, pp. 98–171. See also C. P. Brand, *Torquato Tasso* (Cambridge, 1965), pp. 119–32. Giovanni Getto, *Interpretazione del Tasso* (Naples, 1951), pp. 419–74.

52 Tasso uses Dante in order to correct the opinion of Plato, for whom the rivers of the Underworld were instruments of a temporary purgation, a way station for the soul on its journey to the stars. Tasso insists upon the eternity of damnation: "Ne si ponno purgar le colpe, e l'opre / d'alma crudel ch'irriti eterno sdegno" (12.30).

53 All citations from the *Gerusalemme conquistata* are taken from the edition of Luigi Bonfigli (Bari, 1934), 2 vols.

54 *Del giudizio sovra la Gerusalemme*, in *Opere di Torquato Tasso* (1821-32), 12:284.

55 Origen *Homilies on Genesis* 1.2, *PG* 12.148.

56 Ibid.

57 Augustine *On Genesis according to the Letter* (unfinished) 8. *PL* 34.232.

58 Giovanni Pico della Mirandola *Heptaplus* 5.2. *De hominis dignitate, heptaplus, de ente et uno e scritti vari*, ed. Eugenio Garin (Florence, 1942), 292–95.

59 Thomas P. Roche, Jr., *The Kindly Flame*, pp. 40–43, has argued that Tasso's allegorization of Jerusalem as a figure of civic felicity in the *Liberata* posited a third term between Augustine's two cities. By the *Conquistata*, that middle ground seems to have become untenable.

60 Citations from the *Comedy* are taken from *La Divina Commedia di Dante Alighieri*, ed. C. H. Grandgent (Boston, 1933). For the purely figurative nature of the fiction of the *Paradiso*, see John Freccero, "*Paradiso* X: The Dance of the Stars," *Dante Studies* 86 (1968): 85–111; Marguerite Mills Chiarenza, "The Imageless Vision and Dante's *Paradiso*," *Dante Studies* 90 (1972): 77–91.

61 *Del giudizio*, p. 292.

62 Ibid.

63 For the symbolism of the tree of life and its coupling with the waters of baptism, see Jean Daniélou, *Primitive Christian Symbols*, trans. Donald Attwater (London, 1964), pp. 29–40, 48–57.

64 See Paul A. Underwood, "The Fountain of Life in Manuscripts of the Gospels," in *Dumbarton Oaks Papers V* (Cambridge, Mass., 1950), pp. 43–138.

65 *Del giudizio*, p. 277. See the *Opuscules de Saint Thomas d'Aquin*, Latin text with a French translation by Védrine, Bandel, and Fournet (Paris, 1856–58), 6: 462–83.

66 *Del giudizio*, p. 277.

67 Ibid.

68 Ibid., p. 278.

69 Ibid., p. 279.

70 Ibid.

71 Freccero, "The River of Death."

72 *Dante con l'espositione di M. Bernardino Daniello da Lucca* (Venice, 1568), p. **241**
20. Tasso's note to the "fiumana" of *Inferno* 2. 108 is "La quale non rende
tributo al mare." *Postille di Torquato Tasso alla Divina Commedia di Dante
Alighieri,* ed. Luigi Maria Rezzi (Pisa, 1831), p. 97.

73 Durling plots out a similar movement in Tasso's career; see *Figure of the
Poet,* p. 200 and p. 264, n. 43.

74 Eugenio Donato, in "Tesauro's Poetics: Through the Looking Glass,"
MLN 78 (1963): 15–20, argues that the baroque metaphor grows out of an
epistemological crisis in which the Book of Nature, while perhaps legible
in itself, ceased to possess a legible link to its divine Author: this is the
situation discovered by Tasso's Magus. For Tasso and the beginning of
baroque poetics, see Ulrich Leo, *Torquato Tasso: Studien zur Vorgeschichte
des Secentismo* (Bern, 1951), especially pp. 151–62.

CHAPTER 5

1 *La Galliade ou De la révolution des arts et des sciences* (Paris, 1582), dedicatory
sonnet 8 to the Duc d'Alençon.

2 The sonnet is analyzed by D. P. Walker in *The Ancient Theology* (London,
1972), pp. 84 ff. See also the studies of François Secret, *L'Esoterisme de Guy
Le Fèvre de La Boderie* (Geneva, 1969) and *Les Kabbalistes chrétiens de la
Renaissance* (Paris, 1964).

3 See Werner Goez, *Translatio imperii* (Tübingen, 1958). For *translatio studii,*
see Etienne Gilson, *Les Idées et les lettres* (Paris, 1955), pp. 183–89. Empire
historically follows the course of the sun. Dante describes Constantine
turning the history of empire "contro al corso del ciel" by founding his
eastern capital in Byzantium (*Paradiso* 6. 1–3). Henry David Thoreau's
essay *Walking* is a much later text that rings new changes on many of the
themes of the present chapter. Thoreau calls the sun "the Great Western
Pioneer whom the nations follow." Thoreau notes the association of the
west with the terrestrial paradise and concludes his essay by describing
his walk into the western sunset as the prefiguration of an apocalyptic
enlightenment. Of particular interest to my study is the following passage: "The West is preparing to add its fables to those of the East. The
valleys of the Ganges, the Nile, and the Rhine having yielded their crop, it
remains to be seen what the valleys of the Amazon, the Plate, the
Orinoco, the St. Lawrence, and the Mississippi will produce." See vol. 5,
Excursions and Poems, in *The Writings of Henry David Thoreau* (Boston and
New York, 1906), p. 233. I am grateful to Gordon Braden for bringing my
attention to this passage.

4 *La Galliade,* p. 69. This passage is cited by Claude-Gilbert Dubois in *Mythe
et langage au seizième siècle* (Bordeaux, 1970), pp. 90–91.

5 Columbus, *Four Voyages to the New World,* trans. and ed. R. H. Major (1847;

New York, 1961), pp. 137–38. The Spanish text of Columbus's letters is included at the bottom of the page.

6 Ibid., pp. 141–42.

7 See the cartographical evidence advanced by Roberto Levillier in his controversial study of the voyages of Amerigo Vespucci, *America la bien llamada* (Buenos Aires, 1948), 2: 3–51, 83–161.

8 For a description of de Quiros's Jordan, see *The Voyages of Pedro Fernandez de Quiros*, trans. and ed. Sir Clements Markham (London, 1904), 1: 271.

9 For a seventeenth-century discussion of the flux and reflux of the Thames, see Athanasius Kircher, *Mundus subterraneus*, pp. 140–41.

10 All quotations are taken from vol. 2 of Giovanni Gentile's edition of Bruno's *Opere italiane* (Bari, 1927).

11 Bruno's synthesis of various strains of Renaissance occult thought is the subject of Frances A. Yates, *Giordano Bruno*: "Bruno's truth is neither orthodox Catholic nor orthodox Protestant truth; it is Egyptian truth, magical truth" (p. 239). My chapter is indebted to the discussion of Bruno's thought in A. Corsano, *Il pensiero di Giordano Bruno nel suo svolgimento storico* (Florence, 1940).

12 See *De l'infinito, universo e mondi* in *Opere italiane*, 1: 267–418, and an English translation and commentary in Dorothy Waley Singer, *Giordano Bruno: His Life and Thought* (New York, 1950). See also Sidney Greenberg, *The Infinite in Giordano Bruno* (New York, 1950), which contains a translation of the *De la causa, principio, e uno*; Alexander Koyré, *From the Closed World to the Infinite Universe* (1957; Baltimore and London, 1968), pp. 39–54; Paul Henri Michel, *The Cosmology of Giordano Bruno*, trans. R. E. W. Maddison (Paris, London, and Ithaca, 1973).

13 See Dietrich Mahnke, *Unendliche Sphäre und Allmittelpunkt* (Halle, 1937), pp. 49–59; Yates, *Giordano Bruno*, p. 247. For the relationship of matter and spirit in Bruno's thought, see Michel, *Cosmology of Giordano Bruno*, pp. 108–53, and Gerardo Fraccari, *G. Bruno* (Milan, 1951), pp. 119–76.

14 Yates, *Giordano Bruno*, pp. 287–90.

15 See Nelson, *Renaissance Theory of Love*, pp. 15–66. For a list of some of the notable sixteenth-century commentaries on Petrarch's *Canzoniere*, see William J. Kennedy, *Rhetorical Norms in Renaissance Literature* (New Haven and London, 1978), pp. 201–02, n. 5.

16 Corsano, *Il pensiero*, p. 220.

17 There is an excellent discussion of Bruno's poetics by Giancarlo Maiorino in "The Breaking of the Circle: Giordano Bruno and the Poetics of Immeasurable Abundance," *JHI* 38 (1977): 317-27. See also the brief but pertinent remarks of Rosalie Colie in *The Resources of Kind: Genre-Theory in the Renaissance* (Berkeley, 1973), pp. 108-11. Giorgio Bárberi-Squarotti discusses Bruno's rejection of Petrarchism in "Per una descrizione e interpretazione della poetica di Giordano Bruno," *Studi Secenteschi* 1 (1961):39-59.

18 On this passage, see Corsano, *Il pensiero*, p. 225; Yates, *Giordano Bruno*, p. 277.

19 Cassirer, *The Individual and the Cosmos*, pp. 123–91; on Bruno, pp. 187–91, 97–98.

20 Helene Védreme, in *La Conception de la nature chez Giordano Bruno* (Paris, 1967), pp. 112–14, draws attention to the sense of pain that can be felt in Bruno's description of the destruction of the individual nature, even though he has little use for the individual as such. Her reading of the *Gli eroici furori* is unusually dark and pessimistic.

21 Here, too, the Tree and Well of Life figure the sacraments of the eucharist and of baptism. Spenser could not have known the *Conquistata*, published in 1593, during his composition of the first three books of the *Faerie Queene*. There are, however, remarkable similarities between the two poems: Goffredo's and Redcrosse's respective visions of the New Jerusalem; the witches Armida and Duessa, who are both types of the Whore of Babylon; Spenser's Eden and Clorinda's dream. Both authors are turning to the Book of Revelation for their inspiration.

22 See Thomas P. Roche, *The Kindly Flame*, pp. 104–06, and John Erskine Hankins, *Source and Meaning in Spenser's Allegory: A Study of The Faerie Queene* (Oxford, 1971), p. 279.

23 For the argument that the false Una is the first manifestation of Duessa, see James Nohrnberg's magisterial study, *The Analogy of the Faerie Queene* (Princeton, 1976), pp. 115 ff.

24 *Mondo creato* 7, vv. 670 ff. For the text of the *Mondo creato* cited here and below, see Tasso's *Opere*, ed. Maier, 4: 9–323.

25 All citations of Milton's poetry are taken from *The Poems of John Milton*, ed. John Carey and Alastair Fowler (London and New York, 1968).

26 Augustine *On Genesis according to the Letter* 5. 7, *PL* 34. 330.

27 Philo *Questions and Answers on Genesis* 1. 12. Josephus, *Jewish Antiquities*.

28 *On Genesis according to the Letter* 8. 7, *PL* 34. 378.

29 See Bede *On the Six Days of Creation*, *PL* 93.22; Hrabanus Maurus, *Commentary on Genesis* 1. 11, *PL* 107.473.

30 See Paul A. Underwood, "The Fountain of Life," pp. 47 ff.; Ernst Schlee, *Die Ikonographie der Paradiesesflüsse* (Leipzig, 1937), pp. 28–36, 153–69. Schlee also discusses an earlier tradition, beginning with Philo, which allegorized the four rivers as the four cardinal virtues. The use of this tradition in the *Purgatorio* is discussed by Charles Singleton in *Dante Studies 2: Journey to Beatrice* (Cambridge, Mass., 1967), pp. 158–78.

31 See W. v. Reybekiel, "Der 'Fons vitae' in der christlichen Kunst," *Niederdeutsche Zeitschrift für Volkskunde* 12 (1934): 87–136. For the bleeding cross, see pp. 125–33.

32 See plates 3 and 8 in Konrad Miller, *Mappemundi II* (Stuttgart, 1895), and the plates opposite pages 119 and 126 in Lloyd A. Brown, *The Story of Maps* (Boston, 1949). Joseph Duncan, in *Milton's Earthly Paradise: A Historical Study of Eden* (Minneapolis, 1972), pp. 211–12, cites the opinion of the Swiss divine Johann Heidegger (1667) that the river which flows through Eden in Genesis 2:10 is the Jordan.

33 *Gerusalemme Conquistata* 12. 14–15. The rivers in question are the Nile, Ganges, Tigris, and Euphrates. Josephus, in the *Jewish Antiquities* 1. 40–41, identified the Geon as the Nile and the Phison as the Ganges; his reading became a commonplace. For the Gregory of Nyssa passage, see chapter 3, page 72 and n. 24.

34 The mosaics in churches of SS. Cosma e Damiano (6th-century), S. Prassede (9th-century), and S. Giovanni in Laterano (13th-century) depict the Jordan flowing across the base of the apsidal half-dome. The curve of the dome may suggest the Jordan's oceanic circularity. In SS. Cosma e Damiano, directly under the title identifying the stream as the Jordan, stands the Lamb of God, beneath whose feet spring the four rivers of Paradise. The iconographic pattern is repeated almost exactly in S. Prassede, except that the Jordan, which flowed behind the figures of saints and apostles in SS. Cosmo e Damiano, now lies beneath their feet, and its waters are located immediately above the Lamb and the four rivers. In S. Giovanni in Laterano, by contrast, the four rivers flow from the cross itself, and they lie above the Jordan, which flows across the bottom of the mosaic. Whereas in SS. Cosma e Damiano and S. Prassede the coupling of the motifs might suggest that the four rivers flow out of the Jordan, in S. Giovanni the rivers appear to flow back into the Jordan's stream. See Marguerite van Berchem and Etienne Clouzot, *Mosaïques chrétiennes du IVme au Xme siècle* (Geneva, 1924), pp. 118–24, on SS. Cosma e Damiano; pp. 226–40 on S. Prassede. For the original design of the S. Giovanni in Laterano mosaic, which was reset in 1875–85, see Agostino Valentini, *La patriarcale basilica lateranense* (Rome, 1837), vol. 2, table 30. It should be noted that the little river-gods, Jor and Dan, which are now visible in the mosaic, do not appear in Valentini's drawing.

35 Hankins, *Source and Meaning*, p. 117. See Hankins's general treatment of Spenser and the Book of Revelation, pp. 99–119.

36 A. S. P. Woodhouse, in a seminal and controversial essay, "Nature and Grace in the *Faerie Queene*," *ELH* 16 (1949): 194–228, argued for a more Calvinist Spenser by understanding Book 1 to deal with man's action in the state of grace, while the rest of the *Faerie Queene* deals with man in the fallen world of nature. Woodhouse argues that Spenser did not live to depict a synthesis between the orders of grace and nature which would have centered around the figure of Prince Arthur. I think that such a synthesis emerges in the poem when it contemplates Elizabeth and her reign as a manifestation of divine grace.

37 All citations from Spenser's poetry are taken from the *Poetical Works*, ed. J. C. Smith and E. de Selincourt (London, Oxford, and New York, 1970).

38 Hankins, *Source and Meaning*, p. 107; Nohrnberg, *Analogy of the Faerie Queene*, p. 171. See also Sylvia Barack Fishman, "The Watered Garden and the Bride of God: Patterns of Biblical Imagery in Poems of Spenser, Milton, and Blake," Ph.D. diss., Washington University, 1980, pp. 63–90.

39 *The Book of Common Prayer*, ed. John E. Booty (Charlottesville, 1976), p. 297.

40 *Spenser's Prose Works*, ed. Rudolf Gottfried, in *The Works of Edmund Spenser: A Variorum Edition*, ed. Greenlaw, Osgood, Padelford, and Heffner (Baltimore, 1949), 10: 17.

41 For the history of Spenser's river marriage and its relationship to Camden's *De connubio*, see Jack B. Oruch, "Spenser, Camden, and the Poetic Marriages of Rivers," *SP* (1967): 606–24. A good discussion of the Thames

and Medway episode is contained in Roche, pp. 167–84. Spenser's
treatment of the epic catalogue convention is the subject of Gordon
Braden, "riverrun: An Epic Catalogue in *The Faerie Queene*," *ELR* 4 (1973):
258–67. Alastair Fowler discusses the numerical structure of the episode
in *Spenser and the Numbers of Time* (New York, 1964), pp. 182–96. See also
A. B. Giamatti, *Play of Double Senses: Spenser's Faerie Queene* (Englewood
Cliffs, N.J. 1975), pp. 130–33; Rosemary Freeman, *The Faerie Queene: A
Companion for Readers* (London, 1970), pp. 250–59; Harry Berger, Jr., "Two
Spenserian Retrospects: The Antique Temple of Venus and the Primitive
Marriage of Rivers," *Texas Studies in Literature and Language* 10 (1968): 5–25.

42   Camden, *Brittania* (London, 1600), p. 338.
43   Josephus *Jewish Antiquities* 1. 177. Jerome *Book of Hebrew Questions on
     Genesis* 14. 14, *PL* 23.961.
44   Camden, *Brittania* (London, 1590), p. 282.
45   *Fairie Queene*, IV.xi.20–21. See n. 33 above.
46   *Ruines of Rome* 4.v8.
47   For the gigantomachy as an image of human pride and achievement
     brought to nought, see F. Joukovsky-Micha, "La Guerre des dieux et des
     géants chez les poètes franćais du XVIe Siècle (1500–1585)," *BHR* 29 (1967):
     55–92.
48   See Fishman, "The Watered Garden, pp. 159–81, and, for the Garden of
     Adonis as another version of the enclosed garden of the Song of Songs,
     pp. 111–14. The garden of canticles was frequently associated with Mary
     and contrasted in iconography with Eden: the Eden lost through sin is
     recovered through Mary, who carries the fountain of grace—and dew—in
     her womb. See Stanley Stewart, *The Enclosed Garden: The Tradition and the
     Image in Seventeenth-Century Poetry* (Madison, Milwaukee, and London,
     1966), pp. 38 ff. In the Geneva Bible (1560), the marginal gloss to Song of
     Songs 5:1 makes of the garden an apocalyptic Eden: "The garden
     signifieth the kingdome of Christ where he prepareth the banket for his
     elect. . . ." It is worth recalling that one of Spenser's lost works is a
     translation of the Song of Songs.
49   Roche, *The Kindly Flame*, p. 178, comments: " . . . all Spenser's river
     marriages—with differing emphasis, are myths about love in a fallen
     world. The pattern is the same: Eden—the Fall—love in marriage. Spen-
     ser is trying to show that the only way to retain the vestiges of our pre-fall
     Eden is through the union of lovers, of friends, of rivers." See Nohrnberg,
     Analogy of the Faerie Queene, p. 562, for the analogy between the Garden of
     Adonis and the Marriage of Thames and Medway as matrices of material
     creation, and pp. 579–86, on the physical allegory of the Hall of Proteus.
50   The Blatant Beast is one manifestation of the dragon-Satan of Revelation
     12:9 and 20:2–10, chained and then released again into the world (see
     Nohrnberg, *Analogy of the Faerie Queene*, pp. 695 ff). The Greek word
     diabolos means "calumniator" in its original form, and Renaissance hu-
     manists were aware of the particularly satanic connotations of calumny.
     See M. A. Screech, *Rabelais* (Ithaca, N.Y., 1979), p. 117.
51   See Giangiorgio Trissino, *La quinta e sesta divisione della Poetica del Trissino*
     (1562; Munich, 1969), p. 5 verso; Giovanni Antonio Viperano, *De poetica*

libri tres (1579; Munich, 1967), p. 25. The idea that the first forms of poetry were praise and blame comes from Averroes's commentary on Aristotle's *Poetics*, the first form in which the *Poetics* reached Medieval and Renaissance readers. See O. B. Hardison, Jr., *The Enduring Monument: A Study of the Idea of Praise in Renaissance Literary Theory and Practice* (Chapel Hill, N.C., 1962), pp. 34–39.

52 My remarks on the *Mutabilitie Cantos* are heavily indebted to Nohrnberg, *Analogy of the Faerie Queene* pp. 735–77, to his argument that this fragment puts an end to the "technique of Spenser's allegory." See the appreciative review of this argument by Kitty Scoular Datta in *RenQ* 31 (1978): 647–49. Her comments coincide with my own view that the disruption of allegory in the *Mutabilitie Cantos* is precipitated by its loss of a historical basis. For Nohrnberg (p. 777) the "breaking of the spell of the poem can be taken as evidence for a decisive separation of the 'mind' behind the contemplative subject in the poem, from its union with the 'nature' behind the contemplated object; at such a juncture nature recedes into the wholly other or purely objective, and the mind is left wholly self-possessed or purely subjective." This separation may become imperative when the subjective poetic mind is no longer able to locate itself historically and is in danger of being overwhelmed by its infinite and undifferentiated object. In playing the Neoplatonic game of participation and withdrawal, Spenser might find himself unable to make it back: he does not share Bruno's enthusiastic desire to annihilate his own individuality in the contemplation of the One.

53 See Sherman Hawkins, "Mutabilitie and the Cycle of the Months," in William Nelson, ed., *Form and Convention in the Poetry of Edmund Spenser* (New York and London, 1961), pp. 76–102. For readings of the *Mutabilitie Cantos*, see Thomas M. Greene, *Descent from Heaven*, pp. 311–35; Lewis J. Owen, "Mutable in Eternity: Spenser's Despair and the Multiple Forms of Mutabilitie," *JMRS* 2 (1972): 49–68; Patricia Parker, *Inescapable Romance*, pp. 54–64.

54 See Oliver Elton, *Modern Studies* (London, 1907), pp. 33–34. The *Mutabilitie Cantos* have often been related to Bruno's *Spaccio della bestia trionfante*. For parallels and the possibility of influence between Bruno and Spenser, see also Ronald Levinson, "Spenser and Bruno," *PMLA* 43 (1928): 675–81; Nohrnberg, *Analogy of the Faerie Queene*, p. 751.

55 See A. C. Hamilton, "Our New Poet: Spenser, Well of English Undefyld," in J. Kennedy and J. Reither, eds., *A Theater for Spenserians* (Toronto, 1973), p. 110; Nohrnberg, *Analogy of the Faerie Queene*, p. 163; Parker, *Inescapable Romance*, pp. 78–79.

CHAPTER 6

1 All quotations from the Rabelaisian books are taken from the *Oeuvres complètes*, ed. Pierre Jourda, 2 vols. (Paris, 1962).

2 *The Book of Enoch,* ed. R. H. Charles (Oxford, 1893), pp. 65–66. Erasmus refers to this tradition in *The Praise of Folly:* "Ut igitur inter mortales, ii longisissime absunt a felicitate, qui sapientiae student, nimirum hoc ipso bis stulti, quod homines nati cum sint, tamen obliti conditionis suae Deorum immortalium vitam affectant, et Gigantum exemplo, disciplinarum machinis, naturae bellum inferunt" *Ausgewählte Schriften,* 2: 78.

3 See Françoise Joukovsky-Micha, "La Guerre des dieux et des géants." See also Erasmus on the adage "Gigantum arrogantia," in the *Adagia* 3.10.93, in Erasmus, *Opera omnia* (Louvain, 1703), 2: 948–49.

4 Josephus *Jewish Antiquities* 1. 113–21.

5 *Inferno* 31.67–96. See also Ambrose *Concerning Noah and the Ark* 34; *PL* 14.436.

6 "Et per linguas divise sunt gentes disperseque per terras: que tandem in unitatem fidei ab apostolis variis linguis loquentibus congregate sunt. Hanc aūt Nembroth gigantomachiam et turris erectionem pulchre describit Ovidius montes siquidem montibus gigantes composuisse voluit." *P. Ouidij Nasonis Metamorphoses libri moralizati cum pulcherrimis fabularum principalium figuris* (Lyons, 1510), p. xiii verso. On Lavinius, see Judson Allen, *The Friar as Critic: Literary Attitudes in the Middle Ages* (Nashville, 1971), pp. 81–83.

7 For another literary conflation of Babel and the classical myth of giants that follows Lavinius, see the *Microcosme* (1562) of Maurice Scève, book 2, pp. 1227–1346. It may be possible to see the same typology operating in the device of the androgyne which Gargantua wears on his hat in *Gargantua* 8. In the myth related by Aristophanes in the *Symposium* (190B–C), the original Androgynes are identical to the Aloides who tried to assault the heavens. For this transgression they were split in two, and as human beings seek to find their other halves. Here, then, may be another version of the diaspora of Babel, which is counteracted in human history by the charity enjoined by the Pauline motto on Gargantua's device and— in what is a peculiarly Rabelaisian emphasis—by marriage and the propagation of children which moves that history forward toward its conclusion. The comic obscenity of the device may thus contain an element of apocalyptic promise. See in this light, Jerome Schwartz, "Scatology and Eschatology in Gargantua's Androgyne Device," *ER* 14 (1977): 265–75. I am grateful to Carla Freccero for pointing out to me the Babelic overtones of Plato's myth.

8 For the religious language of this paragraph and of the letter, see Gilson, *Les Idées et les lettres,* pp. 232–36, and see now the important study of Dennis Costa, *Irenic Apocalypse: Some Uses of Apocalyptic in Dante, Petrarch and Rabelais,* Stanford French and Italian Studies 21 (Saratoga, N.Y., 1981), pp. 125–26. My own thinking on Rabelais has been greatly stimulated by Costa's work. Abel Lefranc, in the introduction to his edition of the *Pantagruel* (Paris, 1922), proposed the view of Rabelais as an unbeliever and prompted the response of Lucien Febvre in his magisterial study, *Le Problème de l'incroyance au XVIe siècle: La religion de Rabelais* (1942; Paris, 1968). For Febvre's discussion of Gargantua's letter, see pp. 163–94. For

ironic readings of the letters, see Gerard J. Brault, " 'Ung Abyme de Science': On the Interpretation of Gargantua's letter to Pantagruel," *BHR* 28 (1966): 615–32, and, for a more scholarly treatment, Gerard Defaux, *Pantagruel et les sophistes: Contribution à l'histoire de l'humanisme chrétein au XVIe siècle* (The Hague, 1973), pp. 59–68. For an excellent discussion which focuses upon the praise of marriage in the letter, see Emile V. Telle, "A propos de la Lettre de Gargantua à son fils," *BHR* 19 (1957): 208–33. See also M. A. Screech, *The Rabelaisian Marriage: Aspects of Rabelais's Religion, Ethics and Comic Philosophy* (London, 1958), pp. 14–27.

9   Pliny, *Natural History* 19.1. For Rabelais's possible debt to the *Linelaeon* of Celio Calcagnini, see Screech, *Rabelais,* pp. 289–90.

10 For Rabelais and the Age of Navigation, see Arthur Tilley, "Rabelais and Geographical Discovery," *Modern Language Review* 2 (1906–07): 316–26; 3 (1908): 209-17.

11 Columbus, *Four Voyages to the New World,* p. 148.

12 Ibid., pp. 196–98. Columbus had his friend Fray Gaspar Gorricio compile a "Libro de las Profecias"; it assembled various prophetic and apocalyptic passages from the Bible that seemed to predict his discoveries. It was published by Cesare de Lollis in the *Raccolti di documenti e studi pubblicati dalla R. Commissione Colombiana pel quarto centenario della scoperta dell' America* (Rome, 1894), pt. 1, vol. 2, pp. 75–160.

13 Joachim of Fiore is mentioned in Columbus's "Libro de las profecias," in the *Raccolta* 1.2.83. On the influence of Joachimite thought upon the interpreters of the Age of Discovery, see Marjorie Reeves, *The Influence of Prophecy in the Later Middle Ages* (Oxford, 1969), pp. 269–76, and *Joachim of Fiore and the Prophetic Future* (London, 1976), pp. 126–135. For the link between apocalypticism and the idea of scientific and technological progress, see Ernest Lee Tuveson, *Millennium and Utopia: A Study in the Background of the Idea of Progress* (Berkeley and Los Angeles, 1949). On Egidio da Viterbo and the New World discoveries, see John W. O'Malley, "The Discovery of America and Reform Thought at the Papal Court in the Early Cinquecento," in Fredi Chiappelli, ed., *First Images of America* (Berkeley, Los Angeles, and London, 1976), 1: 185–200. On Postel, see William Bouswma, *Concordia Mundi: The Career and Thought of Guillaume Postel* (Cambridge, 1957), pp. 208–12, 271–73. Despite Postel's denunciation of Rabelais, the two clearly shared in a Joachimite tradition of thought on the Church. As a Franciscan, Rabelais would presumably have been exposed to this tradition, although it is not discussed by A. J. Krailsheimer in his fine study of Rabelais's intellectual milieu, *Rabelais and the Franciscans* (Oxford, 1963). Thomas M. Greene suggests the influence of Joachimite ideas on the fiction of the Abbey of Theleme in *Rabelais: A Study in Comic Courage* (Englewood Cliffs, N.J., 1970), pp. 56–58. See also the remarks of Costa, pp. 123–24.

14 Phelan, *The Millennial Kingdom of the Franciscans in the New World: A Study of the Writings of Gerónimo de Mendieta (1525–1604)* (Berkeley and Los Angeles, 1970), p. 18.

15 For quite a different version of the new Renaissance technology and

discoveries leading to an assault on the heavens, see the *De vita propria* of
Girolamo Cardano, translated by Jean Stoner as *The Book of My Life* (1930;
New York, 1962), pp. 189–90 (chap. 41):

> "On the one hand we explore America—I now refer to the part peculiarly
> designated by that name—Brazil, a great part of which was before unknown,
> Terra del Fuego, Patagonia, Peru, Charcas, Parana, Acutia, Caribana, Picora,
> New Spain, Quito, of Quinira the more western part, New France and regions
> more to the south of this toward Florida, Cortereal, Estotilant, and Marata.
> Besides all these, toward the East under the Antarctic we find the Antiscians
> somewhat like Scythians, and some Northern peoples not yet known, as well
> as Japan. Binarchia, the Amazonas, and a region which is beyond the Island of
> the Demons, if these be not fabled islands—all discoveries sure to give rise to
> great and calamitous events in order that a just distribution of them may be
> maintained.
>
> The conviction grows that, as a result of these discoveries, the fine arts
> will be neglected and but lightly esteemed, and certainties will be exchanged
> for uncertainties. These things may be true sometime or other, but meanwhile
> we shall rejoice as in a flower-filled meadow. For what is more amazing than
> pyrotechnics? Or than the fiery bolts man has invented so much more
> destructive than the lightning of the gods?
>
> Nor of thee, O Great Compass, will I be silent, for thou dost guide us over
> boundless seas, through gloomy nights, through the wild storms seafarers
> dread, and through the pathless wilderness.
>
> The fourth marvel is the invention of the typographic art, a work of man's
> hands, and the discovery of his wit—a rival, forsooth, of the wonders
> wrought by divine intelligence. What lack we yet unless it be the taking of
> Heaven by storm! Oh, the madness of men to give heed to vanity rather than
> the fundamental things of life! Oh, what arrogant poverty of intellectual
> humility not to be moved to wonder!"

In book 6 of the *Os lusíadas*, Luís de Camões implicitly compares the
Portuguese navigators of the Age of Discovery both to the builders of the
tower of Babel (74) and to the aspiring Titans of the classical gigantomachy (78).

16 "Tale enim quiddem videtur dicere dominus, Praedixerunt prophetae
Christum futurum desiderium & expectationem gentium, peccatorum
miserorum, & maxime afflictorum hominum, itaque huiusmodi in ad-
ventu & revelatione Messiae magno cum ardore ad regnum dei ceu
rapiendum, non tantum recipiendum acceleraturos. Nam Michaes ex
Isaiae imitatione, Futurum est, inquit, in novissimo dierum, & erit mons
domus domini praeparatus in vertice montium, elevabiturque ipse supra
vertices, & confluent ad eum populi. Ibunt gentes multae, & dicent,
Venite & ascendamus in montem domini, & ad domum dei Iacobi, &c.
Caeterum novistis a diebum Ioannis Baptisatae, id est, ad eo tempore quo
is Christum praedicare coepit, peccatores, publicanos, milites, meretri-
ces, Ethnicos, & calamitossimos quosque seu acie instructa, ac impetu
quodam facto, irruere & evangelicam gratiam diripere, id est, avidissime
haurire. Hoc enim ipsi etiam pharisaei ac scribae testantur, subinde
indignantes liberum ad Christum & publicanis & peccatoribus aditum

patere. His iam inferendum erit. Agnoscat itaque totus mundus Iesum esse Christum, nec alium porrò expectandum Messiam: illa item tempora in quibus haec proponebat Christus ipsissima esse Messiae tempora, & in his oriri regnum dei, quod per temporum successionem & apostolorum praedicationem per totum terrae orbem est propagatum." Bullinger, *In sacrosanctam Jesu Christi Domini nostri Evangelium secundum Matthaeum, Commentarium libri XII* (Zurich, 1542), p. 111 verso.

17 Cornelius a Lapide, *Commentaria in Scripturam Sacram* (Paris, 1877), 15:286.

18 See M. A. Screech, "The Sense of Rabelais's *Enigme en Prophetie,*" *BHR* 18 (1956): 392–404.

19 See the essays of V. L. Saulnier on the last chapters of the *Quart Livre,* "Pantagruel au large de Gannabin ou la peur de Panurge," *BHR* 16 (1554): 58–81, and "Le Festin devant Chaneph ou la confiance dernière de Rabelais," *Mercure de France* 320 (1954): 649–66.

20 Sir Philip Sidney, *An Apology for Poetry,* ed. Forrest G. Robinson (Indianapolis and New York, 1970), p. 14.

21 "Primus parens peccator factus: & totam posteritatem peccato obnoxiam reddidit: & Cayn fratricidam genuit, cuius successio cunctis sceleribus: ac si ex sanguine peccato scilicet ortum trahens non degenerasset a radice." *Metamorphoses libri moralizati,* (see n. 6 above).

22 Augustine *Commentaries on the Psalms* 61.6:64.2; *PL* 36.733,773.

23 René Girard has offered a new antisacrificial reading of the Matthew passage in "Les Malédictions contre les Pharisiens et la révélation évangelique," *Bulletin du Centre Protestant d'Etudes* 27 (1975): 3–29. Michael Seidel extends Girard's insights to a discussion of the impure origins of the Pantagrueline genealogy in *Satiric Inheritance, Rabelais to Sterne* (Princeton, N.J., 1979), pp. 67–70.

24 *The City of God* 15.1, trans. Marcus Dods (New York, 1950), pp. 478–79, *PL* 41.437.

25 This doubleness has been discussed in different ways by recent critics of Rabelais. See François Rigolot, "Cratylisme et Pantagruélisme: Rabelais et le statut de signe," *ER* 13 (1976): 115–32; Alice Fiola Berry, "Rabelais: Homo Logos," *JMRS* 3 (1973): 51–67.

26 The Babelic overtones of chapter 9 are discussed by Cave in *The Cornucopian Text,* pp. 112–16, and by Costa, pp. 126–28; see also François Rigolot, *Les Langages de Rabelais* (Geneva, 1972), p. 36; Berry, "Rabelais: Homo Logos," p. 51. Gerard Defaux, *Pantagruel et les sophistes,* pp. 172–73, suggests the background presence of 1 Corinthians 12–14.

27 See Erasmus's gloss on "nihil sine voce est" (1 Corinthians 14:10): "Tam multa videlicet sunt linguarum genera in mundo, quorum sua cuique vox est. Ea quidem ab omnibus percipi potest, verum si nihil accedat voci, frustra uterque alteri loquimur." *Paraphrasis in Epistolam Pauli ad Corinthios priorem. Opera omnia* 7.903.

28 See the *Tiers Livre,* chaps. 3–4, 8. The praise of the codpiece plays comically on 1 Corinthians 12:22–23: "Sed multo magis quae videntur membra corporis infirmiora esse neccessariora sunt, et quae putamus

ignobiliora membra esse corporis, his honorem abundantiorem circunda-
mus, et quae inhonesta sunt nostra abundantiorem honestatem habent."
Another Rabelaisian episode which appears to be indebted to the discussion of language in 1 Corinthians is the "ringing" incoherent oration
("omnis clocha clochabilis in clocherio clochando . . .") of Janotus de
Bragmardo, seeking to have the bells ("cymbales") of Notre-Dame returned in *Gargantua* 17–19. The famous Pauline passage which Rabelais
seems to have in mind is 1 Corinthians 13:1: "Si linguis hominum loquar
et angelorum et caritatem autem non habeam, factus sum velut aes
sonans aut cymbalum tinniens."

29 Floyd Gray argues for a double reading of the prologue in "Ambiguity
and Point of View in the Prologue to *Gargantua*," *Romanic Review* 56 (1965):
12–21. Leo Spitzer, however, argues that the prologue discourages any
search for hidden meaning; see "Ancora sul prologo al Gargantua," *Studi
francesi* 27 (1965): 423–34. For D. P. Walker, the prologue announces the
presence of secret meaning, protected from the vulgar and preserved for
the religious initiate; see "Esoteric Symbolism," in G. M. Kirkwood, ed.,
*Poetry and Poetics from Ancient Greece to the Renaissance: Studies in Honor of
James Hutton* (Ithaca and London, 1975), pp. 218–32. See also Cave, *The
Cornucopian Text*, pp. 94–101; Screech, *Rabelais*, pp. 124–30; Costa, *Irenic
Apocalypse*, pp. 111–13.

30 Erasmus, *Ausgewählte Schriften*, 2:206. For Erasmus's discussions of the
Eucharist, see John B. Payne, *Erasmus: His Theology of the Sacraments*
(Richmond, Va., 1970), esp. pp. 126–54.

31 *Ausgewählte Schriften*, 2:206.

32 For readings of the *Convivium religiosum*, see Marjorie O'Rourke Boyle,
Erasmus on Language and Method, pp. 129–41; Cave, *The Cornucopian Text*,
pp. 102–11; Wayne A. Rebhorn, "Erasmian Education and the *Convivium
religiosum*," *SP* 69 (1972): 131–49.

33 For the eschatological dimension of the Sacrament, see Geoffrey
Wainwright, *Eucharist and Eschatology* (London, 1971). See also Jean
Daniélou, *The Bible and the Liturgy* (Notre Dame, Ind., 1956), pp. 152–61,
for a discussion of the typological connections between the Eucharist and
the messianic banquet of the Last Judgment.

34 *Ausgewählte Schriften*, 2:208–10.

35 The Erasmian view of the interpretative community is discussed by James
Kelsey McConica in "Erasmus and the Grammar of Consent," in *Scrinium
Erasmianum*, 2:79–99. For a modern theological discussion, see John
Wilkinson, *Interpretation and Community* (New York and London, 1963).

36 "Hodie vero cum videmus tot opinionibus dissidere philosophorum
scholas, tot dogmatibus tamque diversis digladiari Christianos omnes,
nonne referimus structuram turris Babel?" Erasmus, *Opera omnia*, 4:749.

37 "Si membrum a membro divulsum est, ubi corpus? Si corpus a capite
distractum, ubi vita corporis? Hoc nimirum est quod dicit Paulus nos
vocatos in societatem Filli Dei, quod per fidem insiti sumus illius corpori,
quod est ecclesia: ecclesia vero congregationem sonat, non divisionem.
Quoniam autem non possumus adhaerere capiti, nisi inter nos consen-

tiamus, mutuaque charitate conglutinemur, ideo dicit, *Sitis autem perfecti,* hoc est integrum corpus, neque mutilum, neque convulsum, sed solidum & coagmentatum in Christo, vinculo spiritus ejus. Male habet Paulum quod apud Corinthios hae dissidii voces, *Ego sum Pauli, ego Apollo, ego Cephiae, ego Christi.* Quid diceret, si hoc seculo audiret confusas hominum linguas, Ego sum theologus transalpinus, ego cisalpinus, ego Scotista, ego Thomista, ego Occanista, ego realis, ego nominalis, ego Parisiensis, ego Coloniensis, ego Lutheranus, ego Carolstadianus, ego Evangelicus, ego Papista. Pudet me referre caetera. O domus quam dissipata es, o civitas quam dissecta es. O corpus, ubi nunc illa felix ἑνάς extra quam quisquis est, in Christo non est?" Ibid.

38 "Quin definimus extruere turrim Babel, turrim superbiae ac dissensionis, & incipimus instaurare Hierusolymam, ac templum Domini collapsum" (ibid., 749–50). My chapter repeatedly argues for the influence of Erasmian metaphors and ideas on the fiction of Rabelais. See, in this context, Raymond Lebègue, "Rabelais, the Last of the French Erasmians," *JWCI* 12 (1949): 91–100; M. A. Screech, "Comment Rabelais a exploité les travaux d'Erasme: Quelque details," in J.-C. Margolin, ed., *Colloquia Erasmiana Turonensia* (Toronto and Buffalo), 1:453–61.

39 For commentary on this episode, see Florence Weinberg, *The Wine and the Will: Rabelais's Bacchic Christianity* (Detroit, 1972), pp. 37–44; Costa, *Irenic Apocalypse*, pp. 134–36; Cave, *The Cornucopian Text*, 116–17; Screech, *Rabelais*, pp. 410–39; Jean Guiton, "Le Mythe des paroles gelées," *Romanic Review* 31 (1940): 3–15; V. L. Saulnier, "Le Silence de Rabelais et le mythe des paroles gelées," in *François Rabelais: Ouvrage publiée pour le quatrième centenaire de sa morte (1553–1953)* (Geneva and Lille, 1953), pp. 233–47; Michel Jeanneret, "Les Paroles dégelées (Rabelais 'Quart Livre,' 48–65)," *Littérature* 17 (1975): 14–30.

40 Bernard of Clairvaux *Homilies on "Missus est Gabriel" (Lk. 1 : 26–27)* 2.7; *PL* 183.64.

41 There may also be an analogy between Rabelais's fiction and the description of the Word of God both as a bringer and thawer of ice in Psalm 147, vv. 15–18:

> Emittet eloquium suum in terram,
>   velociter currit verbum eius.
> Dat nivem sicut lanam,
>   pruinam sicut cinerem spargit.
> Proicit glaciem suam et frustula panis;
>   coram frigore eius aquae rigescunt.
> Emittit verbum suum et liquefacit eas;
>   flare iubet ventum suum et fluunt aquae.

42 Bede *Homilies* 2.11. *PL* 94.195.

43 Daniel Russell examines the range of meanings of this figure in "A Note on Panurge's 'Pusse en l'Aureille,' " *ER* 11 (1974): 81–87.

44 Weinberg, *The Wine and the Will*, pp. 41–42.

45 There is, of course, considerable scholarly controversy about the authenticity of the *Cinquième Livre*. The most recent entrants into the debate are

George A. Petrossian, who argues for the book's authenticity in "The Problem of the Authenticity of the *Cinquiesme Livre de Pantagruel:* A Quantitative Study," *ER* 13 (1976): 1–64, and, arguing *contra,* Alfred Glauser in *Le Faux Rabelais* (Paris, 1975). A thoughtful consideration of the problem is provided by John Parkin, who attempts to demonstrate the consistency of the characterization of Frère Jean in the Rabelaisian books, including the fifth one; see "Frère Jean in the *Cinquiesme Livre,*" *ER* 15 (1980): 161–78. My chapter assumes that at least the final episode of the Dive Bouteille is the authentic creation of Rabelais, and attempts to demonstrate some thematic unities in the five Rabelaisian books. I follow the example of Wayne Rebhorn in "The Burdens and Joys of Freedom: An Interpretation of the Five Books of Rabelais," *ER* 9 (1971): 71–90; Rebhorn's essay is an excellent general reading of Rabelais's works.

46 Francis MacDonald Cornford, *Plato's Cosmology: The Timaeus of Plato* (London, 1937), p. 331.

47 Ibid. See also Leonard Barkan, *Nature's Work of Art: The Human Body as Image of the World* (New Haven and London, 1975), pp. 43–44, and Walter M. Kendrick, "Earth of Flesh, Flesh of Earth: Mother Earth in the *Faerie Queene,*" *RenQ* 27 (1974): 533–44.

48 More, *Circulatio sanguinis* (1679), vv. 16–32. *Philosophical Poems of Henry More,* ed. Geoffrey Bullough (Manchester, Eng., 1931), pp. 169–70.

49 See Cave, *The Cornucopian Text,* p. 45.

50 See Weinberg, *The Wine and the Will,* pp. 79–81; George Mallory Masters, *Rabelaisian Dialectic and the Platonic-Hermetic Tradition* (Albany, N.Y., 1967), pp. 59–60. One should, however, distinguish Weinberg's scholarly and often ground-breaking study of Rabelais's Christian symbolism from Masters's occasionally insightful, but generally confused and unreliable account of the traditions of Renaissance occult philosophy.

51 See M. A. Screech's fine reading of this episode, "The Meaning of Thaumaste," *BHR* 22 (1960): 62–72.

52 Pausanias *Descriptions of Greece* IX (Boetia) 39.5–8. The initiate to the oracle of Trophonius drank from two fountains, one of forgetfulness, the other of memory. Philostratus *Life of Apollonius* 8.19.

53 See Erasmus on the adage "In antro Trophonii vaticinatus est," *Adagia* 1. 7.77, in *Opera omnia,* 2:292–94. Pausanias, 9.39.13.

54 Cicero *De legibus* II, 14.36. For Plato, the ability of the mysteries to remove the fear of death made them worthy to serve as metaphors for philosophical initiation (see *Phaedo* 67e–69). Plato's Socrates cites the proverb "There are many who bear the Thyrsus, but few are actually devotees" (69d), implying that the number of true philosophers is small. Erasmus includes this saying, "Multi Tyrsigeri, pauci Bacchi," in the *Adagia* 1.7.6 (*Opera omnia,* 2:263–64), and Rabelais alludes to it when he refers to Pantagruel and his band of companions as "Tyrsigeres" in chapter 34. A similar line of thinking leads Plato to comment in the *Cratylus* (403) upon the similarity between the names of the gods Pluto and Plutus. Both of these gods have their role in the mysteries of Eleusis: Pluto, god of death who rapes Persephone, and Plutus, god of wealth and son of Demeter who,

according to the Homeric *Hymn to Demeter* (487), is sent to the houses of the initiates into her mysteries. For the philosophical Socrates, these are one aptly named god, for the wealth he gives is eschatological in nature: he "will have nothing to do with men while they are in the body, but only when the soul is liberated from the desires of the body" (403e) Rabelais alludes to the *Cratylus* passage in chapter 47: "Pourtant est equitablement le Soubterrain Dominateur presques en toutes langues nommé par epithete de richesses." While roundly condemning the pagan mysteries, Clement of Alexandria applies their language and terminology to Christian worship in the *Protrepticus* 12.120.1–2; *PG* 8.241. For a discussion of the relationship between the mystery cults and the symbolism of *The Praise of Folly*, see Marjorie O'Rourke Boyle, *Christening Pagan Mysteries*.

55 *Les Georgiques de Virgile Maron translatées de Latin en françoys: et moralisées* (Paris, 1519), p. Siv recto: "cest assavoir nouveaux hommes en son sang regenerez sans puissance daller et cheminer en vertu fors que par l'aide de luy qui en fin les fera aller la su en paradis." Michel's allegory is discussed by Raymond Lebègue in "Christian Interpretations of Pagan Authors," in Werner Gundersheimer, ed., *French Humanism 1470–1600* (New York and Evanston, 1969), pp. 197–206, p. 204.

56 Weinberg produces a series of texts on the spiritual significance of drinking; see *The Wine and the Will*, pp. 45–52, 84–85.

57 Augustine *Commentary on the First Letter of John* 7.8; *PL* 35.2033. Per Nykrog, in an excellent essay on the problem of the will in Rabelais, "Thélème, Panurge, et la Dive Bouteille," *Revue d'Histoire Littéraire de la France* (1965), pp. 385–397, suggests that "Fay ce que vouldras" should be related to the "fiat voluntas tuas" of the *Pater noster* (Matthew 6 : 10). It is possible that Rabelais conflates the scriptural verse with the Augustinian tag: to act with charity is to do God's will. Jean Paris, in *Rabelais au futur* (Paris, 1970), p. 212, notes the Augustinian source of the motto of Theleme, but he incorrectly reads irony into Rabelais's quotation.

58 *Commentary on the First Letter of John* 7.1; *PL* 35.2029.

59 Ibid. 7.6; *PL* 35.2032.

60 See the *Ratio seu methodus compendio perveniendi ad veram theologiam* in *Opera omnia*, 5:132: "Ad recte monet Sapiens ille, ut *aquarum de tua bibes cisterna:* & adeo non sit necesse aliunde rogare, ut tu potius de tuo fonte derives in alios." This passage is cited by Cave, p. 85.

61 For a discussion of prophetic interpretation which encompasses many of the ideas of this chapter, see Erasmus, *Hyperaspitae Diatribes*, book 1, *Opera omnia*, 10:1307: "Prophetiam Paulus appellat Scripturae mysticae interpretationem." In this passage, Erasmus counters Luther's claim that Scriptural meaning is single and immediately self-evident; using the text of 1 Corinthians 14, he argues that interpretation is partial and multiple and therefore requires the Church as a community of interpreters.

62 See Edgar Wind, *Pagan Mysteries in the Renaissance* (1958; rev. ed., New York, 1968), pp. 277 ff.

63 Cave, *The Cornucopian Text*, pp. 118–20, wants to see the process of interpretation as endless, one gloss replacing the next, full meaning

infinitely deferred. His reading does not take into account Rabelais's insistence upon the finitude of the history in which interpretation takes place. Cave, however, correctly points to the negative aspects of historical dispersion portrayed in the Rabelaisian books, particularly in the *Quart Livre* (see pp. 194–222); these are also emphasized by Seidel, *Satiric Inheritance*, pp. 65–78, in his discussion of the satirical mode of Rabelais's art. Their readings offer a necessary counterbalance to my own, which stresses Rabelais's positive view of history as a process of reconstitution; for all of its optimism, the Rabelaisian vision offers no escape from the radically contingent and problematic aspects of historical experience.

64 See the preface to *The Great Instauration* which precedes the *New Organon*. (*The New organon and Related Writings*, ed. Fulton Anderson [Indianapolis and New York, 1960], p. 15.) "Non aliter ac si divina natura innocenti et benevolo puerorum ludo delectaretur, qui ideo se abscondunt ut inveniantur; atque animam humanam sibi collusorem in hoc ludo pro sua in homines indulgentia et bonitate cooptaverit" (*Bacon's Novum Organum*, ed. Thomas Fowler [Oxford, 1878], p. 164). Rabelais's evangelical view of scientific progress anticipates Puritan millennial ideas about the restoration of man to a prelapsarian relationship with nature, ideas which inform Bacon's writings. Bacon and Rabelais frequently share the same metaphors, including the typological opposition of Babel to Zion. See aphorism 120 of Book 1 of the *New Organon*: "Nos autem non Capitolium aliquod aut Pyramidem hominum superbiae dedicamus aut condimus, sed templum sanctum ad exemplar mundi in intellectu humano fundamus," p. 317.

65 The "sac" parable alludes to Babel, for this panomphaean word comes from the diaspora from that city when each of its fleeing inhabitants carried a sack behind his or her back. In a world conditioned by the event of Babel, human community and interdependence become all the more vital. See Cave, *The Cornucopian Text*, pp. 119–20, and Greene, *Rabelais*, p. 110.

66 Erasmus *Adagia* II, 4.17, *Opera omnia*, 2:527–28.

67 See Nemours Clement, *The Influence of the Arthurian Romances on the Five Books of Rabelais* (Berkeley, 1926).

68 See Marcel de Grève, *L'Interpretation de Rabelais au XVIe siècle* (Geneva, 1961).

69 See *Les Tragiques* 5 ("Les Fers"), 1447–1532, especially vv. 1497–99:

> Ainsi la mer alloit, faisant changer de course
> Des gros fleuves à mont vers la coupable source,
> D'où sortoit par leur bords un deluge de sang.

The notes of Henri Weber and Marguerite Soulié to Weber's edition of d'Aubigné's *Oeuvres* (Paris, 1969) point out the allusion in these lines to Psalm 114 and cite Beza's poetic translation. See p. 1045, n. 1.

CHAPTER 7

1 See James H. Sims, "Camoens' 'Lusiads' and Milton's 'Paradise Lost': Satan's Voyage to Eden," in Philip Mahone Griffith and Lester F. Zimmerman, eds., *Papers on Milton* (Tulsa, 1969), pp. 36–46. For other cases of Milton's indebtedness to Camões, see by the same scholar, "The Epic Narrator's Mortal Voice in Camões and Milton," *Revue de Littérature Comparée* 51 (1977): 374–84, and "Christened Classicism in *Paradise Lost* and *The Lusiads*," *Comparative Literature* 24 (1972): 338–56.

2 Camões, *Os lusiadas*, ed. Francisco da Silveira Bueno (São Paulo, 1960), p. 454. I have quoted the Portuguese text, although it is likely that Milton also knew Camões's poem through the 1655 translation of Richard Fanshawe; see *The Lusiads*, ed. Geoffrey Bullough (London and Fontwell, 1963), p. 204.

3 See A. B. Chambers, "Chaos in *Paradise Lost*," *JHI* 24 (1963): 55–84, for an excellent discussion of the ancient cosmological doctrine which Milton exploits in his depiction of Chaos.

4 For Milton's knowledge and occasional use of the Vulgate Bible in *Paradise Lost*, see James H. Sims, *The Bible in Milton's Epics* (Gainesville, Fla., 1962), pp. 97–102.

5 See Michael Murrin, *The Allegorical Epic*, pp. 155–58.

6 For a discussion of the marsh gas image, see Kester Svendsen, *Milton and Science* (Cambridge, Mass., 1956), pp. 105–12.

7 For a discussion of Satan as the figure of the modern poet, see Harold Bloom, *The Anxiety of Influence: A Theory of Poetry* (London and Oxford, 1973), pp. 20 ff. Bloom examines Milton's attempt "to make his own belatedness into an earliness, and his tradition's priority over him into a lateness" in *A Map of Misreading* (New York, 1975), pp. 125–43. A discussion of Milton's struggle with tradition is found in Patricia Parker, *Inescapable Romance*, pp. 130–35. The finest recent critic of Milton, Parker suggests that "the poet of *Paradise Lost* may encounter the primal shadow in figuration itself, a representation already preempted by the past, still inextricably wedded to 'Dame Memory and her Siren daughters.' "

8 For the text of Chapelain's *Discours*, see Giambattista Marino, *Adone,* ed. Marzio Pieri (Rome and Bari, 1975), 1:17–50. The passage under discussion here is found on pp. 19–20.

9 See Charles Collas, *Jean Chapelain* (Paris, 1911), p. 279, n. 8. But the comparison of Chapelain to Homer might not be intended as praise; see pp. 288–89. For the Neoclassical Homer, see Kirsti Simonsuuri, *Homer's Original Genius* (Cambridge, 1979).

10 John Dennis, *The Grounds of Criticism in Poetry* (London, 1704), pp. b2 verso–b3 recto.

11 Dennis detaches literature from religion precisely when he may seem to be doing just the opposite: his fifth chapter affirms that "Religion is the Basis and foundation of the greater Poetry." But his argument that grandeur and sublimity may be best attained with a divine subject matter

is concerned not with the poem's authority but with the power of its imaginative effects: religion becomes the handmaiden of poetry. The poet should choose to write about, not the true religion, but "the Reigning one, that both the Poet and the reader may be move'd the more by a Religion in which they were bred." See pp. 113–16.

12 Edward Young, *Conjectures on Original Composition*, ed. Edith J. Morley (Manchester, London, New York, and Bombay, 1918), p. 36.

13 Ibid., p. 17.

14 Ibid., p. 18.

15 See Garin, "La nuova scienza e il simbolo del 'Libro'," pp. 464–65: "la teologia poetica tendeva a farsi poesia; e le immagini s'avviavano a valere per sé. . . . I caratteri mostruosi e terribili dei cieli e degli elementi venivano usati sempre più per imprese, emblemi o livree. Le figure trovavano il loro posto tra retorica e arte della memoria, mentre la nuova scienza dichiarava in formule matematiche il segreto non più segreto della natura." For a discussion of the end of allegory and the emergence of the literary author as creator and original genius, see Michael Murrin, *The Veil of Allegory*, pp. 167–98.

Index of Names

259

261

263